Turkish Social Law

Tankut Centel

Turkish Social Law

Springer

Tankut Centel
Law School
Koç University
Istanbul, Turkey

ISBN 978-3-030-64703-2 ISBN 978-3-030-64704-9 (eBook)
https://doi.org/10.1007/978-3-030-64704-9

This Springer imprint is published by the registered company Springer Nature Switzerland AG.
The registered company address is: Gewerbestrasse 11, 6330 Cham, Switzerland

Preface

The present study is supported by the themes I have been dealing with in my undergraduate lectures at Koç University Law School (Istanbul, Turkey) since 2008.

The idea of writing this book came to me at the beginning of the reform movement of Turkey in the field of social security since 2006. Law No. 5510, enacted in 2006, has managed to gather all social security institutions and employees under a single law. As such, the general health insurance, which was also discussed for years, began to apply by this law in Turkey for the first time.

The Turkish social security system has embarked on a quest for an important reform since 2006. Thus, as of that date, the action has been undertaken to ensure the union of norms and standards in Turkey. Up until then, the social security of employers, self-employed, and public officers was provided by different institutions and different laws, which were subordinate to separate ministries. The reform studies have initially united these institutions under a single roof. Accordingly, regardless of whether the insured is a worker, self-employed, or public officer, their social security services are only carried out by the Social Security Institution under the organization of the Ministry of Family, Labour and Social Services. Thus, previously dispersed social security institutions were gathered under a single ministry and a single roof.

Besides, workers and self-employed and public officers were subject to a large number of social security laws determined by their status. This situation led to dispersed social security legislation and resulted in employees having different standards. All these numerous private laws have been combined in a single text with the Social Insurance and General Health Insurance Act. Thus, it has been ensured that all employees are subject to the same standard norm, as long as their situation does not require them to act differently.

These changes led to the deformation of the reform movement and resulted in a social legislation consisting of a large number of laws.

Furthermore, it is observed that social security institutions have started to lose their autonomous structures in the Turkish social security system. First of all, the general assemblies of social security institutions have been converted to advisory bodies. Then, social party representatives have been made ineffective in taking decisions on the boards of directors of social security institutions. Likewise, the fact that the representatives of the public sector who will serve on the boards of directors are not sought to have a certain experience in the field of social security and that their appointment is held open to political preferences also causes negativity.

Besides, Turkey approved the ILO Social Security (Minimum Standards) Convention, 1952 (No. 102) in 1971 and started to apply in 1974. However, due to the lack of a separate special law for family benefits and in the face of the unemployment insurance was not accepted yet at that time in Turkey, Turkey could not have confirmed Convention No. 102 with all of its provisions.

Since 1999, with the adoption of unemployment insurance, Turkey came to a position to confirm the provisions of Convention No. 102 concerning the unemployment benefits. However, there has not been much progress in the legal area of family benefits. The payment of family benefits is left to be included either in collective labor agreements or in statutory provisions that do not contain significant amounts.

The aim of this book is to provide a comprehensive overview of the social law system of Turkey. It mainly consists of nine parts: an introduction, organization of social insurance, concept of social insurance, social insurance liabilities, social insurance branches, general health insurance, complementary social security institutions, noncontributory regime, and concluding remarks.

Thus, the first part is about the general information on the concept of social law, historical development, and legal sources.

The next five parts focus on the concept and organization of social insurance with social insurance liabilities and social insurance branches including general health insurance.

The seventh part provides information on complementary social security institutions. It consists of charity funds and the private pension system.

The last two parts of the book focus on the noncontributory regime and concluding remarks. The social assistance and social services are inherent in the noncontributory regime.

In the last part, you will find a general evaluation of the Turkish social law system. There you can see an assessment of the whole national social security system.

During the recent COVID-19 pandemic, the need for a strong social security system has once again manifested itself. The accumulated cash in the unemployment insurance fund has made a great contribution to overcome the economic difficulties which have arisen when the pandemic occurred. Thus, those included in the noncontributory system have started to get benefit from the contributory system. It appears to change the understanding up to now that only those who have paid premiums can get benefit from the premium regime.

Besides, special thanks are owed to Springer and especially to *Dr.iur. Brigitte Reschke* for the editorial procedure of the publication.

Finally, I would like to invite the readers—faculty, students, practitioners, and others—to send suggestions and comments as well as any corrections. I will be reached by e-mail at *tcentel@ku.edu.tr*.

I hope that it can contribute to a better understanding of the essentials of the social law system in Turkey.

Istanbul, Turkey
September, 2020

Tankut Centel

Contents

Part VIII Non-contributory Regime

Part IX Concluding Remarks

List of Abbreviations

AD	Act on the Disabled
add.	Additional
art.	Article
C	International Labour Convention (ILO-Convention)
CC	Court of Cassation
Civ. Div.	Civil Division
Const.	Constitution of Turkey (Turkish Republic)
et al.	And others
fn.	Footnote
GDP	Gross domestic product
ILO	International Labour Organization
LA	Labour Act
LCA	Labour Courts Act
OG	Official Gazette
OHSA	Occupational Health and Safety Act
p.	Page
PD	Presidential Decree (governmental decision signed by the President of Turkey)
PPA	Private Pension Savings and Investment System Act
prov.	Provisional
para.	Paragraph
rep.	Repeating
SD	Statutory Decree
SIGHIA	Social Insurances and General Health Insurance Act
SSA	Social Services Act
SSI	Social Security Institution (governmental carrier of social insurances)
TCC	Turkish Code of Commerce
TCO	Turkish Code of Obligations
TLI	Turkish Labour Institution (Turkish Employment Agency)

TPC	Turkish Penal Code
UIA	Unemployment Insurance Act
UIF	Unemployment Insurance Fund

Table of Statutes

Act for Village and Neighbourhood Headmen Allowance and Social Security, Act No. 2108, OG 9.10.1977, No. 16053
Act on Agricultural Workers' Social Insurance, Act No. 2925, OG 10.20.1983, No. 18197
Act on Private Pension Plans Savings and Investment System, Act No. 4632, OG 04.07.2001, No. 24366
Act on the Assessment of Periods Spent Abroad by Turkish Citizens in terms of their Social Security, Act No. 3201, OG 05.22.1985, No. 18761
Act on the Disabled, Act No. 5378, OG 7.7.2005, No. 25868
Act on the Socialization of Health Services, Act No. 224, OG 01.12.1961, No. 10705
Child Protection Act, Act No. 5395, OG 15.7.2005, No. 25876
Constitution of Turkey, Act No. 2709, OG 11.09.1982, No. 17863
Fundamental Act on Healthcare Services, Act No. 3359, OG 05.15.1987, No. 19461
Labour Courts Act, Act No. 7036, OG 10.25.2017, No. 30221
Occupational Health and Safety Act, Act No. 6331, OG 06.30.2012, No. 28339
Private Pension Savings and Investment System Act, Act No. 4632, OG 7.4.2001, No. 24366
Retirement Fund Act, Act No. 5434, OG 06.17.1949, No. 7235
Social Insurance Act, Act No. 506, OG 07.29.1964, No. 11766
Social Insurance Act for the Tradesman, Artisans and Other Self-Employed Persons, Act No. 1479, OG 09.14.1971, No. 13956
Social Insurances and General Health Insurance Act, Act No. 5510, OG 06.16.2006, No. 26200
Social Services Act, Act No. 2828, OG 05.27.1983, No. 18059
Turkish Civil Code, Act No. 4721, OG 12.08.2001, No. 24607
Turkish Code of Obligations, Act No. 6098, OG 02.04.2011, No. 27836
Unemployment Insurance Act, Act No. 4447, OG 09.08.1999, No. 23810

Part I
Introduction

Chapter 1
Concept of Social Law

1.1 Scope of Social Law

The scope and content of social law are closely related with the emergence and development of social security concept. Accordingly, the concept of social security developing in the course of time fundamentally lays the foundation of content to be referred to the term *"social law"*.

As a concept, the social law is defined as the whole of legal regulations regarding the social security that is the whole of institutions given the task of providing the individuals with economic security against certain social risks of life, regardless of their income levels.[1] For this reason, it is important to examine the reasons for the emergence of social policies and social security system constituting the concept of social security, as well as the advancements in these elements.

1.1.1 Emergence of Social Security Concept

The social security concept can be considered as the outcome of modern societies. In fact, the term *"social security"* has been used for the first time in 1935 in *American Social Security Act.*

This concept, which has spread throughout the world, has transformed into a universal principle and become the symbol of today's modern civilization. Accordingly, the social security or social protection having a wider meaning is basically the result of searches for a security solution for the circumstances that would pose a risk for the lives of individuals from economical or physiological aspects.

From this aspect, the reason for social security concept is to provide the individuals, who face with risk, with a minimum security and to ensure the social protection

[1] *See*: Tunçomağ (1990), p. 5.

T. Centel, *Turkish Social Law*, https://doi.org/10.1007/978-3-030-64704-9_1

in this manner. The importance of social security concept gradually increases as a result of the negative effects of economic crises, technological advances, and the transformation in production on the individuals.

The term *"social security"* is mainly considered from the aspect of social policies and social security systems. Among these, the social policies determine the objectives and purposes of social protection, whereas the social security systems cover the legal methods established in order to achieve these objectives. From this aspect, the social law is the whole of legal measures taken against the poverty and deprivation of a country's society.[2]

On the other hand, the social policies that the social security incorporates are considered as the "*narrow-sense social security*". Besides that, the term "*broad-sense social security"* is used for the combination of social policies and social security systems.[3] From this aspect, the social law has a context that both represents the social policies and incorporates the social security systems. Accordingly, the social law consists of the institutions that are involved in broad-sense social security.

1.1.2 Objectives of Social Security

The *"social security"* term incorporates providing the individuals, who lost their capacity of earning their lives in the profession or became dependent due to any reason, with the income that is sufficient for achieving a decent life standard, which fits to the human dignity.

Another field of social security is to offer the medical care and rehabilitation services for healing the individuals, who became disabled due to any disease or disability.

The employees face with the risk of losing their health and even lives during their working life. Ensuring the assurance against the losses that might occur because of occupational diseases and occupational accidents that emerges when the healthy and secure working environment is not provided is one of the objectives of social security.

On the other hand, the individuals might lose his/her job because of the economic problems of the company or country. In this case, compensating the income losses of individuals, who became unemployed, and providing them with new job opportunities are also among the objectives of social security system.

Besides these, the social security has also the objectives such as supporting the families in cases of events putting them into difficult conditions, as well as meeting the housing needs of low-income families. The main objective here is to protect the individuals, who do not have the sufficient income level, from social aspect, as well as eliminating the poverty and deprivation. Thus, the economic inequalities of

[2] Sözer (2019), pp. 1–2.

[3] *See*: Güzel et al. (2020), pp. 5–9.

society are minimized, and the support is provided for ensuring the fairness. Since it is about collecting or creating the income and then distributing it to the society via social security, the social security has also the objective of re-distributing the income within the society.[4]

Given the mentioned objectives of social security, it can be stated that social law is about the social security contributions, and that it aims to secure the individuals from social aspect, to protect the poor individuals from economical aspect, to meet their needs in harmony with the human dignity, and to ensure the social fairness in this way.

1.2 Subject of Social Law

The social security systems consider different risks according to the economic or social conditions or cultural traditions of countries and determine the structure of social security contributions. Besides that, ILO Convention No. 102 is taken as international basis regarding the minimum norms of social security. Accordingly, nine main branches of social security are health (medical care), health (financial aids), occupational accident and occupational disease, maternity, disability, old age, survivor, family allowances, and unemployment insurances.

Turkish social security system is deficient only in terms of family allowances among them, because there is no legal regulation in Turkish law except for the family allowance offered to civil servants and the family allowances paid to workers via collective labour agreements. Besides that, it can be seen that a limited assurance against the unemployment risk was provided in the unemployment insurance founded in 1999.

1.3 Systematics of Social Law

While constructing the rules of social security systems, the social law takes the fundamentals of two different regimes as basis. Some of them cover the legal rules related with the regime running based on the financial contribution of relevant individual. The other legal rules are related with the regime running without the financial contribution of relevant individual.

Thus, the social law is a branch of law covering the rules and institutions related with social security regimes with (*Bismarck*-model incorporating financial contribution) and without (*Beveridge*-model incorporating no financial contribution) premium. The part of social law related with the social security regime with financial contribution is called "*social insurance law*" (*contributory system*). The other part of social law related with regime without financial contribution consists of

[4]Tuncay and Ekmekçi (2019), p. 5.

sub-departments namely "*social benefits law*" and "*social services law*" (*non-contributory system*). From this aspect, the social law concept constitutes the superior concept, whereas the concepts of social insurances, social services, and social support are listed at lower levels in hierarchy.[5]

1.3.1 Social Insurances

The social insurance law is the branch of social law covering the employees. Accordingly, the social insurance law is the branch of law, in which the insurance institution based on the financial contributions that the employees and the employers have paid protects the employees and their families.[6]

Turkish legal system is based on distinguishing the worker and the self-employed at first. For this reason, in the recent past, the social insurances of employees were divided into social insurance for workers and retirement fund for civil servants, whereas the social insurances of the self-employed persons were divided into social insurances of traders, artisans and other self-employed persons. Thus, the social security laws, social security standards, and social security institutions varying between the employee categories have emerged.

However, nowadays, the aforementioned classifications started to be removed following the recent reform based on Acts No. 5502 and 5510 since year 2006. Together with the realization of principles "*single roof*" and "*uniformity of norms and standards*", it is now possible to discuss the uniform social security law in Turkey.

1.3.2 Social Assistances

The social assistances aim to provide the poor individuals with social income. The institutions providing the social assistances are mainly the governmental institutions, and then the charities, foundations, and private companies. At this point, the social assistances provided by the government are funded with the taxes. The other bodies provide these assistances by making use of their own resources.

1.3.3 Social Services

Principally, the social services can be considered as offering poor individuals with the support in forms of goods and services. However, in social services, sometimes the financial aids can be provided for the citizens under specific conditions.

[5] Tunçomağ (1990), p. 6.

[6] Sözer (2019), p. 2.

In Turkey, the social services have been provided in a disjointed manner out of the control of State for a long time. However, the social services are the organized efforts that should be made by the public institutions and various voluntary agencies but under the control of State.

1.4 Role of Social Law in Turkish Legal System

The legal systems are traditionally categorized under the *"public law"* and *"private law"*. The social law is in the category of public law.

In the early periods, in which the social law was not a separate branch of law, it can be seen that the legal regulations protecting the employees were based on the methods of private law. However, when the social security became a public service that the state must offer, the public character of social law became more prominent. Hence, according to art. 60 Const., the State shall take the measures and establish the organization required for providing everyone with social security. According to the aforementioned regulation, the public service character of social security became more apparent. As a result of this, the public authorities play effective role in development and advancement of the social law.

Insurance relationship established within the scope of social law is a public law relationship because the aforementioned relationship occurs by itself as a necessity of law. Similarly, independently from the will of insurance holder, the insurance ownership occurs by itself in accordance with the mandatory provisions of law.

Again, no one may avoid from the rights and obligations of insurance status, and the provisions prepared in order to eliminate, minimize, or transfer these rights and obligations are considered legally invalid (art. 92 para. 1 SIGHIA).

Besides that, it cannot be said that the social law has no relationship with the private law. Especially the general provisions of Civil Code and Turkish Code of Obligations apply also to the social law. For instance, the principle of not abusing the right and the principle of good faith in civil law apply to the social law.[7]

References

Güzel A, Okur AR, Caniklioğlu N (2020) Sosyal Güvenlik Hukuku, 18th edn. Beta Publishing, Istanbul

Sözer AN (2019) Türk Sosyal Sigortalar Hukuku, 4th edn. Beta Publishing, Istanbul

Tuncay AC, Ekmekçi Ö (2019) Sosyal Güvenlik Hukuku Dersleri, 20th edn. Beta Publishing, Istanbul

Tunçomağ K (1990) Sosyal Güvenlik Kavramı ve Sosyal Sigortalar, 5th edn. Beta Publishing, Istanbul

[7]Tunçomağ (1990), p. 177.

Chapter 2
Historical Development of Social Law in Turkey

2.1 Period of Ottoman Empire

*2.1.1 Pre-*Tanzimat *(1839) Era*

Since the Ottoman Empire did not enter into the process of industrialization, an efficient social security system could not be achieved. In this period, it was attempted to meet the individuals' need for social protection through the domestic support, occupational associations, and other religion-based charities. The legal measures that have been taken remained very limited.

Before the reform era of *Tanzimat* (the political reforms made in the Ottoman State in 1839), there were several institutions providing the economic insurance to individuals. In this period, there were several organizations offering social benefits to the poor people. However, these social aids were mainly the religious ones because the charity funds of chambers originated completely from religious reasons and artisans' need for mutual support.[1]

The state has not made any contribution to the relevant funds. These funds were named *"safe-deposit boxes"*. The income sources of these funds were the contributions paid by masters and apprentices on weekly or monthly basis, the donations to the funds, and the fees paid for apprentices promoting to foremanship.[2]

The charity funds supported their patient members during their treatment (based on the condition of poverty), and provided financial aid for the daily needs of the untreatable apprentices, foremen, and the masters, who were old. Moreover, the family members of traders that have become poor were provided with the required support from the funds.[3]

---

[1]Korkusuz and Uğur (2009), p. 95; Şen (2007), pp. 55–56.

[2]Alper (2015), p. 6.

[3]Dilik (1991), pp. 33–34.

T. Centel, *Turkish Social Law*, https://doi.org/10.1007/978-3-030-64704-9_2

The support to poor individuals was made via *zekat* (alms), *fitre* (a special form of Islamic alms), and the other grant and donations that the Islam requires. Besides that, the function of social welfare institution was undertaken by the foundation.[4] However, the foundations in that period were not subject to private law as they are now.[5]

Significant portion of Ottoman foundations focused mainly on the function of social welfare. They have been founded in order to meet the exact and vital needs, which any society cannot stay away from, and to relieve the pains of individuals. Accordingly, the aforementioned foundations aspired mainly after taking care of poor individuals living in neighbourhoods and villages and providing them with healthcare, as well as providing support to individuals, who cannot earn their living because of any disease, as well as protecting the lives of children and orphans.[6]

Thus, in the period before the *Tanzimat* reform era, the poor individuals were provided with support via advanced social instruments such as *fitre*, *zekat*, and especially the foundations without considering if they are poor or employed. On the other hand, the charity funds within the chambers were made use in order to protect only the workers and tradesman members against the significant risks such as old age, disability, and death. This social protection was very important for that period.

2.1.2 *Post-*Tanzimat *Era*

In post-*Tanzimat* era, the social security activities remained very limited and very disjointed, because the Ottoman Empire entered into its regression period. *Fitre, zekat* and especially the foundations lost their significance, and they vanished in the commercial competition with foreign countries. Through the disjointed and significantly insufficient legal regulations, it was attempted to bridge the gap that emerged as a result of existing social security measures' failure in successfully operating.

One of the aforementioned incomprehensive legal regulations is the *Dilaver Pasha Regulation* dated 1865. This regulation was on the coal miners in Eregli region. In this regulation, there was no provision about the social assistances, except for the treatment of workers. However, in the provision set forth in order to prevent the malingering, it was determined under which conditions the health benefits would be provided.[7]

Then, the *Maden (Mining) Regulation* enacted in 1869 draws attention. It set forth that there should be a physician and required medications in the mines. The mine

[4]*See*: Dilik (1991), pp. 37–38; Korkusuz and Uğur (2009), p. 96.

[5]Tunçomağ (1990), pp. 39–40.

[6]Saymen (1952), pp. 1067–1068.

[7]Alper (2015), p. 10; Saymen (1952), pp. 1073–1074; Şen (2007), pp. 63–64.

owners were obliged to pay compensation and allowance, which would be determined by the court, to the families of miners when the worker died at work.[8]

In the period of Ottoman State, there was not another legal measure aiming the social protection. On the other hand, it can be seen that there were several public and private retirement and charity funds aiming to protect the employees of certain institutions (limited to the soldiers and civil servants) especially in the elderliness and sickness periods.[9]

2.2 After the Turkish War of Independence

In the period of government before the proclamation of republic (1921–1923), that is to say during the Turkish War of Independence, two important acts related with the social security were enacted and applied for coal mining areas in Zonguldak and Eregli regions near Western Black Sea.

First of them was Act No. 114 dated 28/4/1921. This law set forth that the coal dusts originating from the coal mining process and left in Zonguldak and Eregli areas by the company shall be auctioned off and the money to be collected shall be used in favour of miners.[10]

The second law was *Act on Rights of Miners of Eregli Coal Mining Area* No. 151 dated 10/9/1921. According to the provisions of aforementioned act, the employers shall have to have sick or injured miners cured free of any charge, to establish a hospital near the mine to employ a physician for this purpose. Moreover, the employers were obliged to pay compensation to the miner with an occupational accident and the family of miner died of an occupational accident. Besides that, Act No. 151 also set forth the establishment of charity funds for the miners. These funds established in mines were joined under the title of "*Labour Union*"; thus, even if they were in limited and primitive form, the first implementation of social insurances in Turkey has been put into practice.[11]

Act No. 151 lost its significance when the social insurance has been established in entire country. Accordingly, after the Cabinet Decree on the implementation of the provisions of health insurance in *Eregli* coal mining area since 15/10/1975, the Labour Union became an institution providing coalminers of Eregli with new rights.[12]

---

[8]Alper (2015), p. 10; Şen (2007), pp. 67–68; Tunçomağ (1990), pp. 41–42.

[9]*See*: Güzel et al. (2020), p. 24 fn. 38; Şen (2007), pp. 70–71.

[10]Şen (2007), p. 76.

[11]Şen (2007), pp. 79–80 and 83.

[12]*See* below Sect. 24.1.

2.3 Republic Period

2.3.1 Period Before World War II

It can be seen that no efficient social security system could be established since the proclamation of republic since 1923 until 1945. Besides that, established between 1930 and 1942, several laws aiming the establishment of retirement and charity funds were similar to the social insurance but they had much narrower contexts in terms of individuals and risks.[13]

In this period, *Code of Obligations* dated 1926 set forth that, as long as the employer make the insurance and the employee pays at least 50% of insurance premium, the worker shall be able to enjoy his/her rights originating from the insurance (art. 112). Moreover, *Act on Protection of Public Health* dated 1930 set forth that specified workers should be provided with the compulsory health benefits.

Then, *Labour Act* No. 3008 dated 1936 set forth the establishment of social insurance for the first time in Turkey, as well as specific fundamental principles of social security, which are still in use. Accordingly, LA regulated the insurance branches to be established, their priorities, the principle of compulsion in insurance, and the scope of insurance for the insured individuals (arts 100–107 LA No. 3008). From this aspect, it was aimed to offer social protection against the risks of occupational accidents and diseases, maternity, old age, unemployment, disease, and death (art. 100 LA No. 3008) and to realize it by establishing "*Directorate of Occupational Insurances*" as a governmental institution.

2.3.2 Period After 1945

The social policy movements appearing after the World War II also influenced Turkey, and it can be seen that the first laws on the social security were enacted. From this aspect, the occupational accident, occupational disease, and maternity insurances were founded at first, and then the social security was added into the responsibilities of Ministry of Labour that was established.

Accordingly, *Act on Occupational Accidents, Occupational Diseases, and Maternity Insurances* No. 4772 was enacted in 1945. In 1949, the old-age insurance was established with Act. No. 5417. However, in 1957, it was joined with the disability and survivor insurances with Act. No. 6900. In 1950, the health and maternity insurance branches were regulated together in Act. No. 5502; and the provisions of previous Act No. 4772 on the maternity insurance were repealed.

In this period, the social insurances were regulated in multiple laws rather than regulating in a single law; the aforementioned regulations were significantly insufficient because the application area of these acts was significantly narrow. Moreover,

[13] *See*: Güzel et al. (2020), pp. 26–27 fn. 48.

providing the spouses and children of insurance holders with health benefit was not taken as basis.[14]

On the other hand, whereas the workers were provided with social security in these laws, Act No. 5434 dated 1949 set forth the establishment of *Retirement Fund* in order to provide the civil servants with social insurance.[15]

2.3.3 Adoption of 1961 Constitution and the Following Period

1961 Constitution gave right to the social security its constitutional character, and it accepted this right as a fundamental human right for the first time in Turkey. According to Art. 48 Const. (1961), "*Everyone shall have the right to social security. The State shall take the necessary measures and establish the organization for the provision of social security*".

During the years after the adoption of 1961 Constitution, many legal regulations were made on the social security. On this subject, Act No. 506[16] that entered into force on 1/3/1965 has gathered the social insurance branches, which seemed disjointed until that day, under its umbrella and enlarged their context in order to provide the workers with social security.

In 1971, in order to provide the traders and artisans and other self-employed persons (except for those working in agriculture), Act No. 1479[17] was enacted. However, in this law, the self-employed persons achieved the protection against only the risks of death, disability, and old age.

In non-contributory regime, the veterans were put on salary in Act No. 1005 in year 1968.[18] Again, in Act No. 2022 enacted in 1976,[19] Turkish citizens, who turned 65 years old and who are needy, weak and forlorn, were granted the right to pension. Similarly, Act No. 2330 in 1980[20] stated that the civil servants that died or injured because of their job shall receive compensation and be put on pension.

[14]Tunçomağ (1990), p. 43.

[15]*See*: Güzel et al. (2020), p. 28 fn. 52.

[16]OG 29.7.1964, No. 11766.

[17]OG 14.9.1971, No. 13956.

[18]OG 24.2.1968, No. 12835.

[19]OG 10.7.1976, No. 15642.

[20]OG 6.11.1980, No. 17152.

2.3.4 Since 1982 Constitution to Date

As well as 1961 Constitution, also the 1982 Constitution adopted the right to social security as a fundamental constitutional right. On this subject, it is stated in 1982 Constitution:

> Everyone shall have the right to social security. The State shall take the measures required for ensuring this security and establish the organization (art. 60).

1982 Constitution take a step forward from the previous constitution, and it assigned a special place for the social assistances and social services that are included in the social security concept.[21] Art. 61 Const. stated that the State should protect the widows and orphans of martyrs of war and duty, together with invalid and war veterans, as well as reintegrating them into the society.

On the other hand, art. 62 Const. imposed the duty of providing the Turkish citizens, who live in foreign countries, with social security to the State and aimed to grant a social protection to the Turkish citizens living abroad.

Moreover, one of the important duties imposed to the State by 1982 Constitution is the duty of "*providing the healthcare services*" (art. 56). Accordingly, the State undertook the responsibility of planning the medical care facilities from a single centre, as well as regulating their service. The State shall fulfil this responsibility by making use of and inspecting the medical care and social assistance bodies in public and private sectors (art. 56 paras 3 and 4 Const.). In order to provide the medical care services in a common manner, the *public health insurance* may be established (art. 56 para. 5 Const.).

1982 Constitution comprehensively recognized the State's responsibility of ensuring the social security and, as 1961 Constitution did, it limited this responsibility to the "*financial power of State*". Accordingly, the State shall fulfil its economic and social duties, which were imposed by the Constitution, to the extent its financial resources allow (art. 65 Const.). At the first glance, this limitation determined regarding ensuring the right to social security might be seen to alleviate the State's duty of social security. However, according to an interpretation of art. 65 Const. in harmony with its purpose, it can be stated that this is only the superficial aspect.[22]

In the years following the adoption of 1982 Constitution, the laws that can be considered important for social insurances were enacted. Some of the milestones in this way are as follows:

- *Act No. 2828 on Social Services and Child Protection Institution* on 24/5/1983,[23]

[21]Tunçomağ (1990), pp. 58–59.

[22]*See*: Tunçomağ (1990), p. 59.

[23]OG 27.5.1983 No. 18059.

- *Act No. 2829 on Combining Services Subjected to Social Security Institutions* on 24/5/1983,[24]
- *Act No. 2925 on Social Insurance of Agricultural Workers* dated 17/10/1983,[25]
- *Act No. 2926 on the Social Insurance for the Self-Employed Persons Working on Their Own Account and on Their Own Behalf in Agriculture* dated 17/10/1983,[26]
- Act No. 3201 on the *Assessment of Periods Spent by Turkish Citizens Abroad in terms of their Social Security* dated 8/5/1985,[27]
- Act No. 3249 on *Encouraging the Social Assistance and Solidarity* dated 29/5/1986.[28]

2.3.5 Social Security Reform Activities

In 2000s, it was seen that the Turkish social security system was significantly complicated and faced with severe problems. This is because no significant change could be achieved in operation and organization of Turkish social security system's structure until that day. In fact, the Turkish social system has consisted for many different components like a mosaic, and there was no harmony or bond between these components.

On the other hand, funding problem was the most important problem faced during this process. The deficits of social security institutions significantly increased year by year, and it was attempted to meet these deficits by making use of the transfers from the general budget. Since 2004, the idea of making a reform in Turkish social security system by standardizing the social security institutions and gathering them under the single roof gained importance as a solution.

On this subject, in order to achieve the single institution at first, the *Social Security Institution Act* No. 5502[29] was prepared. This law terminated the legal entities of Social Insurance Institution, Social Insurance Institution for Traders, Artisans and Other Self-employed Persons and Retirement Fund for Civil Servants (art. 43), and established the "*Social Security Institution*" as a single institution replacing them.

Then, in order to standardize the existing social security norms, the *Social Insurances and General Health Insurance Act* No. 5510[30] was enacted on 31/5/2006. Thus, the social security rights were gathered together under the roof of single

[24]Ibid.

[25]OG 20.10.1983, No. 18197.

[26]Ibid.

[27]OG 22.5.1985, No. 18761.

[28]OG 14.6.1986, No. 19134.

[29]OG 20.5.2006, No. 26173.

[30]OG 16.6.2006, No. 26200.

law. However, the Constitutional Court cancelled some of the important provisions of this law and many others were repealed.[31]

Thereupon, it became inevitable to amend Act No. 5510, and its final form was enacted as of the beginning of October 2008 (art. 108 SIGHIA).

2.3.6 *Some Quantitative Facts About Turkish Social Security System*

As of November 2019, the population is 83,154,997, and 69,932,638 of this population are covered by the social security. Accordingly, the rate of insured population is 85% and the rate of unregistered insured population is 15%. The number of insurance holders is 22,045,985, number of pensioners is 12,949,836, and number of dependents is 34,517,593. Accordingly, the ratio of insurance holders to pensioners is 1.81.[32] Given that this ratio should be minimum 4, it can be stated that the Turkish social security system does not have a positive appearance in terms of active/passive insurance holder ratio.

Similarly, the number of persons registered under the General Health Insurance is 11,424,727. 2,344,506 of them pay their contributions by themselves, whereas the contributions of 9,080,221 individuals are paid by the State.[33]

References

Alper Y (2015) Türk Sosyal Güvenlik Sistemi. Sosyal Sigortalar Hukuku, 7th edn. Dora Publishing, Bursa

Dilik S (1991) Sosyal Güvenlik. Publication of Kamu İşletmeleri İşverenleri Sendikası, Ankara

Güzel A, Okur AR, Caniklioğlu N (2020) Sosyal Güvenlik Hukuku, 18th edn. Beta Publishing, Istanbul

Korkusuz MR, Uğur S (2009) Sosyal Güvenlik Hukukuna Giriş. Karahan Kitabevi, Ankara

Saymen FH (1952) Türkiye'de Sosyal Sigortaların Gelişme Hareketleri ve Yeni Temayülleri. İstanbul Üniversitesi Hukuk Fakültesi Mecmuası 18(3–4):1065–1095

Şen M (2007) Tanzimat ve TBMM Hükümeti Döneminde Sosyal Güvenlik Hukuku Alanındaki Gelişmeler. In: Erzincan University Law School (ed) Atatürk'ün 125. Doğum Yılına Armağan, pp 55–85

Tunçomağ K (1990) Sosyal Güvenlik Kavramı ve Sosyal Sigortalar, 5th edn. Beta Publishing, Istanbul

[31]Constitutional Court, 15.12.2006, 111/112, OG 30.12.2006, No. 26392.

[32]http://www.sgk.gov.tr/wps/portal/sgk/tr/kurumsal/istatistik/aylik_istatistik_bilgileri.

[33]http://www.sgk.gov.tr/wps/portal/sgk/tr/kurumsal/istatistik/aylik_istatistik_bilgileri.

Chapter 3
Legal Sources of Social Law in Turkey

3.1 National Sources

3.1.1 Legislative Sources

3.1.1.1 Constitution

1982 Constitution of Turkey (Turkish Republic)[1] is the first of legislative sources. As in other branches of law, the provisions of Constitution have priority and superiority over the other sources in social security law. So, *"the provisions of the Constitution are fundamental rules binding upon legislative, executive and judicial organs, and administrative authorities and other institutions and individuals"* and *"laws shall not be contrary to the Constitution"* (art. 11 Const.). Thus, the Constitution incorporates the fundamentals guiding all the other sources of law. From this aspect, the regulations about social security (arts 60–61 Const.) between the principle of "*social state*" in Constitution (art. 2 Const.) and the social economic and social rights (arts 41–65 Const.) are the fundamentals guiding the Turkish social security law.

The Constitution has three articles directly related with the social security law. First of them is 60 Const. that grants the right to social security. Accordingly:

> Everyone has the right to social security.
>
> The State shall take the necessary measures and establish the organization for the provision of social security.

By addressing "*everyone*", art. 60 Const. warrants that not only the Turkish citizens but also all the foreigners living in this country shall enjoy the right to social security.

---

[1]OG 20.10.1982, No. 17844, published in the repeating OG 9.11.1982, No. 17863 in the aftermath of its submission to referendum on 7.11.1982 (Act No. 2709).

T. Centel, *Turkish Social Law*, https://doi.org/10.1007/978-3-030-64704-9_3

On the other hand, addressing the right to social security, art. 60 Const. considers the right to social security from a wider perspective and not limited to the social insurances.

Another provision related with the social security is art. 61 Const., which shows the categories that, shall be specially protected in terms of social security. Accordingly:

> The State shall protect the widows and orphans of martyrs of war and duty, together with invalid and war veterans, and ensure that they enjoy a decent standard of living.
>
> The State shall take measures to protect the disabled and secure their integration into community life.
>
> The aged shall be protected by the State. Law shall regulate state assistance to, and other rights and benefits of the aged.
>
> The State shall take all kinds of measures for social resettlement of children in need of protection.
>
> To achieve these aims the State shall establish the necessary organizations or facilities or arrange for their establishment.

About which body shall establish the social security institutions, arts. 60 and 61 Const. have different provisions. Accordingly, art. 60 para. 2 uses the verb "*establish*", whereas art. 61 para. 5 uses the verbs "*establish*" and "*arrange*". It means that there is no provision that exactly holds the State obliged to establish the institutions, which will offer the social security to the public groups that should be especially protected in terms of social security (art. 61 paras. 1–4 Const.).

But, the fact that the State has no obligation of establishing them by it doesn't mean that the State shall remain passive during the establishment of such institutions to offer social security, otherwise the provision in art. 61 Const. would not be a governing provision any longer. Furthermore, there is no obstacle preventing the State from establishing such institutions by itself, because art. 61 para.5 Const. grants the State a chance to choose by using "*and*" rather than "*or*".

Finally, the Constitution took not only those living in this country but also the Turkish citizens living in other countries into consideration. Accordingly, art. 62 of Const. holds the State responsible for taking the necessary measures in order to ensure the social security of Turkish citizens living in foreign countries.

3.1.1.2 Social Security Institution Act

Social Security Institution Act No. 5502[2] terminated the legal entities of previous social security institutions and gathered them (including all the assets of them) under the roof of SSI. Accordingly, it can be stated that Act No. 5502 aims to realize the principle of "*single roof*" for the regime with social contributions in Turkish social security system.

---

[2]OG 20.5.2006, No. 26173.

On the other hand, the unemployment insurance was excluded from SSI and assigned to TLI in *Turkish Labour Institution Act* No. 4904.[3]

3.1.1.3 Social Insurances and General Health Insurance Act

Act No. 5510 on *Social Insurances and General Health Insurance*[4] emerged as a result of reform activities in 2000s. This law was enacted in order to ensure the "*uniformity of norms and standards*".

Accordingly, it was aimed to gather the previous regulations prepared for workers, civil servants, and self-employed persons under a single roof, and to provide all the workers with the standard provisions. However, the civil servants were excluded from the scope of Act No. 5510 in terms of the short-term insurance branches, and the individuals, who become civil servant or public officer for the first time after the effective date of Act No. 5510, were included in the scope of Act No. 5510 after it entered into force. This resulted in the conclusion that the idea of "*single law*" started to lose its validity.[5]

Moreover, the provisions about insured workers, self-employed persons, civil servants, and other public officers, agricultural workers, and farmers that have been partly eliminated by Act No. 5510 will be in force for minimum 50 years for the owners of vested and expectant rights and their insurance holder relatives. Accordingly, the validity of two different law periods (namely the provisions to be applied to individuals that were active before the enactment of Act No. 5510 and the provisions to be applied to those entering into business life after the enactment of Act No. 5510) draws attention. In this case, it is difficult to state that this situation is in harmony with the principle of uniformity of norms and standards.

On the other hand, another important characteristic of Act No. 5510 is that it established the general (public) health insurance, which has been discussed for many years, for the first time in Turkey. On this subject, the services offered within the scope of general health insurance are mainly the protective health services, medical care and treatment services, oral and dental treatment, assisted reproductive therapy methods, and provision of instruments, equipment, and consumable materials (art. 63 SIGHIA). However, since the general health insurance was not regulated in a separate law, Act No. 5510 gained the appearance of "*law in a law*".

[3] OG 5.7.2003, No. 25159.

[4] OG 16.6.2006, No. 26200.

[5] Güzel et al. (2020), pp. 73–74.

3.1.1.4 Social Insurance Act

Social Insurance Act No. 506[6] that has regulated the social insurance rights of workers successfully gathered the insurance branches, which had a disjointed appearance in past, under a single roof. Nowadays, many provisions of aforementioned act were repealed after the Act No. 5510 entered into force.

3.1.1.5 Self-Employed Social Insurance Act

Social Insurance Act for Traders, Artisans and Other Self-Employed Persons No. 1479[7] regulated the social security rights of self-employers in the past. This law, which has provided the traders with the social security for the first time in Turkey, allowed the self-employers to benefit from long-term insurance branches, and then the new healthcare services were added into the list.

Nowadays, many of the provisions of this law were repealed when the Act No. 5510 entered into force.

3.1.1.6 Retirement Fund Act

Public Servants' Retirement Fund Act No. 5434[8] provided the civil servants and other public officers with social security in the past. This act took the organization in form of "*fund*" as basis. It was adopted that the retirement fund shall operate in association with the Ministry of Finance rather than Ministry of Labour and Social Security.

Nowadays, many of the provisions of this law were repealed when Act No. 5510 entered into force.

3.1.1.7 Agricultural Workers' Social Insurance Act

Considering the insurance of agricultural workers, *Social Insurance Act for Agricultural Workers* No. 2925[9] was adopted. However, when Act No. 5510 entered into force, many of the provisions of this law were repealed.

---

[6]OG 29.7.1964, No. 11766.

[7]OG 14.9.1971, No. 13956.

[8]OG 17.6.1949, No. 7235.

[9]OG 20.10.1983, No. 18197.

3.1.1.8 Unemployment Insurance Act

There has not been unemployment insurance act in Turkey until 1999; *severance pay* institution substituted the unemployment insurance. Unemployment insurance could be established as late as early 2000s by means of *Unemployment Insurance Act* No. 4447.[10] The responsibility of implementing the unemployment insurance was given to the Turkish employment agency (TLI) under the *Turkish Labour Institution Act* No. 4904.[11]

3.1.1.9 Village Headmen Allowance and Social Security Act

The village and neighbourhood headmen have vested the social security for the first time in 1977 by means of *Village and Neighbourhood Headmen Allowance and Social Security Act* No. 2108.[12] Among them, the ones that were not working as worker or civil servant were considered within the "*self-employed*" in terms of the implementation of SIGHIA (art. 4 para. 1 Act No. 2108). The social insurance contributions of headmen are borne by the State (art. 4 para. 2 Act No. 2108).

3.1.1.10 Act on Assessment of the Time Spent Abroad by Turkish Citizens with Regard to Social Security Issues

Act No. 3201 on Assessment of Periods spent abroad by Turkish Citizens in terms of their Social Security[13] enable Turkish citizens, who turned 18-year-old, to debt the insurance durations abroad, which can be documented, and the unemployment durations up to 1 year. The same opportunity is given for the time spent as housewife in foreign country (art. 1 Act No. 3201).

3.1.1.11 Promotion of Social Assistance and Solidarity Act

Act No. 3294 *for Promotion of Social Assistance and Solidarity*[14] sets the provision of social assistance to poor and needy citizens and those accepted or having come to Turkey (art. 1 Act No. 3294).

[10] OG 8.9.1999, No. 23810.

[11] OG 5.7.2003, No. 25159.

[12] OG 10.9.1977, No. 16053.

[13] OG 22.5.1985, No. 18761.

[14] OG 14.6.1986, No. 19134.

3.1.1.12 Social Services Act

Act No. 2828 on *Social Services*[15] was adopted in order to regulate the provisions regarding the services offered to families, disabled individuals, elderly individuals, children, and other individuals needing protection, care and/or assistance.

3.1.1.13 Act on the Socialization of Health Services

Act No. 224 *on the Socialization of Health Services*[16] was enacted as the legal basis of health reform, which was attempted in past. The aforementioned act aims that the utilization of healthcare services in Turkey shall be socially fair (art. 1 Act No. 224). However, although the regulations made in this act were effective at the beginning, the problems started to be seen as the area of implementation enlarged.[17] Even though the projected model was successful in rural areas, it could not be activated in urban areas.[18]

3.1.1.14 Fundamental Act on Healthcare Services

Fundamental Act on Healthcare Services No. 3359[19] is important for the provision of healthcare services within the scope of general health insurance. At this point, the aforementioned act regulates the fundamentals to be followed while providing the healthcare services required in general health insurance (art. 3 Act No. 3359).

3.1.1.15 Private Pension Act

Act on Private Pension Plans Savings and Investment System No. 4632[20] accepted the private pension system as a supplementary to the compulsory retirement system. Accordingly, the employees and civil servants shall qualify for pension when stayed in the system for minimum 10 years and turned the age of 56 years (art. 6 para. 1 Act No. 4632).

---

[15] OG 27.5.1983, No. 18059.

[16] OG 12.1.1961, No. 10705.

[17] Okur and Ergin (2008), pp. 618–619.

[18] Okur and Ergin (2008), p. 605.

[19] OG 15.5.1987, No. 19461.

[20] OG 7.4.2001, No. 24366.

3.1.2 Executive Sources

The most important regulation that is directly related with the social insurances act is the *"Regulation of Social Insurances Healthcare Services"*.[21] This regulation was prepared based on the Social Insurance Act. It regulates the fundamentals regarding which diseases shall be considered as occupational disease, as well as vocational incapacity, medical rehabilitation, early aging, and requiring medical care.

Although there are many by-laws about the acts related with the social security law, the most important ones among them are *"Bylaw of Social Security Operations"*[22] about the performance of insurance transactions and the rights and *"Bylaw of Implementation of Public Health Insurance Practice"*[23] about the health insurance operations.

3.1.3 Judicative Sources

Turkish judicial system incorporates no specific social courts in order to make decisions about the disputes regarding the social law. Instead, the resolution of social law disputes was assigned to the labour courts, where the labour disputes are resolved.

On this subject, it is set forth in *Labour Courts Act* No. 7036[24] that, except for the objections to the administrative fines and the disputes of civil servants that began active duty before SIGHIA, the lawsuits arising from the labour and social law, in which SSI or TLI is a party, shall be handled by the labour courts (art. 5 para. 1/b). Similarly, art. 101 SIGHIA assigns the labour courts to resolve the disputes related with the performance of general health insurance and social insurance.

In case of rejection of objection made to SSI about the administrative fines, the administrative courts shall be assigned as the authorized court (art. 102 para. 5 SIGHIA). The administrative courts shall handle the claims of civil servants, who began active duty before SIGHIA, and the claims of their successors (art. 5 para. 1/b LCA).[25]

The persons might refer to the Court of Appeal or Court of Cassation against the final judgments of labour courts on social security (art. 7 para. 3 and art. 8 LCA).

In case of an appeal:

- 9th Civil Division of the Court of Cassation shall be authorized in lawsuits arising from the Unemployment Insurance Act,

[21] OG 22.6.1972, No. 14223.
[22] OG 12.5.2010, No. 27579.
[23] OG 18.4.2014, No. 28976.
[24] OG 25.10.2017, No. 30221.
[25] *See* also: Constitutional Court, 22.12.2011-2010-65/169, OG 25.1.2012, No. 28184.

- 10th Civil Division of the Court of Cassation shall be authorized in lawsuits arising from the social security laws, and especially in recourse lawsuits claimed by SSI in accordance with the social legislation and in debt and declaratory lawsuits claimed against SSI within the scope of social legislation.

It can be seen that these courts actually have significant workload.[26] It is assumed that the actual heavy workload would be reduced by means of courts of appeal being and to be established.

The final authority for the judgments of administrative courts is the Council of State. 11th Chamber of Council of State is authorized for the appeals regarding the retirement procedures of civil servants, whereas 15th Chamber of Council of State is authorized for the appeals regarding the administrative fines originating from the social insurance and public health insurance.[27]

3.2 International Sources of Turkish Social Law

3.2.1 Documents of United Nations

3.2.1.1 Universal Declaration of Human Rights

Universal Declaration of Human Rights accepted by the General Assembly of United Nations on 10/12/1948 is also important for Turkey, which has been the member to United Nations at that date. After accepting that everyone shall have the right to social security as a member of society, art. 22 of Declaration also states that *"everyone is entitled to realization, through national effort and international cooperation and in accordance with the organization and resources of each State, of the economic, social and cultural rights indispensable for his dignity and the free development of his personality"*.

From the aspect of the context of economic, social, and cultural rights specified here, it should be stated that the social security concept is taken from broader aspect and not only the economic security is taken as basis. In this connection, art. 25 Declaration introduces a detailed regulation. Accordingly, it can be seen there that the individual achieved not only the right to have a decent life level but also the right to claim protection against specific risks.[28]

[26] *See:* OG 28.1.2020, No. 31022.

[27] OG 31.12.2016, No. 29935.

[28] Demirbilek (1991), p. 7.

3.2.1.2 International Covenant on Economic, Social and Cultural Rights

Accepted by the General Assembly of United Nations in 1966, the *International Covenant on Economic, Social and Cultural Rights* was accepted by Turkey with the Act No. 4867[29] and put into force by the Cabinet Decree No. 2003/5923 on 10/7/2003.[30] Art. 9 of this Covenant states *"the States Parties to the present Covenant recognize the right of everyone to social security, including social insurance"*. Thus, by warranting the right to social security, a meaning passing beyond the social insurances is pointed out and the concept of social security was not limited to the social insurance.

3.2.2 ILO Conventions

3.2.2.1 Social Security (Minimum Standards) Convention, 1952 (No. 102)

Turkey with Act No. 1451[31] and put into force with the Cabinet Decree No. 7/7964[32] dated 1/4/1974 approved ILO Convention No. 102.

This convention incorporates protection against nine risks. These are the benefits to be offered in cases of disease (healthcare support), disease (sick pays), unemployment, old age, occupational accidents and occupational diseases, disability, death, dependents and family allowances. However, the State to adopt this convention might not provide protection against all the risks specified in convention. Besides that, the State shall provide protection against minimum 3 of specified risks and one of these risks shall be one of the unemployment, old age, occupational accident and occupational disease, disability, and death (art. 2 para. a C 102).

Turkey has approved the provisions of Convention Nr. 102, except for the provisions related with unemployment insurance and family allowances (Sections 4 and 7). However, by accepting the Act No. 4447 in 1999, Turkey started to establish the unemployment insurance since that date. To that date, the *severance pay* was utilized as the substitution of unemployment insurance. On the other hand, Turkey has no specific law specifying the provision of family allowances to the workers. The family allowances and children allowances paid to the public officers are limited in amount. However, the workers seem to be provided family allowance generally via *collective labour agreements* in practice.

[29] OG 18.6.2003, No. 25142.

[30] OG 11.8.2003, No. 25196.

[31] OG 10.8.1971, No. 13922.

[32] OG 15.10.1974, No. 15037.

3.2.2.2 Equality of Treatment (Social Security) Convention, 1962 (No. 118)

ILO Convention No. 118 was approved by Turkey with Act No. 1453[33] and put into force with Cabinet Decree[34] No. 7/6217 on 5/4/1973.

Any State that has approved this convention is responsible for offering the citizens of other member States, who live in that country, with the right to have social security and to benefit from subventions, as well as treating equally in terms of various social security rights (art. 3 para. 1 C 118). However, it can be seen that this provision is conditional upon the reciprocity, except for the refugees and stateless individuals (art. 3 para. 3 and art. 10 para. 1 C 118).

The importance of these provisions, which emphasize the equal treatment in terms of social security, for Turkey that is a country exporting labour force to the other countries has two aspects. Accordingly, if the country in which the Turkish citizens are working has approved C No.118, then they might request to be treated as the citizens of that country. Secondly, as a country that has accepted significant number of refugees due to the Syrian crisis in recent years, Turkey shall not follow the principle of reciprocity for the refugees in terms of equal treatment.

3.2.3 Documents of European Council

3.2.3.1 European Convention on Human Rights

Turkey with Act No. 6366 approved *European Convention on Human Rights and Additional Protocol No. 1.*[35]

However, this convention has no provision directly regulating the right to social security. Besides that, the European Court of Human Rights considers the claims related with the right to social security within the scope of property right as long as they are related with the properties, and the Court also discusses the claims about unjust discrimination in social security within the scope of prohibition of discrimination in art. 14 European Convention on Human Rights.[36] From this aspect, for Turkey that has accepted the compulsory jurisdiction of European Court of Human Rights since year 1989,[37] the European Convention on Human Rights has remarkable importance in terms of the social security.

---

[33] OG 10.8.1971, No. 13922.

[34] OG 9.6.1973, No. 14559.

[35] OG 19.3.1954, No. 8662.

[36] Güzel et al. (2020), p. 37.

[37] Cabinet Decree No. 89/14563 dated 25.9.1989, OG 27.9.1989, No. 20295.

3.2.3.2 European Social Charter

Although Turkey has signed the European Social Charter dated 1961 in 1964, it was approved with Act No. 3581[38] in 1989 and enacted with the Cabinet Decree No. 89/14434 on 7/8/1989.[39]

European Social Charter states that the individuals shall exclusively have:

- The social security right of all the individuals that the workers take care of, as well as the workers themselves,
- The right to social and medical support for all the individuals deprived of sufficient resources,
- The right to enjoy social welfare services (section I nos. 12–14).

Within this context, Turkey is obliged to:

- Keep the social security system at sufficient level that is not lower than required for approving the ILO Convention No. 102, and take the steps that are required in order to gradually improve it to higher levels (art. 12 European Social Charter),
- Provide all the individuals, who do not have sufficient resources and are not capable of obtaining such an opportunity, with the necessary assistance, as well as offering the treatment required in any disease (art. 13 European Social Charter),
- Develop or provide the services that would contribute to the welfare and development of individuals and groups, as well as their adaptation to the social environment (art. 14 European Social Charter).

3.2.3.3 Revised European Social Charter

Revised European Social Charter dated 1996 was approved by Turkey with the Act No. 5547[40] and enacted with the Cabined Decree No. 2007/11907 on 22/3/2007.[41]

The Revised European Social Charter does not incorporate significantly different provisions on social security when compared to the previous form. From this aspect, whereas the ILO Convention No.102 has been taken as minimum basis in previous edition, it is set forth here that the social security system shall be maintained at the level not below the requirements of approving of European Code of Social Security (art. 12 Revised European Social Charter). Regarding providing the social assistances and social services, the previous provisions was repeated (arts. 13 and 14 Revised European Social Charter).

---

[38]OG 4.7.1989, No. 20215.

[39]OG 14.10.1989, No. 20312.

[40]OG 3.10, No. 26308.

[41]OG 9.4.2007, No. 26488.

3.2.3.4 European Code of Social Security

European Code of Social Security dated 1968 was approved by Turkey with the Act No. 2170[42] and enacted with the Cabinet Decree No. 7/17346 on 28/2/1979.[43]

As in ILO Convention No. 102, Turkey approved the provisions of European Code of Social Security other than the provisions of unemployment and family allowances (sections 4 and 7). The reason for this is that the unemployment insurance has not been founded in Turkey at that moment and there was no legal regulation on family allowances except for the civil servants.

As ILO Convention No. 102, also European Code of Social Security classified 9 social risks. But, in order for the member countries to approve the European Code of Social Security, they are obliged to provide social protection against minimum 6 of these 9 risks (art. 2 para. 1/b European Code of Social Security).

3.2.3.5 European Convention on Social Security

European Convention on Social Security dated 1972 and the Supplementary Agreement was approved by Turkey with the Act No. 2023[44] and enacted with the Cabinet Decree No. 7/12537 on 31/8/1976.[45]

Regulating the social security rights of refugees, stateless persons, and immigrants, European Convention on Social Security takes the principles of equal treatment, standardization of rules to be applied, continuing enjoying the rights originating from the social security regulations even when migrating among the participant countries, and the protection of vested or expected rights as basis.[46]

As a labour exporter country, the importance of European Convention on Social Security for Turkey generally concentrates on utilization of the services of Turkish citizens in European countries and their homeland.

3.2.3.6 European Convention on Social and Medical Assistance

European Convention on Social and Medical Assistance dated 1953 was approved by Turkey with the Act No. 1973[47] and enacted with Cabinet Decree No. 7/11753 on 29/4/1976.[48]

---

[42]OG 29.9.1978, No. 16419.

[43]OG 23.7.1979, No 16705.

[44]OG 23.7.1976, No. 15655.

[45]OG 21.2.1977, No. 15857.

[46]*See*: Villars (1983), p. 242.

[47]OG 25.3.1976, No. 15539.

[48]OG 1.8.1976, No. 15664.

Each of the signatory countries of European Convention on Social and Medical Assistance is obliged to provide the citizens of others countries, who are deprived of sufficient means of living, with the social and medical assistance, which are provided to the country's own citizens by the current legal regulations, equally to its own citizens and under the same conditions (art. 1). Thus, the poor citizens of European countries living in Turkey shall have the right to enjoy the social assistance and healthcare services offered in Turkey.

From this aspect, stipulating the Turkish citizenship for the individuals that need of social protection and to be benefit from healthcare services (art. 60 para. 1/c 3 SIGHIA and art. 1 para. 1 Act No. 2022) does not comply with the aforementioned principles of European Convention on Social and Medical Assistance.

3.2.3.7 European Convention on the Legal Status of Migrant Workers

European Convention on the Legal Status of Migrant Workers dated 1977 was approved by Turkey with the Act No. 2257[49] and enacted with the Cabinet Decree No. 8/2006 on 25/11/1980.[50]

It considers the "*immigrant worker*" as another signatory country's citizen, who has been allowed to reside and work in one of the signatory countries (art. 1 para. 1). Through this convention, the signatory states are obliged to treat the immigrant workers in a way equal to their own citizens in terms of the social security rights. Moreover, the signatory States shall also make effort in order to protect the rights of immigrant workers and their family members, which have been vested in other countries via bilateral or multilateral agreements (art. 18).

On the other hand, for the signatory States, European Convention on the Legal Status of Migrant Workers sets the obligation of offering social and medical support to the immigrant workers and their family members living in their country based on the principles set by international agreements and especially the principles of European Convention on Social and Medical Assistance (art 19).

Since Turkey exports labour force to EU countries and has signed social security agreements on this subject, the importance of European Convention on the Legal Status of Migrant Workers is unilateral in practice. In other words, this convention is more important for the workers migrated from Turkey to the European countries. However, it is also obvious that these obligations would apply also to Turkey regarding the EU countries' citizens living in Turkey.

---

[49]OG 6.1.1980, No. 16861.

[50]OG 27.1.1981, No. 17233.

3.2.4 Bilateral Social Security Agreements

By signing bilateral social security agreements, Turkey having many workers abroad aims to enable its citizens to benefit from social protection during the period, in which they live in foreign country. On this subject, art. 62 Const. obliges the State to take measure required for ensuring the social security of Turkish citizens working in foreign countries.

Name of country	Date of signature	Date of entry into force	Scope (branch of insurance)	
			Long-term	Short-term
01. United Kingdom	9/9/1959	1/6/1961	Yes	–
02. Germany	30/4/1964	1/11/1965	Yes	Yes
03. Holland	5/4/1966	1/2/1968	Yes	Yes
04. Belgium	4/7/1966	1/5/1968	Yes	Yes
05. Austria	12/10/1966	1/10/1969	Yes	Yes
06. Switzerland	1/5/1969	1/1/1972	Yes	–
07. France	20/1/1972	1/8/1973	Yes	Yes
08. Denmark	22/1/1976	1/2/1978	Yes	–
09. Sweden	30/6/1978	1/5/1981	Yes	–
10. Norway	20/7/1978	1/61981	Yes	–
11. Libya	13/9/1984	1/9/1985	Yes	–
12. Northern Cyprus	9/3/1987	1/12/1988	Yes	Yes
13. Macedonia	6/7/1998	1/7/2000	Yes	Yes
14. Azerbaijan	17/7/1998	9/8/2001	Yes	Yes
15. Romania	6/7/1999	1/3/2003	Yes	Yes
16. Georgia	11/12/1998	20/11/2003	Yes	–
17. Bosnia-Herzegovina	27/5/2003	1/9/2004	Yes	Yes
18. Canada	19/6/1998	1/1/2005	Yes	–
19. Quebec (Canada)	15/10/1998	1/1/2005	Yes	–
20. Czech Republic	28/6/2001	1/1/2005	Yes	Yes
21. Albania	15/7/1998	1/2/2005	Yes	Yes
22. Luxembourg	8/12/2004	1/6/2006	Yes	Yes
23. Croatia	6/12/2006	1/6/2012	Yes	Yes
24. Slovakia	25/1/2007	1/7/2013	Yes	No
25. Serbia	26/10/2009	1/12/2013	Yes	Yes
26. Italy	8/5/2012	1/8/2015	Yes	Yes
27. South Korea	1/8/2012	1/6/2015	Yes	No
28. Montenegro	15/3/2012	1/12/2015	Yes	Yes
29. Tunisia	28/5/2013	1/4/2018	Yes	Yes
30. Hungary	24/2/2015	1/4/2018	Yes	Yes
31. Moldova	5/5/2017	1/6/2020	Yes	No

Source: www.sgk.gov.tr

Accordingly, Turkey has signed social security agreements with 31 countries at this moment.

In general, the bilateral social security agreements that Turkey has signed with various countries offers right such as:

- Equal treatment for the citizens of both countries in terms of rights and obligations,
- Joining the insurance periods, which have been spent in another signatory country, in determining if the person qualifies for the benefit,
- Enabling the insurance holder and his/her family members to benefit from the healthcare services in case of a disease when they are in another signatory state,
- Even if they live in the other country, enabling the family members to benefit from family allowances (allowance for children and increases),
- Putting any insurance holder on a pension, who turned the age that is required for pension after returning to the other signatory country,
- Enabling any insurance holder, who qualifies for the pension because of his/her services in a signatory State, to continue receiving pension after moving to another signatory state,
- In case of the death of insurance holder, having the insurance holder's family members living in another signatory country to be put on survivor benefits, as well as making a lump sum payment to them.[51]

References

Demirbilek T (1991) İnsan Hakları Evrensel Beyannamesinde Yer Alan Sosyal Güvenlik Hakkının Türk Endüstri İlişkileri Sistemi Açısından İncelenmesi. Kamu-İş İş Hukuku ve İktisat Dergisi 2 (8):3–9

Güzel AG, Okur AR, Caniklioğlu N (2020) Sosyal Güvenlik Hukuku, 18th edn. Beta Publishing, Istanbul

Okur AR, Ergin H (2008) Türkiye'de Sağlık Reformunun Geçmişi ve Geleceği. In: Prof.Dr. Devrim Ulucan'a Armağan. Legal Publishing, Istanbul, pp 599–699

Villars C (çev. Şakar M) (1983) Avrupa Konseyi Çerçevesinde Göçmen İşçilerin Sosyal Güvenliği. Yargıtay Dergisi 9(3):239–252

[51] *See*: http://www.sgk.gov.tr/wps/portal/sgk/tr/emekli/yurtdisi_islemler/sosyal_guvenlik_sozlesmeleri.

Part II
Organization of Social Insurance

Chapter 4
Administrative Structure and Inspection of Social Insurance

4.1 Structural Organization

4.1.1 Organization Models

Nowadays, the social security institutions constitute a remarkable social and economic potential because of the budget they have, the personnel they employ, and the medical care facilities they own. These cannot be taken out of control and be isolated from the democratic order. Accordingly, within the free zone provided by the legal order, the social security institutions' administrative bodies shall be provided with a certain level of freedom. Otherwise, the risks of controlling the power of social security institutions by the central authority and the risk of the use of this power by the central authority in the way not complying with the objectives of social security may arise.

The management of social security system of the State is mainly based on two types of organization.[1] In first of them, the official authorities execute the administration of social security in a hierarchical manner and within the scope of governmental administration. In this system, the insurance holders and employers shall not participate in making the decision related with social security contributions that are directly related with them.

The second social security system appears in the form of indirect management of the State and it is based on the participation of relevant authorities through the autonomous public bodies. Thus, in the autonomous management model, the administration of social security is assigned to the representatives of insurance holders (solely or together with the representatives of employers).

Furthermore, the representatives of central authority and other public institutions are given role in determining the orientation. At this point, the participation of representatives of insurance holders and employers in the management is because

[1]*See* in detail: Centel (1997), pp. 25–37.

T. Centel, *Turkish Social Law*, https://doi.org/10.1007/978-3-030-64704-9_4

they are the parties paying the premiums. The representatives of central authority shall participate because the State is responsible for ensuring the law-abidingness and the provision of social security.

4.1.2 *Turkish Model Having Mixed Character*

The social insurance management in Turkey does not exactly fit to any of aforementioned systems, but it is a system combining various characteristics from both and, thus, it can be called mixed. Accordingly, it can be seen that the central authority plays role in management and the autonomous management model does not exactly apply. Hence, SSI operates within the body of Ministry of Family, Labour and Social Services (central authority) rather than the retirement fund. However, also the representatives of parties playing role in establishment of general assembly and board of management (representatives of insurance holders, employers, civil servants, and those receiving pension from SSI) are given roles within the body of its organs. TLI managing the unemployment insurance has also the similar characteristics.

Besides that, the relevant parties shall have no effect on the decisions regarding the social insurances. Even though the most important and top-level decisions shall be made by the general assembly, the general assemblies of social insurance institutions have generally the character of advisory committees and they have no authority to acquit the boards of management.

Moreover, the head of SSI and the general director of TLI that are not elected but appointed by the political authority and are responsible before the board of management rather than the general assembly naturally presides to the boards of management; in case of equality of votes in making any decision, their position plays the determinant role. In this case, it becomes impossible for relevant representatives to participate in management (making the decisions) in the real manner (the autonomous management model).

4.2 SSI

Within the scope of restructuring in social security system, regarding the management of social insurances, *Social Security Institution Act* No. 5502[2] was enacted on 16/5/2006. This act terminated the presence of the social security institutions (Social Insurance Institution, Social Insurance Institution for Self-Employed, and Retirement Fund) that have fulfilled the management of social insurances in previous period, and it also established *SSI* to undertake their responsibilities.

---

[2]OG 20.5.2006, No. 26173.

SSI is financially and administratively autonomous and has public legal personality; the cases that are not covered by the provisions of Act No. 5502 and PD No. 4 are subjected to the provisions of private law. SSI, headquarter of which is located in Ankara, is in relation with the Ministry of Family, Labour and Social Services (art. 403 para. 2 PD No. 4).

4.2.1 Organs of SSI

4.2.1.1 General Assembly of SSI

The general assembly is not a decision-making body and it is of advisory body character. It has to hold a meeting once every three years under normal conditions. However, the Minister of Family, Labour and Social Services or one third of total number of members might request an extraordinary meeting (art. 407 para. 3 PD No. 4).

The duties of general assembly are specified in art. 407 para. 2 PD No. 4 as follows:

- Providing opinions and suggestions about the social policies and relevant practices,
- Evaluating the budgets and balance sheets of SSI, activity reports, performance programs, mid- and long-term income/expense balances, and recent actuarial costs of SSI, and to provide opinion,
- Offering suggestions regarding the performance objectives of the next period, and
- Selecting the permanent and reserve members of Board of Management.

General assembly consists of 75 members. 21 of them are the representatives of the SSI and government, whereas 54 members were the representatives of workers, employers, union of civil servants, occupational organizations of self-employed persons, and those receiving income or pension from SSI. It can be stated that this body is based on the parity representation and has a democratic structure. Besides that, the advisory organ character of general assembly prevents this tripartite structure from playing determinant role in policies of SSI.[3]

Moreover, since the general assembly holds meeting once every three years and it is authorized for selecting only some of members of board of management (those assigned with election), it can be seen that the general assembly does not have significantly functional role in decision-making mechanism.[4]

---

[3]Güzel et al. (2020), p. 220.

[4]Alper (2006), p. 44.

4.2.1.2 Board of Management of SSI

The board of management is the decision-making body and, as the top management organ of SSI. It undertakes the top management and decision-making authority and responsibility (art. 408 para. 1 PD No. 4).

Board of management consists of 12 members; 6 members representing the central authority and 6 members representing employers, workers, self-employed workers, civil servants, and parties receiving income and pension from SSI. It can be stated that this structure seems to be an equalitarian one. However, although the decisions are made by the majority of votes participating in the meeting, the fact that party incorporating the vote of president shall considered as the majority in case of equality of votes deteriorates this image. Hence, the representatives of social parties constitute the minority in terms of decision-making and management in SSI. It is undoubtedly clear that this does not comply with the democratic and autonomous management perspective.[5]

4.2.1.3 General Directorate of SSI

Head of SSI is assigned by a decision of the President of Turkey (art. 2 para. 2 PD No. 3). He/she also presides to the board of management (art. 408 para. 1 PD No. 4).

Since the political authority makes the assignment of the head of SSI, the political power is enabled to intervene to the management of SSI. However, the position of the head shall be kept away from the political power.

Furthermore, given the background in this regard, it can be seen that the number of honourable individuals, who could resist such arbitrary treatments, remains limited. From this aspect, one of the rare persons is Professor *Hirsch*. In the past, Professor Hirsch rejected the Minister of Labour for paying 1,000,000 TRL for the expense of his ministry from the social security contributions paid by the insurance holders. Then, the Ministry of Labour of that period reminded to Professor *Hirsch* that the Social Insurance Institution is affiliated with his ministry. In response, Professor Hirsch has immediately resigned.[6]

Besides that, the bachelor's degree on a relevant discipline, and required skills, competencies, and experience were not specified among the qualifications that the head should have. On this subject, it was considered sufficient for the head to be graduated from any university offering minimum 4 years of education (art. 3 para. 1 PD No. 3). Thus, the individuals having no experience, knowledge, and specialty on social security might be assigned via the common decree. It is clear that this enables the assignment of unqualified individuals based on the political preferences.

On the other hand, the organization of SSI consists of central and field offices affiliated with the general directorate (art. 410 para. 1 PD No. 4). Among them, the

[5] *See* also: Güzel et al. (2020), pp. 220–221.

[6] Özbek (2006), pp. 170, 237, 294 and 297–298.

central office incorporates the main service units (art. 410 para. 2 PD No. 4). The field offices consist of "*provincial directorate of social services*" and "*social security centres*" affiliated with these directorates (art. 427 para. 1 PD No. 4).

The main service units of directorate incorporate various general directorates and chamber presidencies. Here, the main general directorates playing prominent role are the "*general directorate of pension services*" executing the social insurance operations (art. 414 PD No. 4), the "*general directorate of insurance premiums*" tracking and collecting the premiums (art. 415 PD No. 4), and the "*general directorate of general health insurance*" monitoring the health insurance transactions (art. 416 PD No. 4).

The field organization of this directorate consists of "*provincial directorates of social security*" in every province and "*social security centres*" to be established in affiliation with these provincial directorates (art. 427 para. 1 PD No. 4).

4.3 TLI

4.3.1 Foundation of TLI

In Act No. 4904 *on the Foundation of Turkish Labour Institution* dated 06.25.2003,[7] the unemployment insurance services were separated from SSI and assigned to TLI (Turkish Employment Agency).

The tasks of TLI were determined as assisting the activities aiming to establish the national employment policy, protecting the employment, and preventing the unemployment, as well as executing the unemployment insurance operations (art. 617 para. 1/a PD No. 4).

As well as SSI, TLI is in relation with (not affiliated with) the Ministry of Family, Labour and Social Services; it is a financially and administratively autonomous institution that has a legal entity (art. 65 para. 2 PD No. 4).

4.3.2 Organs of TLI

4.3.2.1 General Assembly of TLI

The general assembly holds its meeting upon the call of Minister of Family, Labour and Social Services once every two years in November. Whenever he/she deems necessary, the Minister of Family, Labour and Social Services is entitled to request an extraordinary meeting (art. 619 para. 2 PD No. 4).

[7] OG 5.7.2003, No. 25159.

In terms of its responsibilities, the general assembly is an advisory organ, because the duties of general assembly are mainly to evaluate, to assist, and to offer suggestions (art. 619 para. 3 PD No. 4).

The general assembly consists of the representatives of central authority and the representatives of relevant parties (worker and employer confederations, union of commodity exchanges, confederation of merchants and artisans, confederation of disabled persons, union of Turkish agricultural chambers, higher education institutions, and unions of civil servants) (art. 619 para. 1 PD No. 4).

This structure of general assembly is based on the parity character of presentation and it may be deemed democratic. However, since the general assembly holds meeting once every two years and it is not given the function of advisory council, this situation prevents the representatives of relevant parties other than the central authority from playing determinant role within this structure.

4.3.2.2 Board of Management of TLI

The board of management consists of three members representing the central authority and three members representing the workers, employers, artisans, and merchants (art. 620 para. 1 PD No. 4). It can be stated that this structure seems equalitarian. However, the fact that party incorporating the vote of president is considered as the majority in case of equality of votes (art. 620 para. 2 PD No. 4) prevents the active participation of the representatives of social parties in the management.

4.3.2.3 General Directorate of TLI

General director of TLI is assigned via a decision signed by the President of Turkey (art. 2 para. 2 PD No. 3) and also naturally presides to the board of management, as well as being a natural member of this board (art. 620 para. 1 PD No. 4).

It was determined to be enough to have bachelor's degree from any higher education institution offering 4-year education (art. 6 para. 1/b PD No. 3). However, since the general director is assigned via a presidential decision, the political authority might play effective role and the practices that do not comply with the principles of social security might be observed.

On the other hand, the organization of TLI consists of central and field offices affiliated with the general directorate (art. 621 para. 1 PD No. 4). Besides the central office consisting of various service units, the field organization consists of *"provincial directorates of labour and employment agency"* and the service units to be established in affiliation with them (art. 624 para. 1 PD No. 4).

Moreover, it was decided to establish *"employment and occupational education commissions"* in the provinces. One of these commissions' most important tasks related with the unemployment insurance is to determine the measures for maintaining and improving the employment and preventing the unemployment, as well as providing the relevant institutions and bodies with suggestions on this subject (art. 625 para. 3 PD No. 4).

It was stated that the decisions of these commissions, in which the representatives of social parties play role, are binding decisions, and they were projected to prepare an action plan about the decisions to be made, to determine the responsible institutions and bodies, and to follow the results (art. 625 para. 4 PD No. 4).

4.4 Auditing of Social Insurance

4.4.1 External Inspection of SSI and TLI

External inspection on the social insurances was completely left to the central authority. Hence, the *"State Supervisory Council"* affiliated with the Presidency of Republic is authorized for inspecting SSI and TLI. Accordingly, upon the request by President of the State, the State Supervisory Council is authorized for performing any sort of investigation, inspection, and examination in SSI or TLI, as well as all other public institutions and bodies (art. 108 para. 1 Const.).

On the other hand, it has been stipulated that financial goals of SSI are to be determined and monitored over time. Accordingly, SSI has been assigned to achieve the transfer amount, namely separate amounts for social insurances and general health insurance allocated in the central administration budget, the three-year transfer projection as well as the long-term retirement and general health insurance financing goals. Within this context, a commission upon recommendation of the board of directors by October of each year, to be implemented for the following year, shall determine SSI shall conduct financing goals and secretariat works of such commission. Such commission consists under the chairmanship of the Ministry of Family, Labour and Social Services, of deputy ministers of Ministry of Treasury and Finance and Ministry of Health, head of SSI and other members to be assigned by the Minister of Family, Labour and Social Services (art. 430 para. 1 PD No. 4).

In this regard, SSI is obligated to take necessary measures of achieving the goals to be set by such commission, submit regulatory amendment proposals to the Ministry of Family, Labour and Social Services, and in cases outside the scope of its authority, to submit necessary measures for relevant institutions as well as their reasons to the Ministry of Family, Labour and Social Services. As such, public administrations are also obligated to confer on SSI for regulations and practices that will directly affect the achievement of SSI's financing goals (art. 430 para. 2 PD No. 4).

Furthermore, the head of SSI is obligated to submit, orally and in writing, a report, including the taken and planned measures for achieving the goals, attained results as well as the recommendations made to public administrations and their outcomes, semi-annually to the President of the State and relevant commissions of the Turkish parliament. And in cases that such set goals are not, or possibly will not be, achieved by the declared date, SSI shall also report and announce the reasons of such failure as well as necessary measures in writing to the Ministry of Family, Labour and Social Services and to the public (art. 430 paras 3 and 4 PD No. 4).

4.4.2 Inspection by SSI

The accurate implementation of legislation provisions regarding the social insurance necessitates an effective inspection activity. Moreover, given the level of unrecorded economy and uninsured workers in Turkey, the importance of inspection to be made by SSI becomes more apparent.

Since the institution that is responsible for ensuring the implementation of previsions of social insurance legislation is SSI, it is clear that SSI would perform these inspections. For this purpose, the *"directorate of guidance and inspection"* was founded within the body of SSI. This unit is responsible for supervising the implementation of provisions related with social security, preventing the unrecorded employment, struggling with the misconduct regarding the social insurance, collecting information and documents related with its tasks, evaluating the reports submitted by the inspectors of SSI, and performing the investigation and examination about the individuals that have signed contract with SSI (art. 418 PD No. 4).

In the professional life, the officers assigned for examination and investigation by SSI inspect the transactions regarding the employment of uninsured workers. However, the inspection and control of insurance transactions by workplaces belonging to the military bodies are to be performed by the military labour inspectors (art. 59 para. 1 SIGHIA).

Social security inspectors, who are the officers authorized with the inspection and control by SSI, are responsible for inspection, control, and investigations regarding the implementation of social security legislation provisions. The official reports to be prepared by these inspectors are valid until proven otherwise. The employers and workers are obliged to obey the call of inspectors and to answer their questions, to provide them with the records, documents, and evidences they request, to assist them in fulfilling their duties, and to meet their demands immediately in this manner. Besides that, while the social security inspectors fulfil their duties, all the civil servants shall assist them and make things easier for them (art. 59 para. 2 SIGHIA).

On the other hand, during the inspections in workplaces, the inspector officers of public authorities also determine if the workers are insured and if the gross amount of income submitted to SSI and the number of days and workers comply with the reality, as well as reporting the underreporting and uninsured employment cases to SSI. Upon these reports, SSI shall take the necessary measures and commence the legal proceedings (art. 59 para. 7 SIGHIA).

4.4.3 *Judicial Inspection*

The labour courts are the courts authorized for resolving all the disputes arising from SIGHIA (art. 101 SIGHIA, art. 5 para. 1/b LCA).

Regarding the disputes arising from SIGHIA and other social security legislations (except for the lawsuits for determining the period of insurance), it is compulsory to apply the SSI before filing a lawsuit. If no response is received from SSI within 60 days after the application, then it means that the application is rejected. Accordingly, in order to be able to file a lawsuit against SSI, it is compulsory for the requests to be rejected or considered rejected. The time spent during the application made to SSI shall not be taken into account when calculating the limitation date and period of prescription (art. 4 para. 1 LCA).

Moreover, before applying to the court regarding the objections to the insurance premiums, the objection shall be discussed and finalized within the body of SSI and then the person might apply to the court (arts 85 and 86 para. 7 SIGHIA). Similarly, regarding the objections related with minimum job rates, the person should apply firstly to the *"minimum labour determination commission"* and then to the court (art. 85 paras 6 and 9 SIGHIA).

On the other hand, against the administrative fines applied by SSI, the person shall apply firstly to SSI and (if SSI rejects the application) then to the administrative court (art. 102 para. 8 SIGHIA).

4.4.4 *Social Insurance Supreme Health Commission*

Regarding the social security practice, some of the subjects require specific expertness. The leading one among them is the issue on medical subjects. Accordingly, in order to resolve the disputes regarding the medical subjects, the *"Social Insurance Supreme Health Commission"* was established.

The supreme health commission consists of 12 physician members consisting of 1 member from each of following parties; Ministry of Defence, Ministry of Health, Ministry of Family, Labour and Social Services, Council of Higher Education, confederations representing the highest number of employers, workers, and civil servants, Turkish Union of Chambers and Commodity Exchanges, Turkish Confederation of Traders and Artisans, Turkish Medical Association, Union of Turkish Agricultural Chambers, and SSI (art. 58 para. 1 SIGHIA). The commission is presided by a member elected from and by its members (art. 58 para. 2 SIGHIA).

This commission examines and finalizes the decisions that have been made by SSI about the disablement and incapacity degrees of insurance holders and then been subject to an objection. The commission has to hear a specialist physician assigned by the commission upon the request of insurance holder or his/her beneficiaries (art. 58 para. 4 SIGHIA).

Supreme health commission finalizes the disputes such as if any disease other than those listed in the list of occupational diseases shall be considered occupational disease. In addition, the supreme health commission also finalizes the objections against the decisions made by SSI based on the health commission reports regarding the vocational incapacity and inability (art. 95 para. 2 SIGHIA).

The decisions made by the supreme health commission are final only from administrative aspect. Accordingly, no one shall object to any administrative organ regarding the decisions of supreme health commission. However, it is also legally possible to file a lawsuit in labour courts against the decisions of supreme health commission.[8]

4.5 Legal Character of Bodies of SSI

4.5.1 Legal Entity of Social Security Institutions

SSI has public legal entity and is administratively and financially autonomous, and it is also subjected to the provisions of private law in cases that are not covered in the provisions of SIGHIA and PD No. 4. It is accepted as the "*relevant institution*" of Ministry of Family, Labour and Social Services (art. 403 para. 2 PD No. 4). The same principles apply also to TLI (art. 615 para. 2 PD No. 4).

Thus, the principle that the social security institutions are among the institutions affiliated with the Ministry of Family, Labour and Social Services was quitted. Hence, the PD No. 4 considers SSI and TLI among the "*relevant institutions*" (arts 403 and 615 PD No. 4).

On the other hand, it is very difficult to determine to which of private and public law provisions the social security institutions are subjected, because the social security institutions both have public legal entity and are subjected to private law provisions (arts 403 and 615 PD No. 4). It is a contradiction that the public legal entities are subjected to the provisions of private law instead of the public law. On this subject, it would be more appropriate to accept that the social security institutions are subject to private law provisions only for their industrial and commercial activities and to the provisions of public law in all other cases.

4.5.2 Operations and Assets of Social Security Institutions

In cases not covered by SIGHIA, the provisions applied to private insurances shall not be taken into consideration while implementing the provisions of SIGHIA (art. 98 para. 1 SIGHIA). Accordingly, the social insurance transactions of social security

[8]Plenary Session of CC, 28.6.1976-6/4, OG 26.7.1976, No. 15658.

institutions are not subject to TCC and the other provisions applying to the insurance companies.

Besides that, the estates and assets of social security institutions and their claims including the bank accounts shall not be seized (art. 35 para. 3 Act No. 5502; art. 1 para. 4 Act No. 4904).

On the other hand, the receivables of social security institutions are among the privileged receivables (art. 35 para. 2 Act No. 5502; art. 1 para. 4 Act No. 4904). Moreover, SSI has been waived from any sort of claims and enforcement procedures and the obligation of making down payment (art. 35 para. 4 Act No. 5502).

References

Alper Y (2006) Sosyal Güvenlik Sisteminde Reform: Sosyal Güvenlik Kurumu Kanunu: Değişiklikler, Yenilikler ve Kurumsal Değerlendirme Analizi. Mercek 11(43):40–55

Centel T (1997) Sosyal Güvenlikte Yapısal Değişim. Publication of Türkiye Metal Sanayicileri Sendikası (MESS), Istanbul

Güzel A, Okur AR, Caniklioğlu N (2020) Sosyal Güvenlik Hukuku, 18th edn. Beta Publishing, Istanbul

Özbek N (2006) Cumhuriyet Türkiyesi'nde Sosyal Güvenlik ve Sosyal Politikalar. Publication of Emeklilik Gözetim Merkezi and Tarih Vakfı, Istanbul

Chapter 5
Financial Structure and Funding of Social Insurance

5.1 Sources of Fund

5.1.1 Funding Practice

Funding a social security system is a complicated subject, which incorporates significantly complex problems, under the economic conditions of Turkey, as in other countries. A significant portion of problems on this subject is related with the sources of income. Accordingly, the ratio of Turkey's social security expenses including the medical care, social assistance, and pension expenses to the gross domestic product exceeded beyond 11%. Thus, the social security expenses of Turkey are between those of countries having mid-level and high level of income. Similarly, Turkey's ratio of public pension expenses to the gross domestic product is very high because of the elderly and dependent population. Hence, the ratio of population turned the age 65 years or higher to the population aged between 20 and 64 years is 10% in Turkey, whereas the ratio of public pension expenses to gross domestic product is about 6%.[1]

The most important source of revenue in Turkish social security system is the premiums collected. These premiums are mainly collected from the insurance holders and employers. Only in the unemployment insurance, the state pays 1% contribution for each of the workers (art. 49 para. 1 UIA).

When compared with the income obtained from the premiums, the direct contribution of state to the system remains insignificant. However, first of all, the State funds the annual budget deficits of the social security institutions. The factors such as difficulties in collecting the premiums, increase in unemployment, ageing of population, and increase in the number of retired individuals indicate that this fund transfer from the Treasury to SSI will continue.[2]

---

[1]Kolçak and Arpa (2015), p. 23.

[2]Tuncay and Ekmekçi (2019), pp. 168–169.

T. Centel, *Turkish Social Law*, https://doi.org/10.1007/978-3-030-64704-9_5

Besides that, SIGHIA emphasizes that the State shall contribute to funding the long-term insurance branches and public health insurance. Accordingly, the State shall contribute to SSI by 25% of the premiums monthly collected by SSI for disability, old age, and survivors insurances and general health insurance. The aforementioned amount to be calculated as the Treasury shall pay the State contribution to SSI within 15 days following the date of request (art. 81 para. 2 SIGHIA).

It should be noted that this is a very important improvement for Turkey,[3] because, in the past, the State in Turkey has preferred utilizing the collected insurance premiums in bridging the deficits of government business enterprises, which have been affiliated with the government, and buying government bonds (in other words, using these funds as a cheap credit) rather than directly supporting the social security institutions.[4]

The indirect contributions of the State to the social security institutions developed as the tax immunity granted to the social insurances in Turkey. It is controversial to what extent and how a government contribution they have been.[5]

Nowadays, it can be possible to say that the same applies to the unemployment insurance funds. Accordingly, it was projected to allocate a significant portion of interest incomes of unemployment insurance funds to the investments within the scope of *South-eastern Anatolia Project* between the years 2008 and 2012 (prov. art. 6 para. 1/a-b UIA). Even though it was projected that the aforementioned funds would be transferred from the revenues to be received from investments back to the unemployment insurance funds (prov. art. 6 para. 1/c), this could not be achieved yet. Besides that, this legal practice was decided to be constitutional by the Constitutional Court.[6]

5.1.2 Funding Methods

In funding the social insurances in Turkey, the methods that are used widely are the capitalization for the long-term insurance branches and pay-as-you-go for the short term insurances branches. Furthermore, it can be emphasized that the capitalization method is the dominant funding method in Turkish social insurance system.[7]

It can be asserted that it is not necessary to implement the capitalization method because the percentage of young population within the general population of Turkey is high and the number of insured workers is increasing. On the other hand, it is not possible to ignore that the social insurance funds are necessary for the economic development in Turkey. Hence, as long as the aforementioned funds are used

[3]*See* also: Güzel et al. (2020), pp. 232–233.

[4]*See*: Tunçomağ (1990), pp. 94–97.

[5]Tunçomağ (1990), pp. 88–89.

[6]Constitutional Court, 4.2.2010, 2008-57/26, OG 22.10.2010, No. 27737.

[7]Çelikoğlu (1994), p. 113; Tuncay and Ekmekçi (2019), p. 171; Tunçomağ (1990), p. 91.

efficiently, they might significantly accelerate the economic development. If the insurance funds are used in ineffective manner, all the weight of economic development is loaded on the insured workers having low level of income and this is not in harmony with the social justice.[8]

On this subject, Turkey could not efficiently make use of the funds achieved form capitalization method and it now faces with gradually increasing funding problems. Thus, the institutions of Turkish social security system have adopted mainly the capitalization method in harmony with the legal regulations. However, the funds of social security institutions have lost their values due to the inflation. The government has utilized the social security reserves as a source of fund, and the use of these reserves has been left to the initiative of social security institutions. When the social security institutions' funds could not receive any revenue higher than the inflation, Turkey has faced with severe funding problems.[9]

5.2 Premiums

5.2.1 Premium Rates

5.2.1.1 Premium Rates of Short-Term Insurance Branches

The premium rate for the short-term insurance branches is 2% of income of the insured worker. This premium is completely paid by the employer. The President of the State is authorized for increasing this rate up to 2.5% and decreasing down to 1.5% (art. 81 para. 1/c SIGHIA).

5.2.1.2 Premiums for Disability, Old Age and Survivor Insurances

The premium for disability, old age and survivor insurances is 20% of the income of insurance holder. The insurance holder pays 9%, and the employer 11% (art. 81 para. 1/a SIGHIA).

5.2.1.3 Premium for General Health Insurance

The premium for general health insurance is 12.5% of the income for the insurance holder subject to the short- and long-term insurance branches. The insurance holder pays 5%, and the employer resting 7.5%. Moreover, those insured only with the

[8]Tunçomağ (1990), pp. 92–93.

[9]Çelikoğlu (1994), p. 125.

general health insurance shall pay 12% of their income as the insurance premium (art. 81 para. 1/f SIGHIA).

5.2.1.4 Premium for Unemployment Insurance

The total premium rate for the unemployment insurance is 4%. The insurance holder pays 1%, the employer 2%, and the State resting 1% (art. 49 para. 1 UIA).

5.2.1.5 Social Security Support Premium

The retirees, who are the insurance holder of previous periods and still working, shall pay the social security support premium. The social security support premium is 30% of the income. The insured worker pays 7.5% of this premium, and the employer resting 22.5%. However, in addition to the aforementioned premium, the employer shall also pay an additional 2% as short-term insurance premium. Accordingly, the premium rate that shall be paid by employer for the working retirees increases to 24.5%.

5.2.1.6 Premium for Agricultural Workers

Insured agricultural workers shall pay totally 32.5% premium, 12.5% of which is the premium for public health insurance (art. 30 Act No. 2925).

5.2.1.7 Premium Rates of Trainees

The premium rate of trainees shall be applied as 5.5%. 1% of this premium is for short-term insurance branches and resting 4.5% is for general health insurance (art. 81 para. 1/d SIGHIA). The premium of trainees shall be paid over minimum wage limit.

5.2.2 *Calculating the Basis*

5.2.2.1 Incomes of Insured Workers

First, the income earned by the insurance holder within that month shall be taken into account while calculating the premiums (art. 80 para. 1/a 1 SIGHIA). Accordingly, the gross amounts paid to the insurance holder, which are paid on hourly, daily, weekly, monthly, and annual basis and are continuous, shall be considered as income (art. 3 para. 1/12 SIGHIA). From this aspect, the Court of Cassation decided that "*the compensation payment for education*" paid to the teachers working at private schools shall be added to the earning subject to premium.[10]

Second, the payments paid to the insurance holder within that month as premium, bonus, and such payments, and the premiums paid to the private retirement insurance and private health insurances shall be taken into account while calculating the premiums (art. 80 para. 1/a 2 SIGHIA).

Moreover, in accordance with the decisions of government and judicial authorities, the payments made to the insurance holder shall be taken into account in calculating the premiums (art. 80 para. 1/a 3 SIGHIA). These payments are the wages, overtime pays, bonuses, and/or the payments having the characteristics of bonus, which are paid because of the decisions of government and judicial authorities.

Besides that, if a decision is made regarding paying the cumulative deficiency payment according to the collective labour contract, this deficiency payment shall be considered within the income of that month, with which they are related, and the premium shall be calculated over that income.[11]

5.2.2.2 Incomes of Self-Employed Insurance Holders

Since the self-employed insurance holders have no constant income, a separate regulation was necessitated for this category. From this aspect, the self-employed insurance holders' earning subject to premium shall be equal to 30 folds of their average daily income declared by the self-employed person's own between the minimum and maximum daily earning. The earning of those, who do not a statement, shall be calculated as 30 folds of minimum daily earning (art. 80 para. 2/a SIGHIA).

5.2.2.3 Incomes of Civil Servants

For the insured civil servants receiving their salaries in accordance with the acts on civil servants, the premiums shall be calculated by taking salaries, special position allowances, occupational allowances, and additional allowances into account. Besides that, the payments made for the deputation or secondary position shall not be taken into consideration (art. 80 para. 3 SIGHIA).

---

[10]CC, 10th Civ. Div., 13.6.2002, 4245/5427, Yargıtay Kararları Dergisi, 11 (2002), pp. 1661–1663, CC, 21st Civ. Div., 11.7.2000, 4716/5504, Yargıtay Kararları Dergisi, 4 (2001), pp. 571–573.

[11]Sözer (2019), p. 211.

5.2.2.4 Incomes of Individuals Subject Only to the General Health Insurance

Since the individuals being protected only by the general health insurance have no income arising from an employment relationship, the calculation of their earning subject to premium is slightly different. Accordingly, the earnings subject to premium for foreigners subject only to the general health insurance and the unemployed and non-dependent citizens shall be calculated by multiplying two-folds of minimum daily income level with 30, whereas the premium of individuals receiving unemployment benefit or part-time wage shall be calculated based on their earning subject to premium (art. 80 para. 4 SIGHIA).

5.2.2.5 Incomes of Insured Agricultural Workers

In determining the insured agricultural workers' earing subject to premium, the minimum daily earning will be taken as basis (art. 31 Act No. 2925). Moreover, the premium to be collected from these workers shall be calculated over 15 day (not 30 days) per month and 180 days per year (art. 32 Act No. 2925).

5.2.3 Incomes Not Included in the Basis

5.2.3.1 Incomes That Shall Be Totally Excluded from the Basis

Art.80 of SIGHIA separately specifies the incomes that shall not be included in calculating the premium. These are:

- Benefits in-kind,
- Death, birth, and marriage benefits,
- Mobile duty allowances,
- Duty travel allowances,
- Severance allowance and lump sum payments having the characteristics of termination compensation or severance pay,
- Exploration payment,
- Notice pay,
- Accident benefit,
- Food, child, and family allowances to be determined annually by the institution,
- Private health insurance and private retirement insurance premium contributions paid by the employers in behalf of the insured workers (monthly total amount shall not exceed 30% of minimum wage) (art. 80 para. 1/b SIGHIA).

5.2.3.2 Incomes That Shall Be Partially Excluded

The incomes that shall be partially excluded from the earning subject to premium are the food, child, and family allowances to be determined annually by SSI and the private health insurance and private retirement insurance premium contributions paid by the employers on behalf of the insurance holder (monthly total amount shall not exceed 30% of minimum wage) (art. 80 para. 1/b SIGHIA).

Accordingly, if the amount of food, child, and family allowance increments paid to the insurance holders by the employer is higher than the amount determined by SSI and the private health insurance and private retirement insurance premium contributions paid by the employers in behalf of the insurance holders is higher than 30% of monthly minimum wage, then the exceeding amount shall be included in the income to be taken as base for premium.

5.2.4 *Determining the Daily Income*

5.2.4.1 Fundamentals

The daily earning subject to premium is calculated by dividing the monthly earning subject to premium by 30. If the insurance holders received an earning subject to premium every day during the month, then the daily earning shall be one thirtieth of his/her income for that month. Regardless of how many days the month took, 30 divide the sum of incomes. If the insurance holders did not work on some days during the month and received no income for the unworked days, then the income subject to premium shall be divided by the number of worked days (art. 80 para. 1/g SIGHIA).

If the insurance holders received an income over an unspecific time and amount such as commission charge or participation in the profits, then the earning subject to premium shall be one thirtieth of minimum monthly income (art. 80 para. 1/e SIGHIA).

5.2.4.2 Working for Multiple Employers

In case that the earning subject to premium works for multiple employers at the same time, then the incomes that the worker earned from separate employers shall be separately taken into consideration and the premiums shall be calculated accordingly. Thus, the premium debts of each employer shall be calculated separately and independently from each other. In these calculations, only the income earned from a specific employer shall be taken into consideration while calculating the premium to be paid for that job.[12]

If the premium is paid at an amount higher than the upper limit of income because the worker works with multiple employers, then the insurance holders shall reclaim refund of exceeding amount. In this case, all sum of the exceeding amount shall be paid to the insured worker in a single sum within the month following the date of reclamation. No default penalty or default interest shall be paid for the premiums paid back (art. 82 para. 4 SIGHIA). Accordingly, as well as the insurance holders shall not be able to reclaim the employer's share in excessive payment, the employer shall not receive back the amounts paid excessively, because the right of reclamation belongs to the insurance holders in proportion to the share of worker.

5.2.4.3 Upper and Lower Limits of Daily Income

The lower limit of daily income (i.e., the minimum daily wage) means that the income to be taken as base for payments and premiums to be collected by SSI shall not be lower than the determined minimum income. As a result of this, if the daily income is below the lower limit, then the premiums and payments shall be calculated by taking the lower limit into account. However, the employer shall pay all of the premiums for the difference between the insured worker's daily income and the minimum daily income. The upper limit (maximum daily income) refers to the maximum income level that might be taken as base for premium. Accordingly, in case that the income of insurance holders exceeds beyond the upper limit of daily income, then the upper limit of income shall be taken into consideration (art. 82 paras 2 and 3 SIGHIA).

The lower limit of income subject to premium (minimum daily income) equals to one thirtieth of minimum wage, whereas the upper limit (maximum daily income) equals to 7.5 times of minimum daily income. However, the upper limit for the Turkish workers to be assigned by the employers for working at countries having no social security agreement is 3 folds of minimum wage (art. 82 para. 1 SIGHIA). The reason for this difference is the idea of increasing the competitive power of Turkish building contractor in foreign countries.[13]

From the aspects of civil servants and other public officials, there is no upper limit to be taken as earning subject to premium. Accordingly, for the insured civil servants, there is no limitation regarding the maximum daily income (art. 46 para. 5 SIGHIA).

Determining the earning subject to premium for the apprentices is different. In fact, the insurance premium is paid from the allowance allocated from the budget of Ministry of National Education over *the half of minimum wage* (art. 25 para. 4 Act No. 3308).

---

[12]Sözer (2019), pp. 206–207.

[13]Güzel et al. (2020), p. 254.

Similarly, for the students subjected to internship during university education, the bursars working at the projects supported by the public institutions and authorities, the students working part-time at the universities, and the course trainees at the courses organized by TLI, the earning subject to premium shall be the minimum daily income (art. 80 para. 1/k SIGHIA).

5.3 Submission of Premium Documents

5.3.1 Preparing the Monthly Premium and Service Reports

5.3.1.1 Submitting the Premium Document to SSI

For the implementation of social insurances, it is very important to report the insurance holders' incomes subject to premium and the number of worked days, because SSI determines if the insurance holders qualifies for receiving the social insurance benefits by taking the insurance holders' incomes subject to premium and the number of worked days into account, and it also determines the level of benefits according to these reports. In case that the employer submitted no document or the employer did not submit the documents completely, then the insurance holders is given the opportunity of filing a declaratory lawsuit against the employer.

Accordingly, the employer is obliged to report the monthly premium and service report involving the names and identity numbers, incomes subject to premium, and numbers of worked days of insurance holders employed during the reported month to SSI on a monthly basis until the day determined by SSI (art. 86 para. 1 SIGHIA). SSI sets the day of submission of documents as follows:

- Until 23rd day of month following the reported month for the private companies,
- Until 7th day of month following the reported month for the public enterprises.

The employer is obliged to deliver the filled monthly premium and service report to SSI via "*e-sigorta (e-insurance)*" system.

5.3.1.2 Notification Obligation of Employers Employing No Insurance Holder

If the employer hires no insurance holder, then the employer shall notify SSI that he/she/it employs no worker, within *15 days* after the end of employing insurance holder (art. 86 para. 13 SIGHIA).

5.3.1.3 Notification of Insurance Holders Employed Less Than Thirty Days

The documents proving that the insurance holders work less than 30 days are submitted by the employer to SSI within the time limit set for monthly premium and service report of reported month (art. 86 para. 4 SIGHIA). Thus, it is aimed to prevent underreporting the number of worked days and paying lower premium.[14]

The medical reports indicating that the insurance holder has been resting, the unpaid or paid leave documents, written part-time employment contract, and the attendance reports involving the signatures of employer and workers might be given as examples for documents proving working less than 30 days.

5.3.1.4 E-Insurance Application

SSI has been authorized for obliging the individuals to submit any sort of information or documents, which shall be submitted to SSI as a necessity of law, via internet, electronic channels, and similar channels (art. 100 para. 3 SIGHIA).

From this aspect, the employers were obliged to submit the monthly premium and service reports to SSI via e-mail. In case that the deadline of period, in which the document shall be submitted, is public holiday, then the employers shall submit the document via e-insurance platform until 23:59 of the first business day following the deadline.

If the employers do not submit the premium and service document to SSI via internet, then they shall be given administrative fine even if they have submitted the hardcopy of document to SSI within the legal period.

5.3.2 Preparation of Premium Document by SSI Directly

5.3.2.1 Right to Prepare Directly

This procedure is about the insurance holders, who have been found to work as a result of the inspections physically made by SSI or the inspections carried out by using the company's records or the documents and information obtained from the public authorities or companies and banks. In this case, the documents are directly prepared by SSI if the documents that shall be delivered as required by the law have not submitted completely or not submitted at all within *a month* after the notification. Then, the premiums are calculated directly by SSI and notified to the employer (art. 86 para. 7 SIGHIA). Accordingly, SSI is authorized for directly preparing the insurance holder employment report and monthly premium and service report, as

[14]*See* also: Can (2000), pp. 34–35.

well as determining the premium to be paid by the employer. Thus, the premiums shall be imposed directly by SSI.[15]

Together with the default penalty and default interest, the premiums to be imposed by SSI shall be communicated to the employer for the payment within a month. The employer is entitled to object to the relevant SSI unit for the premium debt that has been communicated within *a month* after the notification. The objection stops the process. If the objection is rejected, then the employer might apply to the labour court within *a month* following the notification of decision. Application to the labour court does not stop the follow-up and collection of premium debt (art. 86 para. 7 SIGHIA).

5.3.2.2 Determining the Minimum Workmanship by the Insurance Inspector

In case that it is determined that the employer underreported the number of worked days and the income taken as basis for the premium below the required level, the minimum workmanship is determined by taking the characteristics of job, technology used, size of workplace, number of insured workers employed in similar companies, and the opinions of relevant professional and public organizations into consideration. The officers authorized by SSI for inspection and control make these determinations (art. 85 para. 1 SIGHIA).

5.3.2.3 Application to the Minimum Workmanship Determination Commission

Within the body of SSI, the *"minimum workmanship determination commission"* is established in order to examine and finalize the objections made against the minimum workmanship rates, as well as determining the minimum workmanship rates.

This commission has four members from technical staff of SSI, two members from the worker and employer confederations represented in the board of management of SSI, and one member from the Union of Chamber and Commodity Exchanges of Turkey (art. 85 para. 6 SIGHIA). Minimum workmanship rates are determined by the Commission and published in Official Gazette.

5.3.2.4 Accrual of Premiums by SSI

If it is determined after an investigation that the employer has underreported the labour below the required level, then the premiums, default penalties, and default interests to be calculated over the underreported amount shall be notified to the

[15] Güzel et al. (2020), p. 268.

employer for payment within *a month* after the date of notification. If the employer makes a written promise that the premium and relevant default penalties and default interests have been paid or will be paid, then the premium debt is finalized.

The employer might object to the premium debt that has been communicated within *a month* after the notification against the SSI unit. The objection stops the follow-up. If the objection is rejected, then the employer may apply to the labour court within *a month* following the notification of decision. Application to the labour court does not stop the follow-up and collection of premium debts (art. 85 para. 3 SIGHIA).

Moreover, the administrative fines shall be applied to the companies that have been determined to report the values below the minimum labour rate (art. 85 para. 4 SIGHIA).

5.3.2.5 Reconciliation

Reconciliation can be made with the employer before submitting the report, which is related with determining the minimum workmanship and imposing the administrative fine, to the unit of SSI. In case that the reconciliation can be made, then a report shall be prepared with this regard. The reconciled amounts are definite and the employer shall not file a lawsuit against these amounts and make no objection or complaint to any authority. The reconciled premium and administrative fines shall be paid within *one month* following the date of reconciliation statement. The employer shall not benefit from the cash discount for the reconciled administrative fine (art. 85 para. 9 SIGHIA).

In case that the reconciled amounts are not completely paid within the aforementioned time period, then the reconciliation shall be accepted breached and the reconciled amounts shall not be considered as the acquired right. In case that no reconciliation has been made or the settled reconciliation has been breached, then the employer shall request for no reconciliation again (art. 85 para. 9 SIGHIA).

5.3.2.6 Non-submission of Premium Document to SSI

For the cases that the monthly premium and service report are not submitted to SSI within the legal period or the incomes or services of the insurance holders are not reported in summary declaration or the services are underreported or not reported, the employer shall be imposed administrative fine (art. 102 SIGHIA).

5.4 Payment of Premiums

5.4.1 Premium Payment Obligation

The premium payer obliged to pay premium for the workers working based on an employment contract, the civil servants and other public officers are the employers, who employed them (art. 87 para. 1/a SIGHIA).

Self-employed persons, voluntary insurance holders and foreigners, who are considered within the scope of general health insurance since they inhabit in Turkey for 1 year or more and they are not insured in their homeland, are the premium payers obliged to pay the premium (art. 87 para. 1/b SIGHIA).

Besides them, the parties specified below are obliged to pay premium:

- TLI for the individuals receiving unemployment or short-term working allowances and the course attendees participating in vocational courses,
- Ministry of National Education or schools, in which the students have education, for the apprentices, those having vocational education in companies, and those participating in a training course in schools,
- Sponsor public institutions and organizations, private sector organizations or universities for the bursars assigned in the projects sponsored by the public institutions and organizations,
- Higher education institutions for the students subjected to training course during their higher education (art. 87 para. 1/d-e SIGHIA).

5.4.2 Premium Payment Term

5.4.2.1 For the Insured Workers

For the insured workers employed within the scope of an employment contract, the employer is obliged to deduct the premium share of employees, which is calculated over the incomes of insured workers employed during a month, from their wages and to pay the premiums to SSI within the period, which is set by SSI, by adding the employer's premium share to the amount deducted from the workers (art. 88 para. 1 SIGHIA).

The premiums of the insured workers working within the scope of an employment contract consist of the shares of employers and workers (art. 81 SIGHIA). The employer is obliged to pay the employer's premium share to SSI together with the worker's share by deducting the share of employee from his/her wage. If the employer does not deduct the worker's share from his/her wage, then the employer has to pay this share on his/her own. SSI is not authorized for reclaim the unpaid share of worker from the worker.[16]

5.4.2.2 For the Civil Servants

The employers employing insured civil servants are obliged to deduct the premium contribution of employees, which is calculated over the incomes of insurance holder employed during a month, from their salaries, and to pay the premiums to SSI within the period, which is set by SSI, by adding the employer's premium share to the amount deducted from the workers (art. 88 para. 9 SIGHIA). Within this context, the premium payment terms for these employees are set separately for those receiving salary on 1st day of month and those receiving their salary on 15th day of month.

5.4.2.3 For the Insured Self-Employed Persons

Insured self-employed persons are obliged to pay their premiums to SSI on the following month until the end of day, which is set by SSI (art. 88 para. 6 SIGHIA). SSI set this time as the end of month following the month, with which the premiums are related.

5.4.3 Collection of Premiums

5.4.3.1 Collection Fundamentals

SSI is authorized for collecting the premium receivables by setting the premium debts of employers off from its debts to employers (art. 88 para. 14 SIGHIA).

Similarly, SSI is also authorized for fulfilling the obligation of using special payment methods in paying the premiums, as well as determining the collection centres, where the premiums shall be paid (art. 88 para. 15 SIGHIA).

5.4.3.2 Collection Options

The effective collection of social insurance premiums could not be achieved in Turkey. The current economic conditions led the employers to using the insurance premiums, which they shall pay to SSI, as a source of fund for their companies. Besides that, the inefficiency of previous implementations, the practical problems originating from the administrative procedures of SSI, and the insensitivity of unions

---

[16]Güzel et al. (2020), p. 304.

to these problems encouraged this sort of use by the employers. Because of this, the premium receivables that SSI could not collect caused a financial difficulty for SSI.

For this reason, the receivables from social insurance, general health insurance, and unemployment insurance premiums were considered as public receivables and subjected to the private provisions (facilitating and accelerating) of *Act on Collection of Public Receivables* No. 6183 (art. 88 para. 16 SIGHIA).

On the other hand, the legal proceedings shall be initiated for SSI's authorized officers, who have not activated the modus operandi within 1 year after the maturity date of premium receivables, in accordance with the general provisions on this subject (art. 88 para. 21 SIGHIA).

Besides that, before achieving the government aids and government subventions and grants, the employers are required to provide the information and documents indicating that the employer has no debt originating from administrative fines and premium debts (art. 90 para. 6 SIGHIA).

Moreover, the documents prepared by SSI and introducing the administrative fine and premium debts have the force of documents that have been prepared by the official authorities in accordance with the legal regulations (art. 92 para. 2 SIGHIA). Thus, it is aimed to limit the arbitrary objections made by the employers against the premium and administrative fine debts in practice.

5.4.3.3 Deduction of the Premium Debt from Interim Payment and Deposit

The public institutions make the interim payments of employers, who do business via tender, on the condition that the employers have no administrative fine and/or premium debts to SSI. Similarly, the performance guarantees are paid back if it is determined that there is no debt to SSI in relation with the subject of tender. Moreover, any sort of transfer or handover to be performed on the interim payment and deposits shall be made over the resting amount after deducting the amount meeting the premium debts to SSI (art. 90 para. 2 SIGHIA). About the parties making the interim payment and/or paying the deposit back without following these rules, the administrative and criminal actions shall be taken in accordance with the general provisions (art. 90 para. 5 SIGHIA).

5.4.4 Non-payment of Premium Debts

5.4.4.1 Payment of Default Penalty and Default Interest

In case that the premium debts to the Institution are not paid on time and completely, *3% default penalty* shall be applied to the unpaid proportion of debts *per month* for the first three months starting from the maturity date of unpaid amount. Moreover, *default interest rate* to be imposed for each of the month during the period between maturity date and payment date is the average compound monthly interest rate of government debt security (art. 89 para. 2 SIGHIA).

5.4.4.2 Joint Liability

Together with the employer of insurance holder, also the senior managers of companies are jointly liable to SSI for the premium debts. Accordingly, if the insurance premium receivables of SSI are not paid on time without a valid reason, then the officers of public institutions that are charged with the accrual and collection and the legal representatives and senior managers of employers having legal entity including the board members are jointly liable to SSI together with the employers (art. 88 para. 20 SIGHIA).

On the other hand, if the company, where the insurance holder is employed, is sold or inherited or it merges with another organization, then the new employer shall be jointly liable for the previous employer(s)'s premium and default penalty debts to SSI and the debts originating from other accessory obligations. The agreements provisions against this principle are legally invalid for SSI (art. 89 para. 1 SIGHIA).

Moreover, according to the Court of Cassation, the aforementioned responsibility zone shall not be reflected to the previous and/or next employers other than the debtor employer (except for the fraudulent and collusive transactions). Accordingly, introducing the existing company as if it has been sold or handed over or founding new companies in order only to avoid from the previous premium debts or misguiding the third parties do not comply with the aim of law and not prevent the new employer from the responsibility.[17]

However, according to the opinion of Court of Cassation, reopening a previously shut-down company by a new employer as a new company, subcontracting the operations in an organization that are under the responsibility of employer, re-renting the workplace to another entrepreneur after the rental contract has been terminated and the office/workplace has been emptied, selling only the equipment and material in the office/workplace, and terminating the contract of previous contractor and then contracting out the remaining works to another contractor shall not be considered as a handover. Therefore, for the joint liability of new employer, the business must have been handed over to the new employer in functioning conditions and together with the insured workers.[18]

---

[17]CC, 10th Civ. Div., 13.4.1993, 1992-11117/3693, Yargıtay Kararları Dergisi, 1 (1994), pp. 60–64.

[18]CC, 21st Civ. Div., 4.7.1997, 3867/4020, www.kazanci.com.tr.

5.5 Calculating the Number of Premium Payment Days

In calculating the number of premium payment days, only the number of debited days and the durations, premium of which has been paid, is taken into consideration. If the premium of these days has been not paid, then these days shall not be taken into account in determining the number of days worked. In case of a partial payment, only the periods, premium of which has been paid, shall be taken into consideration. Accordingly, in cases that the premium is not paid or the collection by SSI is impossible due to the prescription, neither the number of worked days nor the premium shall be taken into consideration.

On the other hand, if the premium of the days worked before the age 18 has been paid, then these days shall be taken into account only in determining the number of premium payment days but not for determining the insurance period for the long-term insurance branches (art. 38 para. 2 SIGHIA).

On the other hand, the days, which have been worked but the premiums of which have not been paid yet, shall be taken into consideration in determining the number of premium payment days for the insured workers working based on an employment contract and the insured civil servants. Hence, Court of Cassation declared its perspective in the way that claiming that the premiums could not have been collected because of the drop due to prescription does not comply with the principle of goodwill.[19]

Similarly, in cases that the works that have not been reported to SSI were determined at the end of declaratory lawsuit, the premium payment days specified in the court decision shall be taken into consideration (art. 86 para. 9 SIPHIA).

For the insured civil servants, who have been suspended, and those arrested or taken into custody due to a crime (regardless that the crime is related with his/her task or duty), half of these days shall be considered within the number of premium payment days (art. 45 para. 1 SIGHIA). For the civil servants that have been given back to their duty by a court decision, the durations passed in suspension shall be taken into account in determining the number of premium payment days (art. 45 para. 2 SIGHIA).

5.6 Premium Debt Relief

The employers, self-employed persons and voluntary insurance holders, who pay their own premiums on their own, that have suffered from commercial or economic losses due to disasters such as fire, flood, drought, landslide, and earthquake and the factors such as severe accident, imprisonment, and sabotage might delay their debts to SSI for up to *one year* in case that they can document their condition within *3*

[19]CC, 10th Civ. Div., 18.1.1983, 88/99.

months after the disaster or event and on condition that their payment difficulty can be determined as a result of investigation (art. 91 para. 1 SIGHIA).

5.7 Premium Debt Instalment (Restructuring)

The political authorities in Turkey frequently make regulations offering easy terms of payment (premium debt instalment or restructuring) because the insurance premiums cannot be regularly and completely collected on time.[20] However, since such regulations are frequently made, it can be seen that restructuring method is not an efficient method. Thus, the laws on restructuring become the laws encouraging not paying the premium debts on time. This makes the parties, who pay their premiums on regular basis and on time, feel like they are sentenced.[21]

5.8 Premium Incentives

In order to promote the employment and to include the unregistered employment into the formal economy, the premium incentives that are offered are to reduce the premium rates or to have the employer's premium share paid by Treasury.[22]

5.8.1 Partial Payment of Long-Term Insurance Premiums by the State

The Treasury covers 5% of employer's share in premiums of long-term insurances (disability, old-age, and survivor insurance), which shall be paid by the private sector employers. This incentive is the most commonly implemented incentive in Turkey and more than 80% of incentives provided by SSI are provided within this scope.[23]

In order for the employers to be able to benefit from this incentive, they shall submit their monthly premium and service reports to SSI within the legal term, to pay the insurance holders' share in insurance premium to the Institution together with the employer's share that is not paid by the Treasury, and to have no premium or administrative fine debts and no default penalty or default interest debt related with these debts to SSI (art. 81 para. 1/ı SIGHIA).

[20]Öztürk (2016), p. 283.

[21]Güzel et al. (2020), p. 337; Tuncay and Ekmekçi (2019), p. 228.

[22]*See*: Alper (2015), p. 207; Caniklioğlu and Ocak (2009), p. 167; Öztürk (2016), p. 116; Süngü (2008), p. 139.

[23]Alper (2015), p. 208.

If it is proven in the inspections and controls that the employer employs unregistered worker or the registered worker does not work at the relevant workplace, then the employer shall not benefit from this incentive for *one year* (art. 81 para. 4 SIGHIA).

5.8.2 Premium Incentive for Disabled Insurance Holders

Calculated over the minimum wage, the private sector employer's share from premiums of disabled insurance holder employed by the private sector is completely paid by the Treasury (art. 30 para. 6 LA). But, if the employer pays a salary, which is higher than minimum wage level, to the disabled insurance holder, the employer is responsible for paying the premium to be calculated over the difference between paid wage and minimum wage.[24]

5.8.3 Premium Incentive Related with Employment of Unemployed Youth and Women

Based on the condition that they have been unemployed during last six months before the employment, and that they have been employed in addition to the average employment of company, in which they have been employed, for the last six months, the amount that shall be paid by the employer as the employer's share to be calculated over the whole of income subject to premium is covered by the UIF (prov. art. 10 para. 1 UIA).

The employers, who have been found to not register the workers they employed as insurance holder to SSI, shall not benefit from this incentive for *one year* (prov. art. 10 para. 8 UIA).

5.8.4 Premium Incentive for Provinces with Lower Level of Socioeconomic Development

Taking the low socioeconomic development index values of the provinces[25] determined by the President of the State into consideration shall set the premium incentives forth.

This premium incentive is to cover 6 of 11% of employer's share in premiums of disability, old age, and survivor insurances. Moreover, the incentive specified here

[24]Güzel et al. (2020), p. 316; Öztürk (2016), pp. 133–134.

[25]*See*: OG 14.7.2013, No. 28707.

shall be calculated over the minimum wage rather than the full incomes of insurance holders (art. 81 para. 2 SIGHIA).

On the other hand, if it is proven in the inspections and controls that the employer employs unregistered worker or the registered worker does not work at the relevant workplace, then the employer shall not benefit from this incentive for *one year* (art. 81 para. 4 SIGHIA).

5.8.5 Premium Incentive for Employees Working in Research and Development

Except for the civil servants, 50% of employer share in insurance premiums to be calculated over the wage they receive for the R&D and support personnel working in the projects founded in R&D centres and technology companies, public institutions and organizations, foundations established by law, and projects supported by the international funds or carried out by Scientific and Technological Research Council of Turkey (*TUBITAK*), design and support personnel working at design projects, and personnel exempted from wage tax and working at technology development centres is covered by the Ministry of Finance (art. 3 para. 3 Act No. 5746).

5.8.6 Premium Incentive in Investment Incentives

For the insurance holders to be employed in the investments to be made within the scope of incentive certificates, up to all of the employer's shares or up to worker's share in premium (in provinces determined by the President of the State) shall be covered from the budget of Ministry of Economy (add. art. 2 SIGHIA).

If it is proven in the inspections and controls that the employer employs unregistered worker or the registered worker does not work at the relevant workplace, then the employer shall not benefit from this incentive for *one year* (add. art. 2 para. 4 SIGHIA).

5.8.7 Premium Incentive in Employment of Individuals Receiving Unemployment Benefit

Based on the condition that they have been unemployed during last six months before the employment, and that they are employed in addition to the average employment of company, in which they are employed, for the last six months, the general health insurance premiums and the social insurance premiums to be calculated over the minimum wage for the individuals receiving unemployment benefit shall be covered by UIF for the period of unemployment benefit (art 50 para. 5 UIA). The objective here is to have individuals, who receive unemployment benefit, to be employed as soon as possible.[26]

5.8.8 *Premium Incentive in Cultural Investments and Enterprises*

50% (not for more than 3 years during the investment period) or 25% (not for more than 7 years during the operating period) of the employer's premium share to be calculated for the workers to be employed in cultural investments or the Treasury shall cover enterprises (art. 5 para. 1/c Act No. 5225).

5.8.9 *Premium Incentive for Insurance Holders Employed Abroad*

For the insurance holders assigned from Turkey to abroad in order to be employed at the private sector employers' workplaces in foreign countries, only the short-term insurance premium and general health insurance premium shall be paid. The Treasury shall cover 5% of general health insurance premium, which shall be paid by the relevant employers (art. 81 para. 1/i SIGHIA).

In order for the employers to qualify for benefiting from this type of incentive, they shall submit their monthly premium and service reports to SSI within the legal term, pay the insurance holders' share in insurance premium to SSI together with the employer's share that is not paid by the Treasury, and have no premium or administrative fine debts and no default penalty or default interest debt related with these debts to SSI (art. 81 para. 1/i SIGHIA).

5.8.10 *Premium Incentive for Preventing the Occupational Accidents at Very Risky Workplaces*

The employer share of unemployment insurance premium for the employees employed in workplaces, which are in "*very dangerous*" class according to OHSA, where minimum 3 employees are employed and where no occupational accident that resulted in decease or occurred permanent incapacity, shall be collected by 1% for 3 years starting from the next calendar year (add. art. 4 para. 1 UIA).

[26]Caniklioğlu and Ocak (2009), p. 170.

5.9 Limitation Period for Premium Receivables

The premium and other receivables of SSI are subjected to 10-year limitation period starting from the beginning of calendar year following the maturity date. For the premium and other receivables of SSI, this 10-year limitation starts from:

- The date of the finalization of decision, if the receivable arises from a court decision,
- The date of report, if the receivable arises from the determinations made by SSI's officers authorized for control and inspection,
- The date, on which the results are reported to SSI, if the receivable arises from the inspection, control, and investigations performed by the inspectors of public authorities,
- The date, on which the information or document is delivered to SSI, if the receivable arises from the information and document obtained from banks (art. 93 para. 2 SIGHIA).

5.10 Repayment of Unjustifiably Collected Premiums

The premiums that have been collected unjustifiably or by a mistake are the premiums that the insurance holder is not obliged to pay but have paid to SSI because of any reason. The situations such as over-determining the risk class of workplace or over-determining the incomes subject to premium or repetitive payment of premiums might be given as examples.[27]

If the date of payment dates back no more than 10 years, the premiums determined to be collected unjustifiably or by a mistake shall be paid back to the employers, insurance holders, optional insurance holders or general health insurance holders or beneficiaries in proportion to their shares (including the legal interests). The legal interest here shall be calculated for the period from the beginning of month following the date of payment made to SSI to the beginning of month, on which the premium is paid back (art. 89 para. 3 SIGHIA).

References

Alper Y (2015) Türk Sosyal Güvenlik Sistemi. Sosyal Sigortalar Hukuku, 7th edn. Dora Publishing, Bursa

Can M (2000) 4447 Sayılı Yasa'da Kayıtdışı İşçiliğe İlişkin Güvenlik Düzenekleri. Tühis İş Hukuku ve İktisat Dergisi 16(4–5):29–43

[27] *See*: Oral (2007), pp. 134–135; Öztürk (2016), p. 300; Sözer (2019), pp. 225–226.

Caniklioğlu N, Ocak S (2009) 5921 Sayılı Kanun'la Getirilen Teşvikler. Sicil İş Hukuku Dergisi 15:167–182

Çelikoğlu İ (1994) Sosyal Güvenlik Sistemlerinin Finansman Yöntemleri ve Türkiye Uygulaması. Devlet Planlama Teşkilatı, Ankara. yayını No. 2355

Güzel A, Okur AR, Caniklioğlu N (2020) Sosyal Güvenlik Hukuku, 18th edn. Beta Publishing, Istanbul

Kolçak M, Arpa AT (2015) Türkiye ve OECD Ülkelerinde Sosyal Güvenlik Harcamaları. http://torino2015.econworld.org/assets/kolcak_arpa.pdf,l

Oral Aİ (2007) Türk Sosyal Güvenlik Hukuku Açısından Toptan Ödeme. Anadolu Üniversitesi, Eskişehir. yayını No. 1731

Öztürk B (2016) Türk Sosyal Güvenlik Hukukunda Primler. Turhan Kitabevi, Ankara

Sözer AN (2019) Türk Sosyal Sigortalar Hukuku, 4th edn. Beta Publishing, Istanbul

Süngü Y (2008) Yeni İstihdam Paketi ve Sosyal Sigortalarda Uygulanan Teşvikler. Sicil İş Hukuku Dergisi 11:131–141

Tuncay AC, Ekmekçi Ö (2019) Sosyal Güvenlik Hukuku Dersleri, 20th edn. Beta Publishing, Istanbul

Tunçomağ K (1990) Sosyal Güvenlik Kavramı ve Sosyal Sigortalar, 5th edn. Beta Publishing, Istanbul

Part III
Concept of Social Insurance

Chapter 6
Types of Social Insurance

6.1 Compulsory Insurance

"Compulsory insurance" is a type of social insurance that incorporates the emergence of an insurance relationship, which is established without considering the will and request of individual, as well as the non-intervention to the content. Accordingly, within the scope of compulsory insurance, there is a legal relationship, which is regulated by the imperative provisions, between the employer and insurance holder and SSI.

6.1.1 Principle of Insurance Obligation

An important principle of social law is the insurance obligation. This principle incorporates the fundamentals emphasizing the characteristics of social security system. Accordingly, when entered into working life, the individuals are accepted as insurance holder automatically in accordance with their status. From this aspect, the most important point distinguishing the social insurance from private insurances is that the social insurance is compulsory.

On this subject, SIGHIA includes a provision specifying that *"it is compulsory for the individuals, who are within the scope of short- and long-term insurance, to be insurance holder and to have general health insurance and, for the individuals covered by general health insurance, to have general health insurance"* (art. 92 para. 1). Thus, being insurance holder or not has not been left for the preference and will of the individual, and the parties are not allowed to intervene the context of social insurance relationship.

The principle of insurance obligation is also a principle accepted for the unemployment insurance. From this aspect, UIA involves the provision that *"Unemployment insurance is compulsory. Those included in the scope of this Act (UIA) and still*

T. Centel, *Turkish Social Law*, https://doi.org/10.1007/978-3-030-64704-9_6

working shall be insured at the effective date of Act (UIA), whereas those employed recently are insured at the start date of their employment" (art. 48 para. 1).

Since the workers become insured automatically as a result of insurance obligation, registration to SSI by the employer or registration as insurance holder by SSI is not important in terms of gaining the title of insurance holder. Accordingly, even if the employer has not registered the employee, whom the employer has employed, to SSI, the individual that have not been registered benefits from the social insurances (art. 23 para. 1 SIGHIA). Thus, since the unregistered worker gains the insurance status since the first day of employment, the social insurances shall be obliged to offer social insurance benefits.

On the other hand, since the insurance status automatically begins with starting to work, the individual does not need to make any positive or negative declaration of will in order to be insured. Moreover, in order to be insurance holder, there is no necessity of any decision made by a judge or any action taken by SSI.

6.1.2 Content of Insurance Obligation

Insurance status is not only a right of an individual but also a liability. From this aspect, insurance status is independent from the will of individual. The will of individual plays no role in insurance obligation. Accordingly, whether the individual wants or not, he/she shall be insured if the conditions are met.

The insurance obligation has effects that protect the insurance holder even from himself/herself. As well as being a right, insurance status is also an obligation. The insurance holder shall not avoid or waive from this obligation. Hence, art. 92 para.1 SIGHIA declares that the provisions included in contracts in order to remove, reduce, waive, or transfer the rights and obligations of insurance shall be accepted legally invalid. From this aspect, Court of Cassation has declared the quittance via waiver notice specifying that the individual does not work as an insurance holder and prepared in notary null and void.[1]

On the other hand, since the context of social insurances creates a public law relationship regulated by the law, it is not legally possible for insurance holder and employer to intervene in this relationship and modify its context. Accordingly, the insurance holder and employer shall not make an agreement with each other in order to narrow the context of social insurance benefits nor to reduce the social insurance liabilities (art. 92 para. 1 SIGHIA).

[1]*See*: CC, 10th Civ. Div., 1.2.1985, 223/418, Yargıtay Kararları Dergisi, 6 (1985), pp. 831–833.

6.2 Voluntary Insurance

"Voluntary insurance" is a type of insurance, in which the individuals are offered the chance of choosing either being insured or not. In this context, the voluntary insurance is on the contrary with compulsory insurance. Since continuing the voluntary insurance is left to the will and desire of individual, benefiting from this type of insurance or not or waiving this insurance depends on the preferences of individual.

In Turkey, the voluntary insurance has been utilized as a method enabling the individuals, who have never been an insurance holder or lost their qualification to be compulsory insurance holder, to continue the social insurance relationship without working at any organization. In other words, the housewives, who have been working in the past but quitted their jobs when married or had children, started to be put on pension by paying voluntary insurance premium. From this aspect, the voluntary insurance has been established in order to eliminate the deficiencies and gaps that may arise when the compulsory insurance relationship is implemented, as well as preventing the victimization of insurance holder.[2]

Thus, the individuals, who have never worked as an insurance holder and cannot receive any pension because of their previous services as an insurance holder, are granted the option of maintaining the social insurance relationship without working, as well as qualifying for the retirement in the future.

However, benefiting from this method has been left to the will of person. Besides that, the optional point here is only the decision about whether entering into voluntary insurance relationship or not.[3] On the other hand, having voluntary insurance policy is conditional upon meeting the conditions set by the Act. From this aspect, unless the legal conditions are met, no one shall have voluntary insurance.

Besides that, the voluntary insurance incorporates benefiting only from long-term insurance branches and general health insurance. From this aspect, art. 50 para. 1 SIGHIA describes the voluntary insurance as *"the insurance enabling the individuals to benefit from long-term insurance branches and general health insurance by paying voluntary insurance premium"*.

[2]Kutsal (2016), p. 51.

[3]Kutsal (2016), p. 52.

6.2.1 *Conditions of Benefiting from Voluntary Insurance*

6.2.1.1 Residing in Turkey

In order to have voluntary insurance, the individual has to reside in Turkey. On this subject, the *principle of territoriality* applies. Accordingly, the Turkish citizens living abroad are not granted the right to benefit from voluntary insurance.

If the individual resides in Turkey shall be determined according to the provisions of Civil Code. From this aspect, the location, in which the individual resides with the aim of constantly residing at there, is the residence of that individual (art. 19 para. 1 Civil Code). Thus, the ones residing in Turkey with the aim of constantly residing might have the voluntary insurance. However, as an exception, it can be seen that the bilateral social security agreements may modify this principle. Accordingly, in accordance with the social security agreements of Turkey with Sweden and France, the individuals not residing in Turkey may benefit from the voluntary insurance.[4]

On the other hand, the Turkish citizens living in foreign countries, with which no social security agreement has been signed, shall be granted the right to have voluntary insurance when these citizens were living in Turkey. The reason for this is the compensation for exclusion of these individuals from the scope of long-term insurance. Thus, the individuals in such a status are taken into the scope of short-term insurance branches and general health insurance, and it is specified that they might benefit from the provisions of voluntary insurance in terms of long-term insurance branches (art. 5 para. 1/g SIGHIA).

Besides that, the foreigners having no Turkish citizenship might have voluntary insurance, because having voluntary insurance policy is not conditioned to Turkish citizenship in terms of residency, except for the Turkish citizens working abroad.[5]

6.2.1.2 Being Not Subject to the Compulsory Insurance or Working Part-Time

In order to have voluntary insurance, it is required to not work in a position requiring compulsory insurance or to work and have insurance but less than 30 days per month or to not work full-time (art. 50 para. 2/a SIGHIA). Since the compulsory insurance is the primary insurance and the voluntary insurance is secondary, no one shall have both of compulsory and voluntary insurances.

It shall not be important if the individual, who will have voluntary insurance, is an employee (civil servant or worker) or self-employed. The type of employment, which the individual is subject to, is important for the voluntary insurance. Accordingly, the individuals working in a position, which requires compulsory insurance

[4]Güzel et al. (2020), pp. 184–185.

[5]Belverenli (2016), p. 87; Tuncay and Ekmekçi (2019), pp. 372–373.

according to SIGHIA, shall not have voluntary insurance. These are the employees considered fully insured by SIGHIA (full-time employees in general).

The individuals, who work (not full-time) in jobs requiring compulsory insurance, are those working for one or couple of days or one or couple hours per month. From this aspect, the number of premium payment days of part-time employees is determined by summing the hours worked and then by dividing the result by 7.5 (art. 80 para. 1/h SIGHIA). Accordingly, for an insurance holder working for 90 h per month, the number of premium payment days shall be 12 days. In this case, the insurance holder who has been paying premium for 12 days per month can retire in 50 years. In order to overcome this problem and to prevent the victimization of part-time employees, these employees are given option to have voluntary insurance. Thus, the aforementioned individuals shall qualify for long-term insurance branches as full-time employees by completing their number of premium payment days to 30 per month. For this purpose, the individuals to have voluntary insurance shall work for less than 30 days per month or not in full-time manner (art. 50 para. 2/a SIGHIA).

6.2.1.3 Receiving No Pension Because of His/Her Own Insurance Status

In order for an insurance holder to have voluntary insurance, they shall receive no pension, which is related with their work, from SSI (art. 50 para. 2/b SIGHIA), because the voluntary insurance mainly aims to provide security against the long-term risks. Anyone, who has protection against these risks, would ever necessitate voluntary insurance.

Since SIGHIA mentioned about receiving "*pension*", the individual receiving pension from SSI shall be able to have voluntary insurance. Accordingly, an individual receiving survivor pension from SSI may apply to voluntary insurance.[6]

6.2.1.4 Turning the Age of 18 Years

The individual to have voluntary insurance shall have turned the age of 18 years (art. 50 para. 2/c SIGHIA). Although the age of reaching one's majority is 18 in Turkey, attaining majority through alternative ways such as marriage or court decision is not enough for applying to voluntary insurance, because art. 50 para. 2/c SIGHIA clearly states that the person shall have turned the age of 18 years.[7]

---

[6]Balcı (2009), p. 250; Belverenli (2016), p. 110.

[7]Belverenli (2016), p. 112.

6.2.1.5 Applying to SSI

In order to benefit from voluntary insurance, the individual shall apply to SSI by using voluntary insurance application petition, the draft of which is provided by SSI (art. 50 para. 2/d SIGHIA).

Although benefiting from the voluntary insurance depends on the application, it is not a requirement for this application to be accepted by SSI. On the other hand, Court of Cassation declared that the voluntary insurance would not come into existence upon the lump sum premium payment.[8]

6.2.2 Beginning and Termination of Voluntary Insurance

The voluntary insurance begins at the date following the day, in which the application is registered in the records of SSI (art. 51 para. 1 SIGHIA).

The termination date of optional insurance shall be:

- The day following the last day, premium of which has been paid, for the individuals that applied for terminating the voluntary insurance,
- The day of application for those applying for pension, on the condition that they qualify for pension,
- The day of death, for the deceased insurance holders (art. 51 para. 2 SIGHIA).

Similarly, if the voluntary insurance holder starts working in a job requiring compulsory insurance, then the voluntary insurance relationship ends (art. 53 para. 3 SIGHIA).

Finally, if the voluntary insurance holder, who willingly terminated his/her insurance, wants to continue the voluntary insurance again, then he/she shall apply to SSI in written (art. 50 para. 2/d SIGHIA).

6.2.3 Payment of Voluntary Insurance Premium

In order to continue voluntary insurance status, it is compulsory to pay the premiums, which shall be calculated over 30 days a month, uninterruptedly on a monthly basis (art. 52 para. 2 SIGHIA).

The voluntary insurance holders determine their premiums on their own, but the income subject to premium shall be between upper and lower limits. The premiums of insurance holders, who have not applied in written, are collected over the lower limit of income subject to premium.

[8]CC, General Assembly of Civ. Div., 16.3.2005, 10-104/186, www.kazanci.com.tr.

The premium rate of voluntary insurance shall be applied as 32%. The increase of this rate, which has been applied as 25% in the past, to 32% has been conveyed to the Constitutional Court but it has found no breach in this increase.[9]

32% premium consists of 20% for disability, old age, and survivor insurances, and 12% for general health insurance. However, since the individuals that have been assigned to the countries, which have no social security agreement with Turkey, for the purpose of employment are already subject to public health insurance, they shall pay no separate general health insurance according to the provisions of voluntary insurance (art. 5 para. 1/g SIGHIA). Similarly, among the foreign nationals having voluntary insurance, those not residing in Turkey for one year shall do not have to pay general health insurance premium (art. 52 para. 2 SIGHIA).

The periods, premium of which are not paid together with default penalty and default interest within maximum 12 months starting from the month they belong to, shall not be taken into account within the insurance period (art. 52 para. 3 and art. 89 para. 3 SIGHIA).

6.2.4 Legal Consequences of Voluntary Insurance

The periods, voluntary insurance premium of which have been paid, shall be taken into consideration in applying the provisions of general health insurance and disability, old age, and survivor insurance (art. 51 para. 5 SIGHIA). On the other hand, these periods are not taken into account for occupational accidents, occupational disease, health, and maternity insurances.

References

Balcı M (2009) 5510 Sayılı Sosyal Sigortalar ve Genel Sağlık Sigortası Kanunu Döneminde İsteğe Bağlı Sigortalılık Uygulaması Hakkında İnceleme. Sicil İş Hukuku Dergisi 14:249–253

Belverenli D (2016) 5510 Sayılı Kanun Kapsamında İsteğe Bağlı Sigortalılık. Seçkin Publishing, Ankara

Güzel A, Okur AR, Caniklioğlu N (2020) Sosyal Güvenlik Hukuku, 18th edn. Beta Publishing, Istanbul

Kutsal FBS (2016) Türk Sosyal Sigortalar Hukukunun Temel İlkeleri. Beta Publishing, Istanbul

Tuncay AC, Ekmekçi Ö (2019) Sosyal Güvenlik Hukuku Dersleri, 20th edn. Beta Publishing, Istanbul

[9]Constitutional Court, 30.3.2011, 2008-56/58, OG 28.12.2011, No. 28156.

Chapter 7
Relationship of Social Insurance

7.1 Establishing the Social Insurance Relationship

7.1.1 For the Insured Workers

The insurance relationship starts when the individuals started working, having education (technical, vocational, complementary or branch education), internship, or bursarship, for the individuals working based on an employment contract (art. 7 para. 1/a SIGHIA). Accordingly, the beginning of insurance for the individuals within this context is the moment of recruitment.

However, the beginning of insurance rights and liabilities is not the date of signing the employment contract but the date of starting actively working.[1] From this aspect of the start of insurance, Court of Cassation pays importance to working and does not consider the date of sending or delivery of statement of employment to SSI.[2]

On the other hand, readiness for the orders of employer in order to work shall be considered within the scope of concept of "*starting to work*". In such cases, even if the individual does not actively work, readiness for the orders of employer might be enough for the beginning of insurance status.[3]

In cases of debiting the military service or the periods worked abroad, where the actively working is not prominent, the date to be determined by retrogressing from the date of full payment of premiums shall be considered as the beginning of insurance.[4]

---

[1]Tunçomağ (1990), p. 100.

[2]CC, 10th Civ. Div., 21.6.1984, 3455/3579, Çenberci (1985), p. 91.

[3]Akyiğit (1995), pp. 19–20.

[4]CC, 10th Civ. Div., 13.6.1991, 3846/3846, İş Hukuku Dergisi, II/1 (1992), pp. 130–132.

T. Centel, *Turkish Social Law*, https://doi.org/10.1007/978-3-030-64704-9_7

7.1.2 For the Self-Employed Insurance Holders

Since the activity causing the insurance relationship of insured self-employers differ significantly, the beginning of insurance status for these individuals is set separately for each of activities in SIGHIA. Accordingly, the beginning of insurance relationship shall be:

- When the tax liability started, for the persons liable for income tax, the limited and unlimited partners of general companies and limited partnerships, and the partners of association of ship owners,
- When the company is registered at the trade registry office, for the unlimited partners of limited companies and limited partnership, in which the capital is divided into shares,
- The date of election to board membership for the board members of joint-stock companies,
- The date of registration to Registry Office of Traders and Artisans for the self-employers exempt from the income tax,
- The date of registration of agricultural activity for the farmers in case that the notification is made by farmers or occupational organization,
- The date of being elected as village and neighbourhood headman,
- The date of starting actively working based on the license for jockeys and trainers (art. 7 para. 1/b SIGHIA).

The rate of informality among the self-employed persons is very high in Turkey. For this reason, even though they have compulsory insurance, it is very frequent for them not to notify SSI or not to pay the premiums. In order to prevent the self-employed persons from suffering the informality, it is stated in the provisional articles of SIGHIA (prov. arts. 8 and 54) that the unreported periods shall be considered within the insurance period on the condition that the application is made to SSI within the specified time limit and the premiums are paid.

7.1.3 For the Insured Civil Servants

The insurance relationship starts with the date of employment or at the beginning of their education in schools (military schools, non-commissioned officer high school, or police academy) within the scope of art. 4 para. 4/d and e SIGHIA (art. 7 para. 1/c SIGHIA).

7.2 Notification of Established Insurance Relationship

In parallel with the principle of compulsiveness in social insurances, the insurance status does not necessitate any action to be taken. However, in order for SSI to be able to offer insurance benefits and fulfil its legal responsibilities, it should be informed about the insurance holders. For this reason, upon the notification of insurance status to SSI or the direct registration of insurance by SSI, the registration of insurance status is performed.

7.2.1 Notification Period

7.2.1.1 For the Insured Workers

Until 1999, the employers in Turkey had to make the notification to SSI within one month for the insured workers that they employed. Accordingly, the insured worker was employed firstly and then the notification was made. Since that practice was enabling employing unregistered worker and also prevented the imposition of administrative fines, this principle was left in 1999 and the principle that the employer shall firstly make the notification and then start the employment was adopted.

Therefore, for the individuals that do not start working despite they have been registered to SSI, in an amendment made in 2016, the employers are enabled to cancel the notifications, which they have made via e-insurance method, by using e-insurance method until 23:59 of the day following the date of notification. Thus, for the worker deemed to be insured, the employers are obliged to make the notification before the beginning date of insurance to SSI via the statement of employment (art. 8 para. 1 SIGHIA). However, because of several difficulties, specific exemptions were added on this subject.

First, the notification of individuals to be employed in construction, fisheries, and agriculture industries shall be made to SSI until the first day of their employment (art. 8 para. 1/a SIGHIA).

Another exemption is related with those to be recruited for the international transportation vehicles during a trip and with the individuals to be recruited by the companies, which are to be registered to SSI for the first time. The notification of workers, who meet these conditions, to SSI may be made within *one month*. Accordingly, the workers recruited in the transportation vehicles shall be notified to SSI within a month after the first day of their employment, whereas the individuals required in the workplaces, registration statement of which is recently made for the first time, shall be notified to SSI within *one month* following the first day of their employment (art. 8 para. 1/b SIGHIA).

Similarly, the notification of insured foreign nationals to SSI deviated from the general rule. Accordingly, the notification shall be made within *30 days* after the beginning date of work permit certificate. In case that the date of work permit certificate's delivery to employer and the date of work permit certificate are different, then the notifications made within 30 days after the delivery of certificate to the employer shall be considered to be made within the legal time limit.

Similarly, the notification shall be made to SSI within *30 days* for the contracted employees, who are employed by the public authorities and not subject to unemployment insurance, and the employees recruited by the public authorities in order to assign to positions abroad (art. 8 para. 1/c SIGHIA).

Finally, the funds of banks and insurance companies (prov. art. 20 SIGHIA) shall make their notifications within *10 days* starting from the beginning of their participants with the fund until the day, in which they are transferred to SSI (add. art. 1 para. 3 SIPHIA).

7.2.1.2 For the Insured Self-Employed Persons

Except for those involved in agricultural activities, the employment statements of insured self-employed shall be prepared and delivered to SSI within 15 days starting from the dates specified below:

- The date of receiving certificate of election from the board of election for the village and neighbourhood headmen,
- The date of consummation of taxpayer's engagement procedures by the tax office for self-employed, insurance of who starts at the beginning of tax liability (not more than 2 months from the beginning of tax liability),
- The beginning of insurance status (art. 8 para. 3 SIGHIA).

The self-employed persons engaged in agricultural activities shall make their notification to SSI within *one month* from the date of registration to the professional organizations, which have been founded by the law.

The statement of employment of self-employed is not given by the insurance holders, but the relevant institution, body, union, tax office, company representatives, or merchants and artisans registry office are obliged to send these documents to SSI. However, the self-employed persons involved in agricultural activities might make their own notification (art. 8 para. 3 SIGHIA).

On the other hand, it is compulsory to make the notification of jockeys and trainers to SSI by the registration body within *one month* after they started working (art. 8 para. 3 SIGHIA).

Within the date of these notifications, SSI shall announce the beginning of these registrants' insurance rights and liabilities.

7.2.1.3 For the Civil Servants

The employer employing civil servants is obliged to prepare the statement of employment and to make notification to SSI within *15 days* after the beginning of insurance of employees, whom the employer employs for the first time or again. There is no need for notification in appointments and transfers between different units of same public administration (art. 8 para. 5 SIGHIA).

As it can be seen, a different principle applies to notifying the civil servants to SSI. This is because there is no informality in civil service.

On the other hand, the officers that do not fulfil their notification responsibility receive administrative fine. However, the public authority that does not notify the civil servants, who will be registered to insurance, to SSI shall not receive any administrative fine.[5]

7.2.2 *Form of Notification*

Submitting the insurance holder employment report to SSI by using e-insurance fulfils the obligation of notification. The notifications other than the insurance holder employment report would not be considered legally valid.

From this aspect, the delivery of premium notifications shall not hinder the responsibility of employer, who has not delivered the insurance holder employment report.[6] Similarly, imposing fine to the employer shall not hinder the obligation of delivering the insurance holder employment report to SSI (art. 102 para. 3 SIGHIA).

Not submitting the report to SSI within its term that has been set shall not prevent the insurance holder, who faces with social risk, to benefit from aids proposed by SIGHIA. In this case, the provisions and allowances of relevant people arising from occupational accident, occupational disease, disease or maternity that occurred before the date of delivering the report or the date, when SSI revealed that the insurance holder is employed, shall be paid by SSI (art. 23 para. 1 SIGHIA).

However, the sum of any expenses made in the past and to be made in the future by SSI shall be recovered from the employer, as well as the cash asset value of the allowance if paid to the insurance holder (art. 23 para. 2 SIGHIA).

On the other hand, in order to prevent shadow employment, the insurance holders were granted the right to report their insured employment to SSI on their own. Accordingly, within one month starting from the date of employment, the insurance holders shall report to SSI that they started to work as an insurance holder. However, if the employee did not report the insured employment to SSI shall not be considered as evidence against the employee, as well as there is no sanction proposed regarding the insurance holder that has not report his/her employment.

Moreover, by making use of the electronic infrastructure provided by SSI, the banks and public authorities are held responsible for controlling if the individual is registered in terms of insured employment, as well as reporting the individuals determined to be employed without insurance to SSI (art. 8 para. 7 SIGHIA).

---

[5]Keskin (2010), p. 194.

[6]CC, 10th Civ. Div., 9.12.1988, 7391/7456.

7.2.3 Registration Directly

Insurance holders, who have been found to work as a result of the inspections physically made by SSI or the inspections carried out by using the company's records or the documents and information obtained from the public authorities or companies or banks, are registered directly by SSI. Then, the premiums are calculated directly by SSI and notified to the employer (art. 86 para. 7 SIGHIA).

However, the determination regarding the past is not limitless. Accordingly, it is compulsory that the cumulative services of insured employee shall be taken into consideration for maximum one year until the date, when the determination has been made (art. 86 para. 8 SIGHIA).

The determinations to be subject to *ex officio* registration shall be based on material determination or determination from the records of business. Among them, the material determination is the determination made by the personnel of SSI during the inspection in the business. The determination from the business records are the determinations to be made based on the records, which the business is obliged to keep, and the documents, which have proof.

7.2.4 Establishing the Registration Records

The insurance holders are recorded in the "*registration records*" kept in computer medium by making use of TR citizenship numbers in accordance with their statement of employment sent to SSI. As the "*social insurance registration number*", the insurance holders use citizenship number (for Turkish citizens) or the number of ID given by Ministry of Internal Affairs (for foreign nationals) in registration and all other transactions of beneficiaries and dependents (art. 92 para. 4 SIGHIA).

7.2.5 Non-delivery of the Statement of Employment

7.2.5.1 Imposing the Administrative Fine

The non-delivery of statement of employment is subject to the administrative fine. Thus, the accurate implementation of social insurance shall not be limited to the observation and supervision of State, but the State shall also enjoy its right to penalization regarding the aforementioned discrepancy.

In determining the amount of administrative fine, the minimum wage applied when the relevant discrepancy was revealed shall be taken into consideration (art.

102 para. 3 SIGHIA). The date of occurrence of discrepancy shall be the last day of period, which was set for reporting the statement of employment.[7]

Imposing the administrative fine shall not eliminate the responsibility of notification (art. 102 para. 3 SIGHIA).

Imposing the administrative fine applies only to the cases, in which the insured employees and the self-employed persons are not reported. Because, no administrative fine has been proposed regarding not reporting the insured civil servants to SSI.

The administrative fines are subject to 10-year limitation period. The aforementioned limitation period starts at the date of event (art. 102 para. 7 SIGHIA).

7.2.5.2 Amount of Administrative Fine

The amount of administrative fine to be imposed to employers not delivering the statement of employment formally to SSI within the period shall be equal to the minimum wage per insurance holder (art. 102 para. 1/a 1 SIGHIA). If repeated, the administrative fine to be imposed shall be equal to 5 times of minimum wage per insurance holder (art. 102 para. 1/a 3 SIGHIA).

Similarly, if the notification is not made for the self-employed, the administrative fine to be implemented relevant legal entity(s) or company(s) shall be equal to the minimum wage (art. 102 para. 1/g SIGHIA).

7.2.5.3 Objection to Administrative Fines

The administrative fines accrue upon the written notice to the relevant party. The aforementioned fines shall be paid to SSI or transferred to the bank account of SSI within 15 days and the objections shall be made to SSI within the same period. The objection stops the performance. The parties, objections of which have been rejected by SSI, may apply to the authorized administrative court within 30 days starting from the date of notification of the judgment. If the application is not made within this period, then the administrative fine is charged (art. 102 para. 6 SIGHIA).

7.3 Plurality in Social Insurance Relationship

7.3.1 Overlap of Different Compulsory Insurance Periods

The individual may both work based on an employment contract and be a taxpayer because of an independent commercial activity at the same time. This condition is frequently observed among the part-time employees. In such as cases, it is legally

[7] *See*: Özdamar and Çakar (2014), p. 897.

important if the separate insurance relationship shall be established because of both activities.

Whereas the Turkish law adopted the principle of "*singularity in social insurance*" until 2014, Act No. 6111 enabled the insurance holders to have different types of insurance status. Accordingly, if the insurance holder works in the way requiring insurance as more than one of insured worker, insured self-employer and insured civil servant, then the insurance holder shall be accepted as insured civil servant (art. 53 para. 1 SIGHIA). On this subject, the period of working as insured civil servant is prioritized. The reason for such a preference might be that it is forbidden for a civil servant to work at any job other than public service.[8]

In case that the insurance holder works as insured employee based on an employment contract and also as a self-employed at the same time, the period of working as insured worker shall be taken as base (art. 53 para. 1 SIGHIA). For instance, if a physician, who has his/her own clinic and is a self-employed, starts working as a part-time on-site physician at a business, he/she shall be considered to work as insured worker and it would not be discussed if working as on-site physician is a superior form or not. On this subject, it can be seen that the lawmaker granted superiority to the period of working as insured worker.

7.3.2 Overlap of the Period of Compulsory Insurance and Voluntary Insurance

In case that voluntary insurance holder starts working as employee or self-employer or civil servant, the voluntary insurance expires (art. 53 para. 3 SIGHIA). Accordingly, the period of compulsory insurance is taken as basis.

However, as an exception, the part-time workers may have voluntary insurance for the periods other than their compulsory insurance periods. Hence, if a part-time insured worker working for less than 30 days a month or for a couple of hours a day pays premium for voluntary insurance, then the times the premium has been paid for shall be added into the number of compulsory insurance premium payment days and these days shall be considered to be worked as insured worker (art. 51 para. 3 SIGHIA). In this case, the relevant person may have compulsory insurance and voluntary insurance at the same time.

7.3.3 Premium Paid for the Voluntary Insurance Period

The person may have paid premium for a different insurance within a complex structure and may not know the original insurance type. In case that any premium

[8]Akın (2007), pp. 131–132. *See* also: Sözer and Saraç (2008), p. 153.

has been paid for an insurance other than the one of payer, then the premiums that have been paid shall be considered to be paid within the scope of actual insurance; the premiums that have been paid shall not be paid back (art. 53 para. 5 SIGHIA).

7.4 Joining the Social Insurance Relationships

7.4.1 Before SIGHIA

The Act No. 2829,[9] which was in the force before SIGHIA, emphasized the principle of "*the social security institution having the longest active service time during the last 7 years of active service period*". Accordingly, in determining the social security institution to make the pension payment, the social security institution, with which the insurance holder has paid premium for more than 7 years (360 days × 7 years = 2520 days) of actual service period starting backwards from the day of retirement shall make the pension payment half of the whole period.

7.4.2 Period of SIGHIA

SIGHIA gathered the social security institutions of previous period under the same shelter and repealed the Act No. 2829. Besides that, the need for joining the insurance statuses has not ended in Turkey.

The solution offered for this problem is as follows. Regarding the pension requests of insurance holders, who have started working as worker, civil servant, or self-employed firstly after SIGHIA entered into force, the insurance with longest duration of premium payment or the last insurance, if the numbers of premium payment days are equal for all the insurance options, shall be taken as base (art. 53 para. 6 SIGHIA).

7.5 Situations Influencing the Social Insurance Relationship

7.5.1 Service Debt

Paying the premiums of days, premiums of which have not been paid on time, by debiting and then adding these days into retirement insurance period is called "*service debt*".

[9]OG 27.5.1983, No. 18059.

7.5.1.1 Debiting the Maternity Period

If requested, the civil servant, who gave birth, shall be given an unpaid leave for up 24 months after the maternity leave. The civil servant giving birth may also debit this period if desired (art. 41 para. 1/a, c SIGHIA).

Similarly, also the female employees may debit 16-week before and after the birth (in total) and the unpaid maternity leave up to 6 months.[10]

On the other hand, the insured workers, self-employed persons and civil servant women may debit two years after the birth for up to three times (6 years in total) (art. 41 para. 1/a SIGHIA). The maternity debit is conditional upon that woman must have not worked at any job with employment contract or had no voluntary insurance during this period.[11]

7.5.1.2 Debiting the Military Service Period

Debiting the military service period aims adding the military service period to the insurance period or number of premium payment days. Accordingly, the insurance holders may debit their time spent as regular members or as in officer candidate school (art. 41 para. 1/b SIGHIA).

The Turkish citizen immigrants may debit their military service period, which has been spent in foreign country.[12] However, the Turkish citizens working abroad may not debit their paid military service period.[13]

7.5.1.3 Debiting the Unpaid Leave Periods

The civil servant insurance holders may debit their unpaid leave periods (art. 41 para. 1/c SIGHIA).

7.5.1.4 Debiting the Periods of Education for Doctorate and Specialty in Medicine

The insurance holders may debit their time spent as uninsured during education for doctorate and specialty in medicine (art. 41 para. 1/d SIGHIA). However, debiting the time spent in graduate education is not legally possible.[14]

[10] *See*: Özer (2010), pp. 1141–1142.

[11] Özer (2010), pp. 1143–1147.

[12] CC, 10th Civ. Div., 19.11.1985, 6086/6359, Yargıtay Kararları Dergisi, 2 (1986), pp. 230–231.

[13] CC, 10th Civ. Div., 3.3.1988, 1112/1174, Yargıtay Kararları Dergisi, 6 (1988), pp. 795–796.

[14] Güzel et al. (2020), p. 548.

7.5.1.5 Debiting the Period of Law Internship

Regardless of working as civil servant or self-employer, the insurance holder may debit his/her law internship period (art. 41 para. 1/e SIGHIA). However, this right has previously been granted only to the civil servants.

7.5.1.6 Debiting the Period of Imprisonment and Custody

The individuals, who imprisoned or taken into custody while working as insured worker or self-employed and then acquitted of that crime, may debit their time spent in imprisonment or custody (art. 41 para. 1/f SIGHIA).

If they are acquitted of that crime, the insured civil servants meeting the same conditions may add these times into their insurance period and the government is obliged to pay the premiums of those days (art. 45 SIGHIA).

7.5.1.7 Debiting the Strike and Lockout Periods

The insured workers may debit their time spent during strike and lockout periods (art. 41 para. 1/g SIGHIA). Thus, since their employment contracts are suspended during the strike and lockout periods, they may utilize the strike and lockout periods, premiums of which have not been paid and thus not taken into account within the scope of insurance period. However, this debiting shall increase the number of premium payment days but not affect the beginning of insurance relationship.[15]

7.5.1.8 Debiting the Physicians' Period of Voluntary Residency

The physicians may debit their time spent during voluntary residency (art. 41 para. 1/h SIGHIA). This actually applies to the foreign physicians. Hence, the foreign nationals are accepted to specialty education if they provide a document indicating that they will be given scholarship during the specialty education or their expenses in Turkey will be borne.[16]

7.5.1.9 Debit of Civil Servant Resigning for the Elections

The civil servants resigning as required by the act of elections may debit their uninsured and unpaid period between the date of their resigning and the first day of month following the elections (art. 41 para. 1/ı SIGHIA).

---

[15]Güzel et al. (2020), p. 549.

[16]*See*: Güzel et al. (2020), p. 550.

7.5.1.10 Debiting the Missing Days in Part-Time Working Months

The insured workers may debit their missing days to 30 days of month (art. 41 para. 1/i SIGHIA). Although the part-time workers previously had the option of completing by making use of voluntary insurance, they have granted the right to debit since 25/2/2011.

7.5.1.11 Debiting the Period of Education in Foreign Countries

Among the persons, who have been sent abroad for education by the State, the ones that have successfully completed their education and fulfilled obligatory service may debit their time spent as student in foreign countries, to which they have been sent by the state. The period to be debited starts when the students turned 18-year-old (art. 41 para. 1/j SIGHIA).

7.5.1.12 Debit of Persons Having Education on Their Own Account and Then Becoming Officer or Police

After completing education at university on their own account, the persons choosing to be officer or sergeant, those becoming officer after serving as reserve officer and those assigned as deputy inspector or police officer may debit their time spent during the successful education. The same opportunity is also granted to the students studying on the account of Turkish Armed Forces or General Directorate of Security (art. 46 para. 2 SIGHIA).

7.5.1.13 Provisions of Debiting

For debiting, the insurance holder or the beneficiaries shall make the application in written. Without written application, SSI shall not have the insurance holder or beneficiary debited on its own incentive.

The insurance holder or beneficiary making the application for debiting shall pay the premiums, which will be calculated over 32% of income between the minimum and maximum limits of income subject to premium at the date of application, within one month after the notification of debit (art. 4 para. 1 SIGHIA).

However, if the applicant does not make the payment, the right to debit shall not be forfeited. In this case, the insurance holder or beneficiary shall make a new application again. The debit period, premium of which is not paid, shall not be considered as the service period (art. 41 para. 2 SIGHIA).

For the periods before the beginning of insurance, the beginning date of insurance is drawn back by the number of debited days (art. 41 para. 3 SIGHIA).

7.5.2 *Debiting the Services Abroad*

Since 1960s, the labour migration has started from Turkey to the Western Europe, especially to Germany, and Turkey has become a labour-exporting country. The Turkish citizens, who have worked abroad for long years, are deprived of social security when they come back to Turkey before qualifying for retirement and if their service period in Turkey is not enough for qualifying for pension. In order to prevent such a problem, the principle of accepting the insured works in countries other than Turkey (in other words, debiting the services abroad) was adopted.[17]

7.5.2.1 Individuals Qualifying for Debiting

For Turkish citizens and individuals, who were natural-born Turkish citizen but then lost their Turkish citizenship through renouncement, the documented insurance periods abroad as Turkish citizen after 18th age, their unemployment periods (up to one year) and the periods spent as housewife in Turkey shall be considered in their insurance periods (art. 1 Act No. 3201).

In the Act, the "*housewife*" term is utilized. However, it is not clearly specified what is aimed with this term. Considering that they need protection in terms of social security, the term "*housewife*" is interpreted in the way covering unmarried, divorced, and actually married women.[18] Accordingly, regardless of being married or having an occupation, the women turning the age of 18 years and not having any job shall be accepted as housewife.

7.5.2.2 Periods to Be Debited

All or desired portion of the documented foreign services abroad, the unemployment periods (up to one year), and the time spent as housewife abroad may be debited (art. 1 Act No. 3201).

On the condition that their long-term insurance premiums have not been paid for the period, in which they worked abroad, the Turkish employees assigned abroad by Turkish employers to the countries, which have not signed social security agreement with Turkey, may benefit from debiting. On the other hand, if the premiums paid for the period, in which they worked for Turkish employer, are transferred to Turkey, then the debiting shall not be made.[19]

The ones applying for debiting may debit all or desired portion of the period of service abroad. For those requesting partial debiting, the applicant shall specify the period to be debited as days, months, and years.

---

[17]Çelebi (2017), p. 4; Kutsal (2016), pp. 87–88.

[18]Çelebi (2017), pp. 80–81.

[19]CC, 21st Civ. Div., 18.12.2003, 7325/10474.

7.5.2.3 Applying for Debiting

For debiting foreign services, the relevant individual shall make an application. Without an application, it is legally impossible to debit. Returning to Turkey is not required for debiting because of a previous cancellation decision of Constitutional Court. The condition of returning to Turkey for pensioning after debiting shall be accepted constitutional.[20]

The individuals applying for debiting or the Turkish citizen beneficiaries of those lost their lives while working abroad or after permanently returning to Turkey shall apply to the SSI (if the insurance holder has no service period in Turkey) or the last social security institution, which the insurance holder has been affiliated with, in order to benefit from debiting (art. 3 para. 1 Act No. 3201).

7.5.2.4 Paying the Premium for Debited Period

The amount of debt to be charged for every day to be debited is 32% of daily income to be chosen between minimum and maximum daily income subject to premium at the date of application (art. 4 para. 1 Act No. 3201). In the previous period, the principle of debiting on foreign exchange has been adopted. Hence, the amount of debiting has been calculated over 3.5 USD for each day before the amendment.

The debt charged shall be paid within 3 months after the date of notification. For the persons that have not paid the premium debt within 3 months after the date of notification, the application shall be repeated (art. 4 para. 1 Act No. 3201).

7.5.2.5 Legal Consequences of Debiting

The debited days of individuals, who have service periods within the scope of social security laws in Turkey, are added into their number of premium payment days. Accordingly, if the debiting was made for the period before the beginning of insurance, then the beginning insurance is drawn back by the number of debited days (art. 5 para. 2 Act No. 3201). The date of beginning of insurance of individuals having no service period within the scope of social security institutions is determined by drawing the date of full payment of the premium debts by the number of debited days (art. 5 para. 3 Act No. 3201).

If the criteria of total number of premium payment days, the duration of service period, and the condition of age are met, then the insurance holder is put on pension. For this purpose, the insurance holder shall have permanently returned to Turkey and completely paid the debt that has been charged (art. 6 para. 1 Act No. 3201).

---

[20] Constitutional Court, 12.12.2002, 2000-36/198, OG 25.4.2003, No. 25089. *See* also: Çelebi (2017), p. 42.

7.5.3 Applying the Actual Service Term Increment

Another factor affecting the insurance relationship is the "*actual service period increment*". The lawmaker specifies that the actual service periods of those working at specific heavy jobs shall be increased by the nominal service period to be added, and thus it was aimed to allow these individuals to be able to qualify for pension earlier. This type of jobs and workplaces are listed in art. 40 SIGHIA. However, the presence of these jobs and workplaces is not enough, and the insurance holder shall have physically worked at those workplaces and faced with aforementioned risks (art. 40 para. 1 SIGHIA).

For the insured workers or civil servants, who work at the jobs and businesses that are subject to actual service term increment, the number of days corresponding to the job shall be added to the number of premium payment days (per 360 days). The actual service term increment belonging to the durations shorter than 360 days shall be calculated by proportioning the durations (art. 40 para. 1 SIGHIA). Accordingly, the self-employed insurance holders shall not benefit from the actual service term increment.

The jobs and businesses being subject to actual service term increment are arranged in three groups in terms of the days to be added to the number of premium payment days (60 days, 90 days, and 180 days). Accordingly, per 360 days of premium payment, 60, 90 or 180 days shall be added depending on the job of individual or the business, at which the insurance holder works.

On the other hand, in order to benefit from the actual service term increment, the underground miners shall have worked for minimum 1.800 days at the aforementioned businesses and jobs, and the others shall have worked for minimum 3.600 days (art. 40 para. 4 SIGHIA).

7.6 Termination of the Social Insurance Relationship

7.6.1 For the Employees Working Based on an Employment Contract

The insurance status of insurance holders working based on an employment contract shall end as of the termination of their employment contracts (art. 9 para. 1/a SIGHIA). Thus, as of the employment relationship's termination date, the social insurance rights and obligations ends, and the "*insurance holder*" title ends in gradual manner.

On this subject, Act on Social Insurance for Agricultural Workers sets forth a specific regulation. Accordingly, the agricultural worker insurance shall be terminated as of the below-specified dates:

- January 1st of that year for the persons that haven't paid the premium delay fee and the delay fine together with the premiums until the end of February of the year following the year, to which the premiums belong to,
- First day of the year following the date, when the notification is submitted to the records of Institution, for the insurance holders that have notified SSI that they do not want to continue their insurance status,
- The beginning of deduction of premiums for those starting to work in relation with the social security institution (art. 6 para. 1/a, b and c Act No. 2925).

7.6.2 For the Self-Employed Insurance Holders

The insurance status of self-employed insurance holders ends on the date specified below:

- Termination of the activities requiring liability for the income tax payer,
- The date, when the registry in chamber of merchants and artisans is deleting or the monthly income subject to premium decreased below 30 folds of minimum daily income level, for those being exempt from income tax (art. 9 para. 1/b 1 and 2 SIGHIA).

The termination of the insurance status of company shareholders, who have the status of self-employed insurance holder, varies depending on the type of company. Accordingly:

- The date of termination of tax liability (for the limited and unlimited partners of general partnerships and limited partnerships),
- The date of deleting the registry of company in trade register office (for the partnerships limited by the shares),
- The date of decision made by the shareholders about share transfer (for the limited company shareholder insurance holders transferring all of their shares to the other shareholders),
- The date of termination of board membership (for the board members of joint-stock companies) (art. 9 para. 1/b 3 SIGHIA).

On the other hand, the insurances of farmers end when they end agricultural activities or they make the request based on turning the age of 65 years (art. 9 para. 1/b 5 SIGHIA).

Similarly, the insurance of village and neighbourhood *mukhtars* (headman) ends when their duty as *mukhtar* ends. Moreover, the insurance statuses of jockeys and trainers, whose licenses have not been renewed, end as of the end of last year of license (art. 9 para. 1/b 6 and 11 SIGHIA).

Finally, the insurances of individuals residing in foreign countries end 1 day before they join to the social security system of the country, in which they live (art. 9 para. 1/b 7 SIGHIA).

7.6.3 For the Civil Servants

The insurance status of civil servants ends the beginning of month following these dates:

- The date when the payments are stopped in cases of death or requirement of putting survivor pension,
- The expiration date of age limit and the limit of sick leaves (if these limits were exceeded).

In other cases, the date of leaving the job is considered as the termination date of insurance status (art. 9 para. 1/c SIGHIA).

7.6.4 For the Implementation of Illness and Maternity Insurances

In implementation of illness and maternity insurances, the qualification as insurance holder is lost on 10th day of the month following the unpaid leave, participation to strike or being subject to lockout (art. 9 para. 2 SIGHIA).

7.6.5 Notification of the Expired Insurance to SSI

Their employers report the status of workers, whose insurance has expired, to SSI. In case of working self-employed, the status shall be reported to SSI within 10 days by themselves or the institutions or tax offices by submitting the "*notification of employment's termination*" (art. 9 para. 3 SIGHIA).

If the aforementioned notification is not submitted, then the administrative fine that equals to 1/10 of minimum wage shall be imposed for each insured worker, whereas the administrative fine shall equal to the minimum wage for the self-employed. For the civil servants and the other public officials, no penal sanction has been set forth.

7.6.6 Reactivating the Terminated Insurance

By making a mass payment, it is legally available to reactivate the terminated insurance period for the retirement and survivors' insurances. Accordingly, the individuals, for whom the lump sum payment has been made, may qualify for receiving pension by reactivating their terminated insurance period by making the lump sum payment back to SSI.[21]

First of all, in order to reactivate the expired service periods, the person shall have started working as an insurance holder after receiving the lump sum payment. In this case, it is compulsory to pay the amount, which shall be calculated by updating the lump sum payment that has been made, back to SSI. For this purpose, by applying to SSI in written, the individual shall request the revival of previous service periods (art. 31 para. 2 SIGHIA).

On the other hand, by debiting or joining the service periods in a foreign land or adding the periods, which were gained via action for fixing of service period, to the service periods, the beneficiaries of deceased insurance holders may legally complete the number of premium payment days required for benefiting from the survivor insurance. Accordingly, after adding the reactivated duration to the previous service terms, the beneficiaries qualify to receive survivor pension. For this purpose, the beneficiaries of deceased insurance holder shall pay the amount, which equals to the updated lump sum payment, back to SSI and then make written request for revival (art. 36 para. 4 SIGHIA).

References

Akın L (2007) Sosyal Güvenlik Hukukunda Bağımlı Çalışanların Maluliyeti. Yetkin Publishing, Ankara

Akyiğit E (1995) İşverenin İşi Kabulde Temerrüdünün 506 Sayılı Sosyal Sigortalar Kanunu Açısından Değerlendirilmesi. Çimento İşveren Dergisi 9(3):15–24

Çelebi D (2017) Türk Sosyal Güvenlik Hukukunda Yurt dışı Hizmet Borçlanması. Adalet Publishing, Ankara

Çenberci M (1985) Sosyal Sigortalar Kanunu Şerhi. Olgaç Matbaası, Ankara

Güzel A, Okur AR, Caniklioğlu N (2020) Sosyal Güvenlik Hukuku, 18th edn. Beta Publishing, Istanbul

Keskin M (2010) Sosyal Güvenlik Mevzuatında İşveren Yükümlülükleri. Sicil İş Hukuku Dergisi 18:193–201

Kutsal FBS (2016) Türk Sosyal Sigortalar Hukukunun Temel İlkeleri. Beta Publishing, Istanbul

Oral Aİ (2007) Türk Sosyal Güvenlik Hukuku Açısından Toptan Ödeme. Anadolu Üniversitesi, Eskişehir. yayını No. 1731

Özdamar M, Çakar E (2014) Sosyal Güvenlik Kurumuna Yasal Süresi Dışında Verilmesine Rağmen İdari Para Cezasına Konu Edilmeyecek Bildirimler. Marmara Üniversitesi Hukuk Fakültesi Hukuk Araştırmaları Dergisi 20(1):895–915

Özer HD (2010) Doğum Borçlanması. In: Prof.Dr. Ali Güzel'e Armağan, vol 2. Beta Publishing, Istanbul, pp 1137–1157

Sözer AN, Saraç C (2008) Sosyal Sigorta İlişkisinde Çokluk: Sigortalılık Hallerinin, Tiplerinin ve Sürelerinin Birleşmesi. Sicil İş Hukuku Dergisi. 12:152–159

Tunçomağ K (1990) Sosyal Güvenlik Kavramı ve Sosyal Sigortalar, 5th edn. Beta Publishing, Istanbul

[21] Oral (2007), p. 131.

Chapter 8
Scope of Social Insurance

The scope of social insurances (as person) is limited to the individuals covered by the SIGHIA. The first category in this group is the insurance holders. However, the relatives (family members) of insurance holders shall also be involved in this category. These individuals benefit from the social insurance law not because of their professional services but as the dependents of insurance holders.

8.1 Those Considered as Fully Insured

8.1.1 Workers and Individuals Deemed to Be Worker

8.1.1.1 Those Working Based on an Employment Contract

Art. 4 para. 1/a SIGHIA principally covers the workers employed based on the criterion of *"employment contract"*. However, because of the complexity of business relationship, it is not always easy to determine if the legal aspect of these relationships is established by the employment contract.

For both of TCO and LA, the presence of employment contract and also the factors "*working, wage, and dependence*" are sought together. From the aspect of insurance concept, the presence of wage factor is not an absolute necessity. On the other hand, working dependently is the determinant factor for the insurance according to art. 4 para. 1/a SIGHIA.

The presence of employment contract has been determined in the past by the Court of Cassation as one of the factors *"time"* and *"dependence"*. The point to start here is whether a work or art is produced as a result of employment and if the individual is working under the authority of another individual. According to these that are still valid today, the professional soccer players, trainers and managers, translator guides, village watchmen and imams, cooperative presidents receiving payment, nude models modelling to the academy students, and physicians working

T. Centel, *Turkish Social Law*, https://doi.org/10.1007/978-3-030-64704-9_8

at a private polyclinic were accepted to be the insured employees working on an employment contract.[1]

Again, in the past, Court of Cassation sought after the fulfilment of condition of working at the business owned by the employer in order for one to be accepted as an insured worker.[2] But, as a result of the technological and economic advancements of today, the ones needing to work outside the workplace because of the characteristics of job shall be considered among the employees working at the workplace. From this aspect, it would be more appropriate to seek after the condition of working within the business organization of employer, rather than working at the workplace.

The duration of working on an employment contract is of no importance for the social insurances. Accordingly, even if they work on an employment contract for only 1 day, the individuals are principally considered within the scope of social insurance. For this reason, the classification is made based on working for less or more than 10 days. Thus, the housekeepers working for 10 days may have voluntary insurance, whereas those working for more than 10 days may benefit from all the branches of social insurance.

8.1.1.2 Foreign Workers

Until 2003, the foreign workers were taken into the scope of social insurance as an obligation from the aspect of short-term insurance branches and voluntarily from the aspect of long-term insurance branches. And then, in order to treat the citizens and non-citizens equally from the aspect of social security, as a necessity of ILO Convention No. 118 approved and enforced by Turkey, the Act No. 4958 granted the foreign citizens with the right to benefit from all the insurance branches, except for the unemployment insurance.

Nowadays, SIGHIA incorporates a different principle for the foreigners. Accordingly, based on the principle of reciprocity, the foreign nationals working on an employment contract, except for the nationals of countries that international social security agreement has been signed with, are accepted within the scope of art. 4 para. 1/a SIGHIA (art. 4 para. 2/c SIPHIA).

The foreigners, who are the nationals of countries having an international social security agreement (especially those having mutual social security agreement with Turkey) shall benefit from the provisions of aforementioned agreement primarily. But, if there is no related provision in that social security agreement or if there is a reference to Turkish social law, then the provisions of SIGHIA shall be applied.[3]

On the other hand, without prejudice to the provisions of international social security agreements, among the employees sent by and in the name of any company, which is established in any foreign country, to Turkey for less than 3 months for

---

[1] *See*: Güzel et al. (2020), pp. 83–86.

[2] Güzel et al. (2020), p. 89 fn. 56.

[3] Güzel et al. (2020), pp. 93–94; Sözer (2019), p. 71.

business purposes, the ones residing abroad and being subject to the social security system of foreign country (this shall be documented) are excluded from the scope of social insurance. After the temporary time (maximum 3 months), they are subject to the Turkish social insurance regulations (art. 6 para. 1/e SIGHIA).

Similarly, the foreign workers working at free zones are also subject to Turkish social security regulations (art. 10 Act No. 3218).

Moreover, the individuals that are the citizens of foreign but have Turkish origins may benefit from the social insurances as Turkish citizens do (art. 5 Act No. 2527). From this aspect, it can be stated that there is no difference between the Turkish citizens and foreign nationals having Turkish origins in terms of social security since 1980.

Finally, the foreign nationals working for special services of embassy and consulate personnel in Turkey shall be excluded from the scope of social insurance if they document that they have insurance in the country, which has sent them, or in any third country. On the other hand, if they cannot document their insurance, then they shall be subject to the Turkish social insurance regulations (art. 9 para. 2 Bylaw on Social Insurance Operations).

8.1.1.3 Agriculture and Forestry Workers

SIGHIA includes the agricultural and forestry workers continuously or discontinuously working at public agencies and the agricultural and forest workers continuously working at private sector companies within the scope of compulsory insurance. However, those discontinuously working at private sector companies (even if for a certain wage) are not within the scope of compulsory insurance (art. 6 para. ı).

However, being excluded from the scope of compulsory insurance doesn't mean being excluded from the scope of social insurance (being deprived of social security). Thus, the agricultural workers, who have worked for less than 30 days in private sector companies before in the period of Agricultural Workers' Social Insurance Act, now continue their voluntary insurance in SIGHIA period (prov. art. 12 para. 10 SIGHIA). Again, the ones that have started working discontinuously in agriculture or forestry industry in the period of SIGHIA have been included within the scope of social insurance in terms of certain voluntary insurance branches (add. art. 5 para. 4 SIGHIA).

8.1.1.4 Presidents and Board Members of Labour Unions

The ones elected as president or board member of labour unions, confederations, and union branches were considered as insured even though there is no employment contract-based relationship between them (art. 4 para 2/a SIGHIA).

8.1.1.5 Artists, Philosophers and Authors

The movie, theatre, performance, show, vocal, and musical instrument artists and those working on music, painting, decoration, and similar branches, as well as the philosophers and authors are accepted to be insured (art. 4 para 2/b SIGHIA).

This population has been taken to the scope of social security for the first time in Turkey with an additional article (add. art. 1) brought by art. 14 Act No. 2167 dated 29/6/1978.[4] And then, SIGHIA continued the same social protection. Among them, the part-time workers and the artists working for 10 days or less per month may benefit only from the specific insurance branches (add. art. 6 paras 1 and 3 SIGHIA).

8.1.1.6 Security Guards

The security guards employed according to the *Act on Protecting the Farmers' Products* No. 4081 dated 2/7/1941[5] are accepted as insurance holders (art. 4 para. 2/d SIGHIA). They are not employed based on an employment contract but are assigned by the governors or district governors (art. 7 Act No. 4081).

8.1.1.7 Prostitutes

The prostitutes specified in *Act on Protection of Public Health* No. 1593 on 24/4/1930[6] are considered as insured (art. 4 para. 2/e SIGHIA).

An SSI memorandum issued in 1974 clarified that, since there is no employment contract between the prostitute and the owner of fornix, they shall not be deemed insured.[7] This population named "*prostitute*" in Act on Protection of Public Health has been granted the social security with an addition provision (add. art. 4) brought by art. 14 of Act No. 2167 dated 29/6/1978.[8] SIGHIA that has been enacted later continues the same social protection.

8.1.1.8 Qualified Instructors Those Working on Course Payment and Provisional Personnel

The individuals employed as qualified instructors in courses organized by the Ministry of National Education are considered insured (art. 4 para. 2/f SIGHIA).

[4]OG 11.7.1978, No. 16343.

[5]OG 10.7.1941, No. 4856.

[6]OG 6.5.1930, No. 1489.

[7]*See*: Centel (1978), p. 12.

[8]OG 11.7.1978, No. 16343.

They are the instructors offering the in-service course and seminar trainings in formal and mass education institutions.[9]

Since SIGHIA stated only the courses organized by the Ministry of National Education, the courses organized by the other institutions and corporations shall not be considered within this scope.[10]

Similarly, the individuals employed by public authorities based on a certain course payment are considered insured. These individuals are generally the personnel working at public schools (not listed as permanent) and offering training or education services.

Moreover, those employed as "*temporary personnel*" in accordance with the Civil Servants Law benefit from the provisions of social insurance (art. 4 para. 2/f SIGHIA). Since these individuals are employed for a period less than 1 year or for a season, they are employed at the positions determined by the Council of Ministers at determined wages but are not deemed personnel (art. 4 para. C Act No. 657).

8.1.1.9 Those Participating in Public Service Employment Program

TLI organizes "*public service employment programs*". These programs are those aiming to offer short-term employment and training for unemployed individuals in the periods, when the level of unemployment is high.

Within this context, the premiums of the participants of public service employment programs are borne by TLI (art. 73 para. 3 Bylaw on Active Labour Services). Accordingly, the participants of these programs are deemed employee, they shall be within the scope of social insurance (art. 4 para. 2/g SIGHIA).

8.1.2 Self-Employed Persons

The individuals working on own name and account without employment contract are considered to have social insurance (art. 4 para. 1/b SIGHIA). Within this context, SIGHIA requires the self-employed to be Turkish citizen in order to be insured. Accordingly, the self-employed foreigners living in Turkey in accordance with the formal requirements are under the social protection against the risks of work life.

---

[9]Sözer (2019), pp. 77–78.

[10]Korkusuz and Uğur (2009), p. 113.

8.1.2.1 Village and Neighbourhood Headmen

The village and neighbourhood headmen have been granted the right to social security since 1977. Accordingly, Act No. 2108 enacted on 29/8/1977[11] provided what village and neighbourhood headmen with the social insurance (art. 4 para. 1). The same provision was also included in art. 4 para. 1/b SIGHIA.

But, art. 4 para. 1 Act No. 2108 required the village and neighbourhood headmen not to work in another job. Accordingly, any headman to work based on an employment contract (in addition to their task as headman) shall not benefit from the security offered by Act No. 2108 but they shall benefit from the social security provided to the employees by SIGHIA.

8.1.2.2 Income Taxpayers

In order for independent workers to be accepted as insured, they shall be income taxpayer in small business taxation or real taxation system. These are the individuals being taxpayer because of business income or self-employment income (art. 4 para. 1/b 1 SIGHIA).

The lawyers and notaries, who are in the self-employment income groups, have been excluded from the scope of social insurance of previous period. Among them, the independent lawyers shall benefit from the social security according to art. 4 para. 1/b 1 SIGHIA. Accordingly, those employed by any employer in any law office shall benefit from the social security according to the provisions of art. 4 para. 1/a SIGHIA.[12]

8.1.2.3 Artisans and Traders

As an exemption among the self-employed individuals, the traders and artisans being no income taxpayer are considered insured (art. 4 para. 1/b 2 SIGHIA). These are the individuals earning no trading profit since they have not sufficient capital for earning trading income from the aspect of income tax. In order for these individuals to be able to benefit from social insurance, they shall be registered in "*artisans and traders register*".

On the other hand, the traders and artisans that can document that they have been registered in registry of traders and artisans, but their income is less than 30 times of minimum wage limit shall not be accepted as insurance holder (art. 6 para. 1/k SIGHIA). It is clear that, because of the size of underground economy in Turkey, this situation would not accord with the insurance compulsion.

---

[11]OG 10.9.1977, No. 16053.

[12]Caniklioğlu (2010), pp. 962–963.

8.1.2.4 Company Shareholders

The shareholders of joint-stock companies, who are the board members, the working partners of limited partnerships divided into shares, and all the shareholders of other companies and association of ship owners are accepted as insurance holder (art. 4 para. 1/b 3 SIGHIA). However, the shareholders, who are not the members of joint-stock company's board, and the non-working shareholders of limited partnerships are not within the scope of social insurance.

The founder shareholders of joint-stock companies, who are not the board member, were not accepted insured (on the contrary with the previous period). However, the founder shareholders of joint-stock companies, who have been insured in previous period, were granted the right to continue their status in SIGHIA period (prov. art. 22 SIGHIA).

8.1.2.5 Farmers

Those independently running agricultural activities are accepted as insurance holder (art. 4 para. 1/b 4 SIGHIA). These individuals operate in producing the herbal, forest, animal, and aquaculture products and/or storing, transporting or marketing these products. These activities of aforementioned individuals are performed in their own properties or in form of partnership in properties of others or in public spaces (art. 3 para. 1/19 SIGHIA).

On the other hand, the individuals, who document that their average monthly income is lower than the 30-x minimum daily wage, are not considered insurance holder (art. 6 para. 1/ı SIGHIA). It is clear that this does not comply with the insurance obligation in Turkey, where the underground economy reached at high levels.[13]

8.1.2.6 Jockeys and Trainers

Subject to the provisions of *Act on Horse Races* No. 6132 dated 10/7/1953,[14] the jockeys and trainers are considered self-employed insurance holders (art. 4 para. 3 SIGHIA).

On the other hand, although they are in relation with the horse races, the individuals working as jockey apprentices or stableman work based on a labour agreement and they are deemed insurance holder (as an employee).[15]

---

[13]Güzel et al. (2020), p. 107.

[14]OG 15.7.1953, No. 8458.

[15]Sözer (2019), pp. 89–90.

Similarly, even the jockeys and trainers working at the horse races, which are not within the scope of Act No. 6132, are not deemed self-employed insurance holders.[16]

8.1.3 *Civil Servants*

The individuals started working as permanent employee at public institutions for the first time since the day SIGHIA entered into force (1/10/2008) and not included in worker or self-employed insurance holder classes or working under a contract but not obliged to have insurance are deemed insurance holder as civil servant or other public officials (art. 4 para. 1/c SIGHIA).

In addition to those specified above, the following parties shall be deemed insurance holder as public officials:

- Those taking office in public institutions as a result of an election or appointment and being granted the pension right as civil servants have,
- Prime ministers, deputies of the President of the State, ministers, parliamentarians, deputy ministers, majors, elected members of provincial committee,
- Persons, who were elected as the chairperson of public unions and confederations and as the chairperson of union branches and boards and taking leave without pay,
- Military students and individuals in basic military and police training in order to be appointed as sergeant, police or gendarmerie (art. 4 para. 4 SIGHIA).

Moreover, besides SIGHIA, Act No. 6191 dated 10/3/2011[17] provides that, once the preliminary contract is signed, the contracted private candidates and specialized sergeants shall be treated as insurance holders as public officials (art. 7 para. 1).

8.2 Those Deemed Partially Insured

There are individuals, who are not actually engaged in activities requiring being insurance holder but are facing with social risks because of the tasks they fulfil. The lawmaker does not deem it necessary for them to be taken under social security against any sort of social risk but provides that they shall be deemed partially insured and they shall benefit only from the specific branches of social insurances. The individuals in this group shall be named "*partially insured*" instead of "*fully insured*".

[16]Korkusuz and Uğur (2009), p. 146.

[17]OG 22.3.2011, No. 27882.

8.2.1 Convicted and Arrested Prisoners

The convicted and arrested prisoners, who have to work, are not deemed worker since their business relationship is not based on their freewill and they are not working under an employment contract. Principally, only the provisions of occupational accident, occupational disease, and maternity insurances shall be implemented for these individuals, who need social protection. Accordingly, the convicted and arrested prisoners employed in facilities, ateliers, and similar units established within the body of penal institutions and prisons shall partially benefit from the social insurance (art. 5 para. 1/a SIGHIA).

The employer is the penal institutions and institution of prison workshops, and the representatives of the employer are the manager directors and supervisors of these institutions (art. 12 para. 5 SIGHIA).

8.2.2 Apprentices and Students Having Vocational Education

Turkish legal system adopted the principle that the apprentices and students having vocational education in businesses shall be employed based on apprenticeship contract instead of employment contract and they shall not be deemed employee and insurance holder. However, the individuals that may face with social risks in businesses are not completely kept away from the social security.

Accordingly, in *Act of Vocational Education* No. 3308 dated 5/6/1986,[18] it is set forth that the provisions of only the occupational accident and occupational health insurances and the provisions of general health insurance shall be applied to the apprentice candidates, apprentices, and students having vocational education in businesses (art. 5 para. 1/b SIGHIA; art. 25 para. 4 of Act No. 3308).

8.2.3 Interns

The provisions of occupational accident and occupational health insurances and general health insurance shall be applied to the students, who are subject to internship obliged to compulsory internship during occupational and technical secondary education and higher education (art. 5 para. 1/b SIGHIA).

From this aspect, the students studying at 6th grade of medical schools are paid monthly income for their services during education (add. art. 29 Act No. 2547). Regardless of earning the income that is lower than the lower limit of income subject to premium, these intern students shall benefit from the provisions of occupational accident and occupational disease insurances.

---

[18]OG 19.6.1986, No. 19139.

8.2.4 Students of Vocational and Technical Education

The students having supplementary education or branch education during vocational and technical education shall be subject to the provisions of only the occupational accident and occupational disease insurances and the provisions of general health insurance (art. 5 para. 1/b SIGHIA). Different from the interns, these students are those, who have to complete their education or direct themselves to a certain occupational or technical domain.

8.2.5 Bursars Employed in Supported Projects

Since 2016, the bursars (i.e., the students receiving scholarship) are partly taken into the scope of social insurance. However, it can be seen that not all the bursars are covered within this scope. Accordingly, only the bursars employed in projects supported by the public institutions and organizations shall benefit from the provisions of occupational accident and occupational disease insurances and the provisions of general health insurance (art. 5 para. 1/c SIGHIA).

8.2.6 University Students Working Part-Time

The Act of Higher Education grants the university students with the opportunity of part-time employment by considering the difficulties in employing personnel in universities (art. 46 para. 1/k). Among these employees, the ones having income level lower than the minimum level subject to premium shall be subject to the provisions of occupational accident and occupational disease insurances and the provisions of general health insurance (art. 5 para. 1/b SIGHIA). The ones having income level higher than the lower limit shall benefit from all the insurance branches.[19]

On the other hand, since the medical benefits are borne by the medico-social services of universities, the students working part-time in the universities are not in the need for benefiting from the provisions of general health insurance.

[19] Gerek (2009), pp. 235–236.

8.2.7 Disabled War Veterans and Those Disabled on Active Duty

Among the disabled war veterans and those disabled on active duty, the allowances paid to those, who started working as an insurance holder, shall not be stopped. The provisions of long-term insurance branches shall apply to those working as civil servant without having their allowance stopped, whereas the clauses of occupational accident and occupational disease insurances shall apply to those working as worker or self-employed. However, those benefiting from the occupational accident and occupational disease insurances may request the implementation of long-term insurance branches (art. 5 para. 1/c SIGHIA).

8.2.8 Trainees

The trainees attending to the vocational courses organized by TLI in order to provide, improve, and change the profession of individuals shall benefit from the clauses of occupational accident and occupational disease insurances and the provisions of general health insurance (art. 5 para. 1/e SIGHIA). From this aspect, since the trainees participating to the courses organized by TLI were specified, the others participating to the courses organized by other institutions or organizations shall not benefit from the provisions of insurance.

8.2.9 Those Assigned Abroad for Working

The Turkish employees assigned abroad for employment in businesses, which are located in countries having no social security agreement with Turkey, by the employers shall be subject to the provisions of short-term insurance branches and general health insurance. However, when requested by the relevant employee, these employees may optionally benefit from the long-term insurance branches (art. 5 para. 1/g SIGHIA).

On the other hand, the workers assigned abroad for temporary duties or self-employed individuals residing in foreign countries for a temporary period are not in this category. Accordingly, the rights and obligations regarding the social insurance in Turkey continue for these temporary periods (art. 10 SIGHIA).

8.2.10 *Those Receiving Job Loss Indemnity Payment as a Result of Privatization*

The provisions of law on short-term insurance branches shall not be applied to those, who have lost their jobs and received "*job loss indemnity payment*" because the institution at which they have worked has been privatized (art. 21 Act No. 4046). On the other hand, they shall be granted the right to benefit from provisions of long-term insurance branches and general health insurance (prov. art. 13 para. 1 SIGHIA).

8.2.11 *Those Receiving Pension*

Since 1986, the retirees are granted the right to work legally without their pension stopped. However, they were obliged to pay "*social security support contribution*". But, enacted in 2006, SIGHIA abolished the workers' option for working by paying social security support contribution.[20] On the other hand, by placing a provisional article for those have been insured before the SIGHIA entered into force, these people are granted the right to work by paying the social security support contribution.

Accordingly, the individuals working as worker or civil servant before SIGHIA entered into force and the retirees working by paying social security support contribution at the date, when SIGHIA entered into force, shall maintain their present status. But, although they would pay short-term insurance premium in addition to 30% social security support contribution, these individuals shall benefit from only the occupational accident and occupational disease insurances (prov. art. 14 para. 1/a SIGHIA).

8.2.12 *Drivers and Artists Working Part-Time*

The individuals working for less than 10 days per month in affiliation with one or more employers in taxicabs, buses, minibuses, and similar urban transportation vehicles shall be deemed insured only if they pay their insurance premium over 30 days per month by themselves (add. art. 6 para. 1 SIGHIA). Based on this regulation, the drivers and helpers working in taxicabs and private public transportation buses, who have been working without social security, were granted the right to social security to a certain extent.[21]

[20]See: Caniklioğlu (2008), p. 165.

[21]Tuncay and Ekmekçi (2019), pp. 340–341.

Similarly, the artists employed by one or more employers based on a part-time employment contract for less than 10 days per month shall benefit from the provisions of social insurance once they pay their own social insurance premiums over 30 days per month (add. art. 6 para. 1 SIGHIA).

The drivers, helpers, and artists employed part-time may benefit from the social insurance partly, because only the provisions of long-term insurance branches and (upon their request) those of the unemployment insurance shall be applied to these employees (add. art. 6 para. 3 SIGHIA).

8.2.13 Workers Working at Impermanent Agricultural and Forestry Activities

For the impermanent agricultural and forestry workers, only the provisions of occupational accident and occupational disease insurances and long-term insurance branches (disability, old age, and survivor insurances) are applied. Accordingly, the provisions of disease and maternity insurances shall not be applied to impermanent working agricultural and forestry workers (add. art. 5 para. 4 SIGHIA).

8.2.14 Those Working at Domestic Services for Less Than 10 Days Per Month

Those employed by one or more employers in domestic services for less than 10 days per month shall benefit only from the provisions of occupational accident and occupational disease insurances (add. art. 9 para. 2 SIGHIA).

Accordingly, the aforementioned individuals may not benefit from the long-term insurance branches and disease, maternity, and general health insurances. However, once these workers pay their premiums by themselves, they may benefit from the other insurance branches (disability, old age, and survivor insurances and public health insurance) as well (add. art. 9 para. 2 SIGHIA).

8.3 Those Accepted Uninsured

8.3.1 Employer's Spouse Working Without Receiving Any Wage

The spouse of employer, who works at the business without receiving any payment, fulfils the mutual help anticipated in the family law and pursues the aim of improving the family's quality of life (art. 151 para. 1 Civil Code). Because of the fulfilment of a duty arising from family law, the employer's spouse working without receiving an income is deemed uninsured (art. 6 para. 1a SIGHIA).

The term "*spouse*" here refers to one of individuals defined as wife and husband in Civil Code. For this reason, the ones living together without marriage are not within the scope of this principle. It also refers to both woman and man.

On the other hand, since working without receiving any payment is taken as base, the spouse to work for a payment in the business of other spouse shall have social insurance. In determining if the spouse works on a payment, the characteristics of works done by spouse and if the qualifications of spouse are suitable for that job shall be taken into account. From this aspect, it would be necessary to separately analyse under which conditions the spouse shall be deemed insured.[22]

8.3.2 Those Working in Indoor Jobs

The individuals working indoors are not accepted as insurance holders (art. 6 para. 1/b SIGHIA).

However, principally, they shall be living together in the same house and be relatives up to third degree (including the third-degree relatives). Moreover, these individuals shall receive no assistance from outside. Finally, the job done shall be one of those fulfilled in spaces used as settlement such as house, apartment, residence, etc.

On the other hand, the tasks fulfilled shall not have to have certain qualifications. Thus, once the tasks are fulfilled within the borders of house and the relatives fulfil the jobs, the workers working in jobs other than the handcrafts shall not be deemed insurance holders.[23]

8.3.3 Those Working at Domestic Services

According to art. 6 para. 1/c SIGHIA, the workers working at domestic services are not deemed insurance holders.

However, it should be stated that this article is misleading and inconsistent, because add. art. 9 SIPHIA sets the insurance conditions of those working at domestic services. Accordingly, if a paid employee is employed in domestic services for longer than 10 days per month, he/she shall benefit from all of the insurance branches. On the other hand, if they work for less than 10 days per month, these workers shall benefit only from the occupational accident and occupational disease insurances.

[22] Alper (2015), p. 117.

[23] Alper (2015), p. 118; Güzel et al. (2020), p. 112; Tuncay and Ekmekçi (2019), p. 348.

8.3.4 Those Fulfilling Military Service

The individuals fulfilling their military services as private and non-commissioned officer, and the students of officer candidate school are not accepted as insurance holders (art. 6 para. 1/d SIGHIA).

This is because the military service is an obligation that is fulfilled within the scope of public law. For this reason, the individuals fulfilling this obligation shall not work based on an employment contract or be engaged in an activity establishing an insurance relationship. On the other hand, Court of Cassation declared that the individuals, who are employed by an employer with an employment contract during their leave from military service, should be deemed insurance holder.[24]

8.3.5 Those Documenting That They Are Insured in a Foreign Country

The workers, who have been working for a company established in a foreign country, appointed to Turkey for less than 3 months are able to document that they are insured in foreign country, and the self-employed individuals residing in foreign country and being insured in that country within the scope of that country's social security system shall not be deemed insurance holder (art. 6 para. 1/e SIGHIA).

The aforementioned regulation reserves the provisions of international social security agreement. Accordingly, if Turkey has bilateral social security agreement with the country, in which the company appointing the worker is established, and if the contract of employee projects the continuity of worker's insurance for a certain period during his job in Turkey, then the worker shall not be deemed insurance holder for a period specified in contract instead of the 3-month period specified in art. 6 para. 1/e SIGHIA.

8.3.6 Students Working in Production and Manufacturing

The students actively working in practical production and manufacturing jobs during the normal education periods of college shall not be deemed insurance holders (art. 6 para. 1/f SIGHIA).

This is because the students fulfil these duties as a natural consequence of their education. In this case, since there is not any activity creating an insurance relationship, these individuals shall not be deemed insurance holders.[25] On the other hand,

[24]CC, 9th Civ. Div., 3.5.1979, 1474/3970, IHU, SSK art. 3 No. 4.
[25]Çenberci (1985), p. 69.

the production and manufacturing activities that are unlikely to be deemed as a natural consequence of education and that aim to benefit from the labour of students shall require the students to be insured.[26]

8.3.7 *Patients and Disabled Individuals in Orientation*

The individuals, who became disabled because of a disease or a disability, shall be oriented (corresponding to rehabilitation from medical aspect) to their previous job or adapted to a new job that is compatible to the previous job. Among these individuals, the ones taken to treatment in medical facilities or rehabilitation centres shall not be deemed insurance holder (art. 6 para. 1/g SIGHIA) because their work during orientation period does not cause a relationship in terms of professional activity.

On the other hand, the disease or disability does not solely hinder anybody from being insurance holder. Similarly, if those completing the orientation period are employed, then the insurance relationship emerges.

8.3.8 *Civil Servants and Self-Employed Individuals Aged Less Than 18 Years*

Among the independent workers and civil servants, those aged less than 18 years shall not be deemed insurance holder (art. 6 para. 1/h SIPHIA). On the other hand, if those completing vocational school or art school and declared adult by the court work in a job that is related with the education, then these individuals shall not wait to turn 18-year-old for being insurance holder (art. 6 para. 2 SIPHIA).

8.3.9 *Agricultural Workers Working at Impermanent Jobs and Farmers Having Low Level of Monthly Income*

The agricultural and forestry workers working at impermanent agricultural or forestry businesses shall not be deemed insurance holder. Similarly, the independent workers being engaged in permanent agricultural or forestry activities but being able to document that their monthly income is low shall not be deemed insurance holder (art. 6 para. 1/ı SIGHIA).

On the other hand, the farmers engaged in agricultural activities may terminate their insurance status after turning the age of 65 years (art. 6 para. 1/ı SIPHIA).

[26]*See*: CC, 21st Civ. Div., 29.6.2015, 8956/14976, www.kazanci.com.

8.3.10 Self-Employed Persons Having Low Level of Monthly Income

Among the individuals working on their own name and account, those being exempt from income tax but being recorded in registry of traders and artisans and documenting that their monthly income is lower than minimum wage limit shall not be deemed insurance holder (art. 6 para. 1/k SIPHIA).

These are small business owners and artisans. Such a regulation may be seen socially suitable. However, in an environment where the real income levels of individuals cannot be determined accurately because of the failures of inspection system, it is clear that such a regulation would contribute to the grey economy. For this reason, the suitability of such a regulation for the countries having large grey economy such as Turkey is controversial.

8.3.11 Persons Employed in Foreign Missions of Public Agencies

Among the Turkish contracted personnel employed in foreign missions of public agencies and having permanent residential permit or citizenship in that country, those proving that they have insurance from the social security organization of that country and the contracted personnel employed in public agencies' foreign missions and insured by their employees in that country shall not be considered insurance holder within the scope of SIGHIA (art. 6 para. 1/l SIGHIA). Thus, it can be understood that, with such a regulation, it was aimed to prevent the double insurance.

8.3.12 Persons Assigned to Youth and Sport Activities

Those impermanent appointed in camp, training, and preparation activities and any youth and sport activity organized by Ministry of Youth and Sport, General Directorate of Sport, Turkish Football Federation, and independent sport federations shall not be deemed insurance holder (art. 6 para. 1/m SIGHIA).

The main reason for such a regulation is that these activities are not professional ones but they are performed with an amateur spirit. Thus, because there is no professional work, no insurance relationship shall emerge in such cases.

8.3.13 Self-Employed Persons Continuing Activity While Receiving Pension

The individuals continuing working as self-employed while receiving pension shall not be deemed insurance holder (art. 6 para. 1/n SIGHIA).

The main purpose of this regulation is to prevent the individuals, who continue working while receiving pension, from being subject to occupational accident and occupational disease insurances, because the obligation of paying social security support contribution of the retired self-employed persons was abolished if they continue working.

8.4 Family Members of Insurance Holder

The idea of social security is not limited only to the insurance holders. Accordingly, in addition to the insurance holders, the modern social security systems aim to provide the family members of insurance holders with a certain level of social protection as well.

While taking the family members of insurance holder into the scope of insurance, differences may appear depending on if insurance holder is alive or not. Based on this difference, SIGHIA names the insurance holder's family members as "*dependent*" or "*beneficiary*".

8.4.1 Dependents of Insurance Holder

The family members of insurance holder are within the scope of social insurance as the dependents as long as the insurance holder is alive. However, the aid to be provided during this period is limited to the general health insurance. Accordingly, as long as the insurance holder is alive, the family members shall not be provided with a financial aid.

The term dependent refers to the:

- Spouse, who is not an insurance holder, has no voluntary insurance or has no income or pension arising from his/her own insurance,
- Non-married children, who are single and didn't turn 18 year-old or 20 year-old for those having education in high school or apprenticeship training or occupational training in companies or 25 year-old for those having higher education, as well as the non-married disabled children (regardless of their age),
- Parents of the general health insurance holder who keeps them (art. 3 para. 1/10 SIGHIA)

Thus, according to SIGHIA, the dependents that insurance holder is liable to look after are spouse, children, and parents. And, it is not possible for another such as grandparents, grandsons or granddaughters of insurance holder to benefit from the medical aids.

It can be clearly seen that there is no distinction made here between the sons and daughters. Accordingly, the daughters will also lose the title of "*dependent*" when they turn the specified age.

When started working, the dependent gains the title of "*insurance holder*" and loses his/her rights as dependent. Principally, working part-time or full-time does not make any difference. However, as an exemption, those working part-time or those working in domestic services for 10 days per month or longer but less than 30 days per month shall keep their rights as dependent from the aspect of public health insurance (art. 3 para. 3 and add. art. 9 para. 1 SIGHIA).

8.4.2 Beneficiaries

The spouse, children and parents, who are put on income or pension or who receive lump sum payment from the Institution when the insurance holder or individuals receiving pension from SSI dies, are named "*beneficiary*" (art. 3 para. 1/7 SIGHIA). Moreover, art. 34 SIGHIA specifies who shall be beneficiary and how the survivor pension shall be divided between the beneficiaries.

Daughters lose their rights as dependent when they turn the age specified in the law. However, it can be seen that there is no such limitation for being considered beneficiary. Accordingly, as long as the daughters do not work or do not receive any income or pension from SSI in return to their works, they qualify for receiving income or survivor pension from SSI as beneficiary. Thus, the daughter of insurance holder, whom the insurance holder is not obliged to look after, gains the right to survivor pension after the death of insurance holder, and she qualifies for benefit from general health insurance. It is not seen consistent from the aspect of policy of the law that the dependents and beneficiaries as the family members are subject to different provisions.[27]

References

Alper Y (2015) Türk Sosyal Güvenlik Sistemi. Sosyal Sigortalar Hukuku, 7th edn. Dora Publishing, Bursa

Caniklioğlu N (2008) 5510 Sayılı Kanun ve İş Sözleşmesine Göre Çalışanların Sosyal Güvenlik Destek Primi Ödeyerek Çalışmaları. Sicil İş Hukuku Dergisi 10:164–177

[27] Güzel et al. (2020), p. 194.

Caniklioğlu N (2010) 5510 Sayılı Kanuna Göre Bağımsız Çalışan Avukatların Sosyal Güvenliği. In: Prof.Dr. Ali Güzel'e Armağan, vol 2. Beta Publishing, Istanbul, pp 957–993
Çenberci M (1985) Sosyal Sigortalar Kanunu Şerhi. Olgaç Matbaası, Ankara
Centel T (1978) Genelev Kadınının Sosyal Güvenliği. Günümüzde Yargı 23:11–13
Gerek N (2009) Üniversitelerde Kısmi Zamanlı Olarak Çalıştırılan Öğrencilerin Sosyal Güvenlik Sorunları. Sicil İş Hukuku Dergisi 14:233–238
Güzel A, Okur AR, Caniklioğlu N (2020) Sosyal Güvenlik Hukuku, 18th edn. Beta Publishing, Istanbul
Korkusuz MR, Uğur S (2009) Sosyal Güvenlik Hukukuna Giriş. Karahan Publishing House, Ankara
Sözer AN (2019) Türk Sosyal Sigortalar Hukuku, 4th edn. Beta Publishing, Istanbul
Tuncay AC, Ekmekçi Ö (2019) Sosyal Güvenlik Hukuku Dersleri, 20th edn. Beta Publishing, Istanbul

Part IV
Social Insurance Liabilities

Chapter 9
Liabilities of Employer

9.1 Registering the Workplace

9.1.1 *Objective of Registration*

The employees may benefit sufficiently from their rights arising from SIGHIA, and SIGHIA may be implemented in desired manner only when SSI knows the workplaces and employees working at these workplaces. It is impossible for SSI to detect all the workplaces throughout Turkey. For this reason, the companies are held responsible for registering their workplaces to SSI. Accordingly, the objective of obligation to register the workplace to SSI is to determine the workplaces, where the insurance holder is to be employed, and the employer/employer's representative of these workplaces, as well as enabling the registration of workplaces.[1]

9.1.2 *Submission's Range of Implementation*

The notification to be made by the employer is related with the workplace. From this aspect, it is important to have information about the meaning and content of "*workplace*" given in SIGHIA.

9.1.2.1 Primary Workplace

The primary workplace is defined as the places, where the insurance holders work, by taking the concept of insurance holder as basis (art. 11 para. 1 SIGHIA). From this aspect, once the insurance holder starts working at a place, then that place gains

[1]Güzel et al. (2020), pp. 209–210.

T. Centel, *Turkish Social Law*, https://doi.org/10.1007/978-3-030-64704-9_9

the character of workplace. Accordingly, from the aspect of SIGHIA, it is not possible to define a place, where no insurance holder is employed, as a workplace.

9.1.2.2 Places Affiliated with the Workplace

The places qualitatively affiliated with the goods and services produced in workplace and organized under the same management are included in the concept of workplace (art. 11 para. 2 SIGHIA). However, it is not always easy to determine the aforementioned affiliated places. For this reason, the most useful method is to determine these places by considering the characteristics of each physical place.

9.1.2.3 Outbuildings of Company

The outbuildings such as resting areas, nursing rooms, dining halls, sleeping rooms, showering areas, examination and maintenance areas, physical and vocational training areas, offices, and halls are included in the concept of workplace (art. 11 para. 2 SIGHIA). The aforementioned places are not limited to those specified in the law. Accordingly, any place that is related with the fulfilment of business tasks or with the workplace may be included within the concept of workplace.[2]

9.1.2.4 Means of Workplace

The means are also included in the concept of workplace (art. 1 para. 2 SIGHIA). Since the term "*vehicle*" is used with its broader meaning, the machines and instruments such as cranes, bulldozers, dozers, and graders are included in the concept of workplace, in addition to the vehicles such as trucks, automobiles, and buses belonging to the company.

In order for the means to be included in the scope of workplace, they are not expected to belong to the employer. For this reason, the means rented or operated by the employer are included in the concept of workplace.

9.1.3 Term of Notification

9.1.3.1 Declaration of Opening

The employer is obliged to submit the "*workplace notification*", the template of which will be prepared by SSI, to SSI until the day of employing the insurance

[2]Tunçomağ (1990), p. 131.

holder (art. 11 para. 3 SIGHIA). However, if the last day of the term of notification is a holiday, then the notification may be submitted to the business day following the holiday period.

If the workers and officers are employed in the same company or institution, then the workplace notifications shall be separately prepared for workers and officers and separate registrations shall be made.

The public authorities and banks are obliged to submit the names and addresses of contractors undertaking any type of tasks contracted out to SSI in *15 days* (art. 90 para. 1 SIGHIA). Besides that, the governorates, municipalities, and legal entities authorized for granting licenses are obliged to submit all the documents and information related with the building license and other licenses to SSI in *one month* (art. 11 para. 6 SIGHIA). Upon these notifications, if it is revealed that the aforementioned place or construction is not registered to SSI, the Institution shall directly register the workplace.

The subcontractor shall register the employees, who the subcontractor employs in the workplace of primary employer, to SSI by means of a number, which will be given by the SSI, through the registry of primary employer by submitting the contracts signed between primary employer and subcontractor (art. 11 para. 8 SIGHIA). The objective here is to enable SSI to track the relationship between employer and subcontractor.

On the other hand, the employers to submit the number of insurance holders, who will be employed during establishing the company, and the start day of employment to the trade registry authorities shall be considered to make their notification to SSI. Hence, the trade registry authorities are obliged to submit the notifications, which have been made to the trade registry authorities, to SSI in *10 days* (art. 11 para. 3 SIGHIA).

Each workplace, for which a workplace notification has been made, is given a registration number by SSI, and this number is notified to the employer. All of the transactions related with the workplace are executed by using the given registration number. For this reason, the registration number shall be written on any document submitted to SSI.

9.1.3.2 Registration of Changes Related with the Transfer and Transportation of Workplace

In case that the workplace is transported from the actual address to another address in another city or the business or workplace, where the employees are employed, is transferred or inherited to another employer, a workplace notification shall be submitted to SSI for this change (art. 11 para. 5 SIGHIA).

In case of an address change within the borders of same city, there is no obligation to submit a new workplace notification. In this case, it is enough to submit the address change in written (art. 11 para. 5 SIGHIA).

In such cases, the workplace notification shall be submitted in *10 days* after the transportation of workplace or the transfer of business or workplace to a new employer. In case of the transfer of workplace by inheritance, the inheritors are obliged to submit the workplace notification to SSI in 3 months after the date of death (art. 11 para. 5 SIGHIA).

Similarly, a workplace notification shall be prepared in case that the change of company type or the merge of company with another one. The workplace notification shall be submitted to SSI in 10 days after the registration of aforementioned changes to the trade registry or after the date of taking a new partner (in case of taking a partner to an ordinary partnership) (art. 11 para. 4 SIGHIA).

9.1.4 Cancellation of the Registration

If it is revealed that the workplace has been registered wrongly or unduly, then the relevant unit of SSI cancels the relevant registration.

If it is understood that two or more registration numbers have been assigned to a single workplace or business, then the relevant department directly cancels the numbers given afterwards.

The cancelled numbers shall not be assigned to another workplace. However, if using the subsequently given number has made any transaction, then the numbers used in transactions are joined in the registration number of workplaces.

9.1.5 Direct Registration of Workplace by SSI

In case that the employer has not submitted the notification within the specified term, then the workplace is registered directly by SSI. Although the registration may be made based on the inspections performed by the inspector assigned by SSI for inspection and control or based on the results obtained from the records of business, it may also be made based on the results obtained during the inspections performed by the inspector of public institutions. Thus, the workplace that has never been registered to SSI would be registered directly by SSI based on the information obtained by the public institutions and organizations authorized for licensing or the decisions of labour courts.

9.1.6 Imposing Administrative Fine

If the workplace notification is not submitted at all or not submitted within the specified term in the specified form and procedure, then the administrative fine shall be imposed to those responsible for submitting this notification (art. 102 para. 1/b SIGHIA).

9.2 Liability of Submitting the Insured Employees

9.2.1 Content of the Notification Obligation

The employer is obliged to notify SSI about the insurance holders employed, the end of employment, or that no insurance holder is employed. Since these subjects were discussed in detail while explaining the establishment of insurance relationship and the termination of that relationship, the relevant obligations are not re-explained here.[3]

9.2.2 Non-submission of Insurance Holders to SSI

Not registering the insurance holders to SSI and the unregistered employment are the important problems in Turkey, where the unregistered economy reached at remarkable levels. Besides that, the utilization of legal options such as imposing administrative fine or directly registering the workplace by SSI may sometimes be ineffective because of the troubles and inefficacies in State's inspection organization.

Besides that, it is necessary to detect the insurance holders in order to protect the rights of uninsured workers and to prevent them from the negative consequences from the aspect of long-term insurance branches. The administrative options may be used for this purpose or the judicial remedy can be used in determining the uninsured employment.

9.2.2.1 Determination of Insurance by SSI

In case that the insurance holders are not notified to SSI or the premium documents of registered insurance holders are not submitted to SSI, SSI is authorized to prepare the premium documents directly (art. 86 para. 7 SIPHIA). It means that SSI determines the insurance relationship and the services offered as an insurance holder.

However, the services of uninsured workers, who have not been registered to SSI, shall be taken into account only for up to 1 year backwards from the date of determination (art. 86 para. 8 SIGHIA).

9.2.2.2 Detecting the Insurance by Means of Judicial Decision

If the insurance holders, premium document (monthly premium and service report or summary and premium document) of whom has not been submitted by the employer or cannot be detected by the company employing them, apply to the labour court in 5

[3]*See*: above Chap. 6.

years starting from the end of their working period in that company and if they prove their receivables by means of judicial decision, then the sum of their monthly incomes specified in the judicial decision shall be taken into account in calculating the number of premium payment days (art. 86 para. 9 SIGHIA).

The beginning of period for filing a lawsuit starts from the termination date of employment. Accordingly, the insurance holder may file a declaratory lawsuit for 5 years starting from the end of the last year of employment. In case that the insurance holder dies, then the beginning date of 5-year period for the inheritors starts from the date of insurance holder's decease unless the period of filing lawsuit has lapsed when the insurance holder was alive.[4]

Declaratory lawsuit for detecting the services insurance holder shall be filed against the employer, who employs the insurance holder. However, this lawsuit to be filed against the employer shall be directly notified to SSI by the court. At the end of trial, SSI, which will participate in the proceedings upon the notification, may go to the law even when the defendant employer does not. SSI is obliged to implement the finalized decision of court (art. 7 para. 4 LCA).

Court of Cassation decided that, in the declaratory lawsuit, the proceedings should be against all the employers, who employed the insurance holder, together with SSI.[5] Accordingly, in addition to the primary obligator employer, the aforementioned lawsuit shall be filed against the other responsible parties. Thus, in case that the business has been handed over or inherited to a new employer, the new employer that is responsible for the premium debts together with the previous employer shall be in defendant position. Similarly, since the primary employer is held responsible for the premium debts of sub-employer, the lawsuit shall be filed against also to the primary employer.

Because of its nature, the declaratory lawsuit for determining the period of service is subject to the principle of investigation. Accordingly, not limited to the proofs provided by the parties, the judge of labour court shall make any type of investigation and research in order to reveal the truth. Hence, the decision shall not be made solely based on the abstract statements of witnesses.

If the court decides the presence of services offered by the plaintiff insurance holder, the sum of monthly incomes specified in the court's decision shall be taken into account while calculating the number of premium payment days (art. 86 para. 9 SIGHIA). Accordingly, in parallel with the court decision regarding the determination, SSI shall collect the premium (including the shares of insurance holder and employer) and the default penalty and default interest from the employer. Regarding the premium debt collected from the employer for the previous periods, the employer may recourse to the insurance holder in proportion to the share of insurance holder. However, if the employer has deducted the premium share of insurance holder but

[4]CC, 21st Civ. Div., 7.10.1996, 5611/5402, Yargıtay Kararları Dergisi, 5 (1997), pp. 775–776.

[5]CC, 10th Civ. Div., 26.9.1991, 4998/7272, Yargıtay Kararları Dergisi, 12 (1991), pp. 1826–1827.

not paid the premium to SSI, then the employer is not entitled to recourse to the insurance holder anymore.[6]

On the other hand, if the premiums have not been collected from the employer by SSI despite the court's decision, then this would have no effect on income replacement to the insurance holder and SSI shall use the number of premium payment days specified in the court's decision.[7]

Moreover, depending on the court's decision, the insurance holder shall gain the right to receive the payments that would be paid for the maternity and health insurances (art. 86 para. 10 SIGHIA).

9.3 Liability of Premium

Employer's liability of premium refers to preparing the premium documents and paying the premium debts. Accordingly, the employer is obliged to prepare the premium documents for the insurance holders being employed by the employer and to submit them to SSI. Moreover, the employer is also obliged to dock the premium share of employee from the salary of insurance holder specified in the premium documents, and to pay the premium to the Institution by adding the employer's share of premium.

Since the detailed information about the abovementioned premiums was given when discussing the premiums as the funding source of social insurance, these subjects are not discussed again.[8]

9.4 Obligation of Medical Certification for Employing Insurance Holder

There are jobs, for which the labour legislation obliges taking medical certification. In case that SSI pays a temporary incapacity allowance to an insurance holder working in one of these jobs without obtaining the specified medical certification or in any job, to which the insurance holder is physically unsuitable, because of any disease that the insurance holder had before the employment or any disease that the insurance holder got because being employed in a physically unsuitable job, the allowance paid to the insurance holder shall be reclaimed from the employer (art. 21 para. 3 SIGHIA).

---

[6] Güzel et al. (2020), p. 300.

[7] CC, 10th Civ. Div., 20.3.2006, 12426/2934, Çalışma ve Toplum Dergisi, 12 (2007/1), pp. 335–337.

[8] *See* above Chap. 8.

From this aspect, in order to prevent such a consequence, the employer shall not employ an insurance holder in these jobs without receiving the required health report. Moreover, the employer is also obliged not to employ the insurance holder in any position that does not comply with content of health report.[9]

In this case, SSI shall be obliged to pay temporary incapacity allowance to the insurance holder, who has been employed in a job that is not physically suitable to the insurance holder, because of his/her disease. This payment, which has been made by SSI because of employing the insurance holder without health report or on the contrary to the current health report, shall be recovered by the responsible employer. The employment inconsistent with the report may also cause healthcare costs in addition to the temporary incapacity allowance. In this case, the healthcare costs borne by SSI shall also be recovered by the responsible employed (art. 76 para. 3 SIGHIA).

9.5 Obligation of Archiving and Submitting the Documents

The independent business owners and employers retaining workers and officers shall archive the workplace records and documents for *10 years* starting from the beginning of year after the year, which the records belong to, and submit these documents in *15 days* if requested by SSI's officers authorized with the inspection and control (art. 86 para. 2 SIGHIA).

The term of obligation of archiving is *30 years* for the public authorities. The officers of Department of Bankruptcy and Liquidation are obliged to archive the documents throughout their term of office. The private sector, public bodies, and bankruptcy and liquidation officers are obliged to submit the relevant document, which they are obliged to archive, in *15 days* when requested by SSI's officers authorized with inspection and control (art. 86 para. 2 SIGHIA).

In case that the obligation of archiving for specified period and submitting in 15 days after the written notification by SSI is fulfilled without force majeure, an administrative fine shall be imposed (art. 102 para. 1/e SIGHIA).

9.6 Obligation of Protecting the Insurance Holder

The short-term insurance premium being paid does not abolish the employer's responsibility arising from the insurance holder's losses arising from the occupational accident and occupational disease. On this subject, in order to avoid from possible compensation, the employers shall take all the necessary measures (art. 4 OHSA).

[9]Turan (2009), p. 198.

From the aspect of act of social insurance, the responsibility of employer arising from the occupational accident and occupational disease arises from SSI's right to recourse. The employer's obligation of protecting the insurance holder lays the foundation here.

The employer's default in obligation of protecting the insurance holder legally evokes the mechanism of recourse. Accordingly, if the occupational accident and occupational disease occurred because of the deliberation or any action of employer against the occupational health and safety legislation, then the employer shall pay the sum of the cash capital values of the payments made and to be made by SSI to the insurance holder or his/her beneficiaries in accordance with SIGHIA. However, in case that the employer is found responsible, then the *principle of inevitability* shall be considered (art. 21 para. 1 SIGHIA). In order to avoid from such recourse by SSI, the employer shall take all the measures specified by the occupational health and safety regulations (especially, OHSA).

9.7 Obligation of Notifying the Accidents and Diseases to SSI

9.7.1 For the Workers

The occupational accident shall be immediately notified to the authorized law enforcement agency by the employer of insurance holder and in *three business days* after the accident by directly submitting or sending the "*occupational accident and occupational disease notification*" to SSI via registered mail. If the occupational accident occurs in places that are out of the control of employer, then this term starts from the date, when the employer is informed of the accident (art. 13 para. 2/a SIGHIA).

The employer, as in reporting the occupational accidents, reports the occupational diseases that the insured workers get. Although there is no requirement as to form of the notification, it would be useful to place the notification by using the template prepared by SSI for reporting the occupational accidents and occupational diseases. In this form, the first section following the identification is allocated to the occupational accident, whereas the last section is allocated to the occupational diseases. In this notification, the diagnosed occupational disease, the date of diagnosis suspicion, and the method of making diagnosis shall be specified in the notification form. There is no need for reporting the occupational diseases to the law enforcement agencies.

9.7.2 *For the Civil Servants*

When the duty disability occurs, the employing public institution, and the insurance holder and his/her beneficiaries shall report the case to relevant authorities.

Accordingly, the public body shall firstly notify the law enforcement agencies, because it may be needed to submit the case to the jurisdiction if it has legal aspects. Then, according to the specific regulations of public body, the event shall be immediately reported to the authorized body, if any. Thus, the internal discipline and inspection procedures can be initiated. Hence, in order for the obligation of performance to be fulfilled, the event shall be reported to SSI within *15 business days*.

On the other hand, considering that the public employer may be neglecting, the insurance holders and beneficiaries are granted the right to report. In this case, the report shall be performed within the same period (15 business days). The notification made by the insurance holder and beneficiaries does not abolish the public administrations' obligation of notification (art. 47 para. 3 SIGHIA).

9.7.3 *Default in Fulfilling the Obligation of Notification*

In case that the occupational accident is not timely notified to SSI, then the temporary incapacity allowance to be paid to the insurance holder until the date of notification shall be collected from the employer by SSI (art. 21 para. 2 SIGHIA).

The default of public servants in fulfilling the obligation of notification within the specified period does not pose an obstacle in putting the incapacity allowance of officer. However, SSI shall be informed in order for this procedure to be accomplished. The permanent incapacity might have been treated as ordinary incapacity since the notification has not been timely made. In this case, the required correction shall be made, and the relevant public authority by SSI shall collect the sum of allowance differences (art. 47 para. 6 SIGHIA).

9.8 Obligation of Offering Healthcare Service After the Accident

The employer is obliged to provide the general health insurance holder, who had occupational accident or got occupational disease, with the required healthcare service. The costs of healthcare services, which have been borne by the employer for this purpose and which can be documented, shall be compensated by SSI (art.

76 para. 1 SIGHIA). Since the term "*employer*" includes the public employers, they also are obliged to offer healthcare services to the employees.[10]

The employer, who or which does not provide the necessary healthcare services immediately, may lead SSI and insurance holder to suffer. In this case, the employer shall compensate the loss that they suffer. For this purpose, the delay shall cause a prolongation of duration of the therapy of general health insurance holder or an increase in the degree of disablement. In such events, the employer is obliged to pay any type of healthcare expenses that SSI had to bear (art. 76 para. 2 SIGHIA).

9.9 Obligation of Easing the Workplace Inspection

SSI has the right and authority to inspect if the liabilities undertaken depending on the social insurance relationship between employer and insurance holder are fulfilled as necessary. During exercising this authorization, the employer and insurance holder shall ease the procedure for SSI.

Accordingly, the employers, insurance holders, workplace owners, and the officers of bankruptcy and liquidation agency, as well as the legal entities and real persons related with this procedure, shall:

- Inform SSI's officers authorized with the control and inspection when requested,
- Submit and show the necessary documents, evidences, and records,
- Provide the necessary convenience without any delay in order for them to fulfil their tasks. Moreover, all the civil servants are obliged to provide the officers of SSI, who are authorized with control and inspection, with necessary convenience, as well as helping them while they are fulfilling their task (art. 59 para. 2 SIGHIA).

The employers, insurance holders, workplace owners, and the other persons related with this procedure are obliged not to prevent the officers of SSI, who are authorized with control and inspection, from doing their duties while there are executing the inspection and investigation procedures. Otherwise, the ones preventing the officers without using force and violence shall be imposed an administrative fine up to 5 folds of minimum wage (art. 102 para. 1/ı SIGHIA). In case of using force and violence, both the criminal action shall be taken against them (art. 265 para. 2 TPC) and they shall be imposed an administrative fine up to 10 folds of minimum wage.

[10]Sözer (2019), p. 165.

References

Güzel A, Okur AR, Caniklioğlu N (2020) Sosyal Güvenlik Hukuku, 18th edn. Beta Publishing, Istanbul

Sözer AN (2019) Türk Sosyal Sigortalar Hukuku, 4th edn. Beta Publishing, Istanbul

Tunçomağ K (1990) Sosyal Güvenlik Kavramı ve Sosyal Sigortalar, 5th edn. Beta Publishing, Istanbul

Turan E (2009) 5510 Sayılı Yasa Kapsamında Rücuan Tazminat Davaları. Sicil İş Hukuku Dergisi 15:193–211

Chapter 10
Obligations of the Insured

10.1 Obligation to Declare Employment to SSI

In order to prevent informal employment and especially the application of uninsured employment, the legislator has obligated the insured with protecting his/her right. Accordingly, the insured are obliged to inform the Institution that they have started insured employment within one month from the date they start (art. 8 para. 2 SIGHIA).

There is no distinction between the employees in this regulation text. In this regard, not only insured workers but also public officials and self-employed individuals are included in the scope of the notification. However, this obligation is of particular importance in terms of informal economy, particularly in respect of insured workers. On the other hand, uninsured employment is not an intense situation in terms of public officials and insured self-employed persons in practice.

The obligation to declare employment has been accepted by the legislator as an opportunity recognized to the insured, instead of a liability. In this respect, it is understood that the declaration in question is of an arbitrary nature. As a matter of fact, while the fact that the employer does not provide declaration for the insured necessitates the application of administrative fines, the fact that the insured do not declare themselves is not sanctioned.

Accordingly, it is foreseen that the fact that the insured do not declare themselves will not provide evidence against the insured (art. 8 para. 2 SIGHIA). Thus, in service declaratory cases, it is prevented the use of the failure to fulfil the declaration obligation against the insured.[1]

[1]Alper (2015), p. 136.

T. Centel, *Turkish Social Law*, https://doi.org/10.1007/978-3-030-64704-9_10

10.2 Obligation to Bear Premium Deductions

If insurance conditions are created, it is mandatory that individuals are insured, and it is not possible for them to waive their insurance rights and obligations. Accordingly, it is not legally possible for employees to eliminate the obligation to be insured in order to make a profit. As a matter of fact, the provisions to be put into contracts to eliminate, reduce, waive or transfer insurance rights and obligations are legally invalid (art. 92 para. 1 SIPHIA). Thus, employees lack the opportunity to eliminate the obligation to be insured by making an agreement with their employers to make a profit by avoiding premium deductions. In this respect, the insured is under the obligation to bear insurance premium deductions.

10.3 Obligation Not to Cause Insurance Incidents

While the employer is obliged to protect the insured against occupational accidents and diseases, the employees are obliged to comply with the health and safety measures to be taken. In this sense, employees are obliged to protect themselves and thus not to cause insurance incidents. In fact, employees are under the obligation not to endanger the health and safety of themselves and of other employees affected by the work they do, in line with the training they receive regarding occupational health and safety and the employer's instructions on this matter (art. 19 para. 1 OHSA).

It is seen that the same principle is accepted as the "*obligation of the insured to protect themselves*" in terms of the social insurance legislation.[2] As a matter of fact, SIGHIA recognizes that the incapacity to work related to the insurance incident and consequential damages means a violation of the obligation of the insured to protect themselves. Accordingly, the insured should not suffer from an occupational accident due to his/her defect, should not suffer from an occupational disease or any disease and should not cause prolongation of the treatment period or increase in the incapacity to work.

In case of a violation of this obligation, a reduction is made in the temporary incapacity allowance or the permanent incapacity allowance. Accordingly, if there is a serious defect, the aids in question will be reduced down to one third based on the level of defect of the insured (art. 22 para. 1/b SIGHIA). In the case of insured persons who have suffered an occupational accident or disease or a disease due to intended actions, this reduction is made at half rate (art. 22 para. 1/c SIGHIA).

However, if the insured is deceased as a result of an occupational accident or disease due to the defective action of the insured, SSI cannot recourse the right holders cannot be for the allowances. Similarly, the same recourse prohibition is applicable when the death in question occurs as a result of the defect of the insured's

[2] Sözer (2019), p. 183.

right holders (art. 21 para. 5 SIGHIA). The defect here is the non-compliance with the relevant provisions of the occupational health and safety legislation.[3]

10.4 Obligation to Eliminate the Negative Consequences of Insurance Incidents

10.4.1 Obligation to Accept the Proposed Treatment

When an insurance incident occurs, the insured must accept the treatment proposed by the doctor in order to eliminate their temporary or permanent incapacity to work. Accordingly, the insured is obliged to eliminate the negative consequences of an insurance incident, such as occupational accident and disease and disease and accident.

The obligation to accept the proposed treatment is legally binding for the insured in the event of written notification by SSI. On the other hand, the treatment to be applied must be of a generally accepted nature and one that the insured can bear. In this respect, where there is no written notification or where the proposed treatment is not bearable for the insured, the legal liability of the insured will no longer be in question.[4]

The insured may not accept the proposed treatment, despite the written notification of SSI and the acceptable nature of the treatment. In this case, the prolongation of the period of treatment or the increase of incapacity to work will require the temporary incapacity allowance or the permanent incapacity allowance to be paid in half (art. 22 para. 1/c SIGHIA).

10.4.2 Obligation to Follow Physician Instructions

It is not enough for the insured to accept the proposed treatment in order to avoid the reduction in insurance allowances. In addition, the insured is also required to comply with the doctor's recommendations for the treatment being applied. Because the success of a treatment being applied is often only possible, for example, by complying with specific doctor instructions, such as taking prescribed medications on a timely basis and in recommended doses, performing the necessary examinations at regular intervals or following recommended diets. Failure to do so means a violation by the insured of the obligation to eliminate the negative consequences of insurance incidents.

---

[3]Sözer (2019), p. 184.

[4]*See*: Sözer (2019), p. 185.

Violation of the obligation in question arises in the event of occurrence of negative consequences such as prolongation of the period of treatment or increased incapacity to work or disability. If these negative consequences occur, reductions will be made in the allowances to be given to the insured. In fact, the reduction in question occurs as reduction of the temporary incapacity allowance or permanent incapacity allowance paid after the occupational accident or occupational disease or disease down to one fourth. When making this reduction, factors such as the prolonged period of treatment or the increased rate of incapacity to work will be taken into consideration (art. 22 para. 1/a SIGHIA).

10.4.3 Obligation Not to Work Without Receiving Recovery Report

The insured must not be employed in works requiring a recovery report unless this report is received, and if a recovery report is received, he/she must not be employed in a way contradictory to the content of the report in question (art. 21 para. 3 SIGHIA). The view of this obligation arising for the employer in terms of the insured is the obligation for employees who have taken medical leave not to work without regaining their health. As a matter of fact, in order for the insured to return to work, he/she is required to submit a document to the employer indicating that the treatment is over and that he/she is capable for work (art. 22 para. 1/d and art. 76 para. 3 SIGHIA).

Obligation not to work without receiving recovery report mainly concerns insured workers and public officials. In this case, the insured will not be paid the temporary incapacity allowance if he/she works without receiving a document from the physician indicating that the treatment is over and that he/she is capable for work. The paid temporary incapacity allowances will also be recovered from the date of the unpaid payment (art. 22 para. 1/d SIGHIA).

In addition, the treatment costs for the same disease will be requested from the insured (art. 76 para. 3 SIGHIA).

References

Alper Y (2015) Türk Sosyal Güvenlik Sistemi. Sosyal Sigortalar Hukuku, 7th edn. Dora Publishing, Bursa

Sözer AN (2019) Türk Sosyal Sigortalar Hukuku, 4th edn. Beta Publishing, Istanbul

Chapter 11
Obligations of Legal Entities and Third Parties

11.1 Obligations of Public and Private Legal Entities

11.1.1 Obligation of Self-Employed Person to Declare Employment

The obligation of the insured to declare employment to SSI also applies to self-employed individuals. However, self-employed individuals are not left with an arbitrary obligation. In addition, some obligors are determined for them. The obligor person in question varies depending on whether relevant self-employed has a tax burden or on the professional organization to which he/she is addressed.

Accordingly, the insurances of income taxpayers begin as of their liability. Tax offices will make insurance declaration for them. The insurances of those who are exempt from income tax begin as of the registration date to the registry directorates of tradesmen and craftsmen. The registration date will be declared to SSI by the registry directorates of tradesmen and craftsmen.

The obligors of company shareholders to declare to SSI vary according to the type of the company. Accordingly, the tax offices make the declaration for the shareholders of general and limited partnerships and associations of ship owners. For the shareholders who are members of the board of directors of joint stock companies, the date of election will be declared to SSI by the company authorities. The declaration for limited liability companies must be made by the registry directorates at the date of the registration; in share transfers, it must be made by the company authorities as of the date of the decision of transfer.

On the other hand, the declaration obligation for the village and neighbourhood headmen to SSI is upon the provincial or district governors.

Finally, the *Jockey Club of Turkey* must fulfil the declaration obligation for jockeys and coaches.

In the event that the employment declarations for the said independent workers are not submitted to SSI, an administrative fine is imposed on the institutions and

T. Centel, *Turkish Social Law*, https://doi.org/10.1007/978-3-030-64704-9_11

organizations and legal entities not fulfilling this obligation by the amount of the monthly minimum wage (art. 102 para. 1/g SIGHIA).

11.1.2 Obligation of Self-Employed Person to Declare the Termination of Insurance

The office to declare the termination of insurance is the same office that declares the beginning of insurance. However, in cancellation, unlike registration, it is deemed that the insured himself/herself is obliged to provide declaration.

In the event that the termination declarations for the said independent workers are not submitted to SSI, an administrative fine is imposed on the institutions and organizations and legal entities not fulfilling this obligation by the amount of the monthly minimum wage (art. 102 para. 1/g SIGHIA).

11.1.3 Obligation to Declare Works Done by Tender

Official institutions are obliged to submit the identity information and addresses of those who undertake all kinds of work done by tender to SSI within 15 days at the latest (art. 90 para. 1 SIGHIA).

This obligation brought to the official institutions is a precaution to prevent unregistered (uninsured) work. Thus, SSI will be able to monitor the workplace records and the insured job entry declarations of the contractors who will undertake works from the official authorities.[1]

On the institutions and organizations and legal entities that do not declare the works they are undertaking by tender will be imposed an administrative fine (art. 102 para. 1/g SIGHIA).

11.1.4 Obligation to Provide Information and Documents to SSI

It is mandatory to provide some information and documents to SSI in order to ensure that persons can provide their social security and to follow up their receivables effectively. Some of them are carried out at the time of the procedure and others at the request of SSI.

[1]Sözer (2019), pp. 191–192.

11.1.4.1 Providing Regular Information

Public and private legal entities and natural persons must provide all kinds of information and documents required by SSI, provided that they do not violate the confidentiality obligation. As a matter of fact, SSI has been authorized to require natural and legal persons to send all kinds of documents and information to be provided through Internet, electronic and similar media in accordance with the law (art. 100 para. 3 SIGHIA). The framework of the information to be given is limited to the providing of social security of persons and the follow-up and collection of the receivables of SSI.

In this regard, the official institutions provide information within the framework of the protocols to be made with SSI and others undertake to provide information directly without any protocol.

Contrary behaviour, that is, not giving any information or giving it late, requires the application of administrative fines (art. 100 para. 6 and art. 102 para. 1/I SIGHIA).

11.1.4.2 Control of Insurance Registration

For public offices and banks, the obligation to control whether the persons they do procedures for are registered in terms of insurance is foreseen. Accordingly, the said organizations are obliged to inform SSI of the persons they have determined to be uninsured as a result of their control. The control task here will be carried out in the transactions to be determined by SSI by utilizing the electronic infrastructure to be provided by SSI (art. 8 para. 7 SIGHIA).

In case of violation of the obligation to control insurance registration, an administrative fine of one tenth of the monthly minimum wage per insured will be imposed (art. 8 para. 8 and art. 102 para. 1/g SIGHIA).

11.1.4.3 Providing the Minimum Labour Information

If it is concluded that the organizations have not paid sufficient premiums at the time of their activity, SSI subjects them to minimum labour practices. In order to determine whether minimum labour will be needed and the possible amount, the official authorities need data on the workplace in question. In this case, if SSI requests information, the public offices must submit the information and documents related to the determination of minimum labour to SSI no later than one month in writing (art. 85 para. 5 SIGHIA). Otherwise, an administrative fine of twice as much as the minimum wage is imposed on the personnel in the public offices (art. 102 para. 1/f SIGHIA).

11.1.4.4 Providing the Information on Registration Procedures

Governorships, municipalities and other public and private legal entities authorized to issue licenses are obliged to inform SSI of the information and documents related to the construction license and any other license or procedures with the qualities of a license and, if any, the information related to the employment which is the basis of their issuance within one month from the date of issue (art. 11 para. 6 SIGHIA). Otherwise, an administrative fine shall be imposed on the institutions and organizations that fail to fulfil the declaration obligation (art. 100 para. 1/h SIGHIA).

11.2 Obligations of Third Parties

Third persons arise as the result of the Institution offering social security allowances to the insured if they cause to suffer an occupational accident, become disabled, die or receive health care. SSI has the right to receive (recourse) these allowances from third parties. Therefore, third parties are under the obligation to protect the insured by avoiding actions that will harm them and not to cause insurance incidents for the insured.[2]

11.2.1 Obligation to Avoid Short-Term Risks

If the occupational accident, occupational disease and disease occur due to the fault of the third person, the payments made or to be made to the insured and the right holders and half of the advance capital value of the allowances shall be recourse to the third person causing the damage and, if they have a fault, to their employers (art. 21 para. 4 SIGHIA).

11.2.2 Obligation to Avoid Long-Term Risks

Half of the advance capital value of the allowances to be given to the insured disabled due to the intention of third persons or to the right holders in the event of the death of the insured shall be recourse to the third person causing the damage by SSI (art. 39 para. 1 SIGHIA).

[2] Sözer (2019), p. 195.

11.2.3 *Obligation to Avoid Damaging the Health of the Insured*

The third person's action may also constitute a health risk under the general health insurance. According to this, besides the financial allowances, it is also necessary to provide health aids to the insured. In this case, if SSI needs to provide health services or the duration of treatment is prolonged due to a defective action of the third person, SSI may recourse to the third person for the health expenses it incurred (art. 76 para. 6 SIPHIA).

Reference

Sözer AN (2019) Türk Sosyal Sigortalar Hukuku, 4th edn. Beta Publishing, Istanbul

Chapter 12
Obligations of SSI

12.1 Obligation to Conduct Insurance Audits

The social security legislation foresees different legal obligations to employers and insured persons. The authority and duty to control the fulfilment of these obligations have been left to SSI. As a matter of fact, the auditors and control officers of SSI must document the cases that they have identified during their work, which contradicts the social insurance legislation, and the transactions that create receivables in favour of SSI.

This documentation can withstand any evidence, except for oath. Accordingly, workplace records and official institution records and the event reports to be kept will help with this documentation. In this regard, the minutes to be kept by the officers shall be deemed to be legally valid until proven otherwise (art. 59 para. 2 SIGHIA).

Apart from the auditors and control officers of SSI, the auditors of some other official authorities also have the duty to audit. In this context, the authorities (ministries and local administrations) of public offices are obliged to determine whether insured employees are employed in the workplaces they audit, during the audits and inspections they will perform in accordance with the provisions of their legislations. Accordingly, if these authorities find out of unregistered employment or missing income or day notice, they are obliged to report this to SSI within one month at the latest (art. 59 para. 7 SIGHIA).

12.2 Obligation to Follow Insurance Receivables

SSI is under the obligation to follow up the insurance receivables. In this respect, it is seen that SSI has been given authority such as issuing documents ex officio and minimum labour determination.

T. Centel, *Turkish Social Law*, https://doi.org/10.1007/978-3-030-64704-9_12

On the other hand, the insurance receivables of SSI are public receivables and their follow-up is subject to the procedure foreseen in *Act on Collection of Public Receivables* No. 6183.[1] This procedure is a method that accelerates and facilitates the follow-up and collection of receivables under the privilege granted to state receivables.

The premium receivables of SSI are subject to a 10-year statute of limitation as of the due date (art. 93 para. 2 SIGHIA). In the past, a significant number of premium receivables of SSI could not be collected on time due to different factors. In order to solve this problem, it has been foreseen to prosecute the authorized personnel of SSI that does not apply for collection of premium receivables within one year at the latest after the due date (art. 88 para. 21 SIPHIA).

12.3 Obligation to Issue Documents Ex Officio

In order to prevent unregistered work, SSI has the authority to issue premium documents ex officio for insured persons who it has determined to be employed. This authority applies not only to unissued premium documents, but also to the amount of missing days and income in issued documents.

SSI officers essentially determine the uninsured employment in charge of audits and controls. As this determination can be performed as a result of the audits carried out in the workplace, the examination of the workplace records can also yield a possibility of determination.

In addition, uninsured employment cases can be uncovered during the works carried out by auditors of public offices in accordance with the provisions of their own legislation. Similarly, documents or information issued by public institutions and organizations and banks may also uncover uninsured employment.

In all these cases, SSI has the authority to create a premium receivable by issuing a certificate of premium ex officio. This seems to be an effective method of preventing uninsured employment.[2]

12.4 Obligation to Determine Minimum Labour

SSI can determine minimum labour to prevent unregistered employment. The minimum labour determination here means that if the premiums paid for any workplace are lower than what they should be, it means the determination and collection of the difference from the employer by SSI.

[1]OG 28.7.1953, No. 8469.

[2]Sözer (2019), pp. 168–169.

In order for minimum labour to be determined, in general, the nature of the work carried out, meaning the intensity of the labour or technology, the status and volume of the work against the correspondent work are taken into consideration. According to these criteria, the number of employees to be employed, their working hours and their premium earnings are estimated. The estimated result is compared with the employer's declaration. If there is a negative difference, SSI determines the minimum labour required for the execution of the work (art. 85 para. 1 SIGHIA).

The "*minimum labour determination commission*" within SSI carries out the minimum labour determination work. This commission both examines whether an adequate amount of labour has been declared to SSI and evaluates any objections to its decisions. The commission consists of seven members, four from the technical staff of SSI, two appointed by the workers' and employers' organizations and one from the Union of Chambers and Commodity Exchanges of Turkey (art. 85 para. 6 SIGHIA).

When it is determined that an adequate amount of labour has not been declared as a result of the investigation, the premium amount that is required to be paid according to the amount of labour reported as incomplete is calculated. The calculated premium amount is added the delay fine and late fee and is notified to the employer. The employer has to pay the total accrued debt to SSI within one month (art. 85 para. 2 SIGHIA).

Outside paying the premium debt accrued by SSI in this way, employers have different options such as making a commitment to pay, appealing or settling. In the event that a commitment is made to, the notified debt shall be considered final. If the employer does not comply with the aforementioned commitment and does not pay his/her debt, the provisions regarding the collection of premiums together with delay fine and late fee will be applied (art. 85 para. 2 SIGHIA).

The employer who does not pay the premium debt accrued and does not commit to payment may appeal to SSI within *one month* from the date of notification. Appeal stops tracking. In case SSI rejects the appeal, the employer can apply to the labour court. The application must be made within *one month* after the date of notification of the refusal to the employer. The lawsuit does not stop the follow-up and collection of the premium debt (art. 85 para. 3 SIGHIA).

For the accrued premium debt, the employer can also apply for a settlement with SSI. However, the way of settlement can only be used in cases where which insured employee the incomplete labour belongs to cannot be determined. The settlement here is made before the report, as a result of the minimum labour investigation carried out by the officers in charge of inspection and control, is sent to the relevant department of SSI. According to this, the amount to be paid agreed on by the parties together is determined by a minute. The amount of debt reached by settlement must be paid within one month of the arrangement date of the settlement minute. Otherwise, the settlement is considered to be broken and the agreed amounts do not constitute vested rights. If no settlement request is made in time, no negotiation can be reached as a result of the negotiations or the agreement reached is broken, the employer cannot request a settlement on this issue again (art. 85 para. 9 SIGHIA).

12.5 Confidentiality Obligation

SSI obtains some personal data belonging to the insured while performing its social security duties. The information in question is related to the working life, assets and health status of the persons. Some of these are present in own records of SSI and the rest are obtained from private and official institutions. Thus, the data are accumulated in the records of SSI, especially through the auditors and attorneys of SSI and physicians who provide health services.

In this regard, each of the professional staff employed by SSI is under the obligation of confidentiality in accordance with the special regulations to which they are subject. However, it is necessary to assume that SSI also has the obligation of confidentiality as a legal person, including its entire staff. Otherwise, the transfer of these data to the hands of third parties shall mean the interference with the private life of the persons. Therefore, SSI must prevent such interference by means of confidentiality.

SIGHIA includes the provision of *"the confidentiality of the health information of the general health insurance bearer and the patients he/she is obliged to treat is essential"* as regards the confidentiality obligation of SSI (art. 78 para. 2). In order to complete this arrangement, the provision of *"SSI cannot share the personal data and the data with the nature of trade secret data it processes with the purpose of carrying out the duties assigned by SIPHIA and other laws with natural or legal persons without the notarized approval of the data owner"* was adopted (art. 35 para. 6 Act No. 5502).

Another norm on the subject is the access of SSI to the information required to perform its duties. Accordingly, SSI has the right to request from real or private persons or official persons the information necessary to ensure the social security of persons.

However, some limitations are accepted here. In fact, the first limitation is that information and documents cannot be requested individually. The second limitation is that information is not given in case of serious consequences against the security and fundamental external benefits of the State. Finally, the provisions on the privacy of private life and family life and the right to defence are reserved. In this way, persons who are in the scope of providing information are obliged to provide all kinds of information and documents that will be requested as long as the limitations are followed (art. 100 para. 1 SIGHIA). If the employees of SSI use in such a way as to harm the insured and such information that may be requested, damages required to be compensated by SSI in accordance with the general provisions.

12.6 Obligation to Inform

Insured people need information about whether their employers are fulfilling their duties regarding them. Therefore, all data available in the insurance file should be kept open to the information of the insured upon request. Similarly, it is the most natural right of the insured to learn about their allowances and obligations related to the insurance.

In order to meet this need, the insured were given the right to request information and documents from SSI, and it is foreseen that SSI is obliged to inform the insured. According to this, the *General Directorate of Social Insurance* is obliged to inform the insured, their right holders and employers through all kinds of communication tools about their rights and duties arising from social security legislation (art. 13 para. 1/g Act No. 5502). Similarly, the *General Directorate of General Health Insurance* is obliged to inform the insured, their right holders and employers through all kinds of communication tools about their rights and duties arising from social security legislation (art. 14 para. 1/c Act No. 5502).

The information provided here takes place as questions asked on the Internet being answered on the same media, as is the same in application in written media. SSI should be careful when fulfilling the obligation to inform the insured and should avoid making incorrect informing and defective transactions that could lead to the loss of rights of the insured. Otherwise, if the insured is damaged due to the errors of the information given, SSI shall be held responsible.

In this respect, Court of Cassation found the request for pecuniary damages against SSI valid in the case where the insured, who has left his/her job after SSI gave information that he/she was entitled to retirement, but who did not receive a pension on the grounds that the information given was incorrect and who was not accepted back to his/her former job.[3] Likewise, in the case where SSI, who first noticed that someone else's information had been entered in the records of an insured and then assigned pension to the insured who had previously warned SSI, but then requested that the pensions be cancelled and reinstated, Court of Cassation recognized that the insured has been enriched in good faith.[4]

12.7 Obligation to Impose Sanctions

SSI is authorized to impose sanctions if the obligations foreseen in the social insurance legislation are not fulfilled. The sanction imposed by SSI is mainly to impose administrative fines.

[3]CC, 10th Civ. Div., 13.7.2009-2008-11781/12872.

[4]CC, 10th Civ. Div., 20.10.2009-11103/15867.

When SSI detects a violation of obligation, it notifies the related person of the fine corresponding to the action. After the notification, the penalized person either pays the amount notified to him/her and/or use the right to appeal.

The appeal is first made to the "*administrative fine appeal commission*" of SSI. This commission consists of the chief of the unit or his/her deputy, the relevant chief and file officer and, if applicable, a lawyer.

If the payment is made in advance within 15 days, only three quarters of the fine will be collected, and one quarter will be waived. The appeal stops the follow-up. It is also possible for individuals to appeal to SSI without making any payment. However, in this case, the right to benefit from the quarterly discount is eliminated.

If the appeal to SSI is rejected, it is possible to file a lawsuit in the administrative court within 30 days of the date of notification. Otherwise, the administrative fine will be finalized. Upon the refusal of the court, the unpaid quarter of the fine is charged to the concerned person.

Administrative fines not paid within 10 years from the date on which the offense is committed are dropped due to prescription (art. 102 para. 7 SIGHIA).

Reference

Sözer AN (2019) Türk Sosyal Sigortalar Hukuku, 4th edn. Beta Publishing, Istanbul

Part V
Social Insurance Branches

Chapter 13
Occupational Accident and Occupational Disease Insurance

13.1 Occupational Accident Concept

The number of people who lost their lives as a result of occupational accidents in Turkey, as set forth by the mine tragedy in Soma in 2014, has reached scary dimensions. Given the fact that not all of the occupational accidents were reported to SSI and the uninsured employment of many workers, the numbers in the official statistics cannot be said to be realistic. Nevertheless, even the number of official statistics on the loss of life of 1252 insured workers in 2015 seems frightening.[1]

In 2014 and 2015, occupational accidents were seen more among male workers group of 26–35 ages. Most of fatal accidents were seen among unskilled workforce. Construction sites, opencast quarries, opencast mines and industrial sites were the most dangerous places as of accident risks. Production, manufacturing, processing, storing excavation, construction, repair and demolition are the second most dangerous works. Regarding work experience, most occupational accidents were seen among workers with a work experience of 1 month-1 year in 2014 and 2015. Workers with at least five-year experience were more careful at work.[2]

13.1.1 Definition of Occupational Accident

Occupational accident is defined in art. 13 para. 1 SIGHIA. Accordingly, an occupational accident is the event that has occurs in the following ways;

- When the insured is at work,

[1]Gümüş (2017), pp. 281–282.

[2]*See*: Gümüş (2017), pp. 277 and 282–283.

T. Centel, *Turkish Social Law*, https://doi.org/10.1007/978-3-030-64704-9_13

- If the insured is working independently on his/her own behalf and account because of the work being carried out by the employer, because of the work being carried out,
- During the times when an insured does not do his/her main work, due to the fact that the insured employee working in connection with an employer is sent to another location outside the workplace as an official,
- At times reserved for insured nursing mothers to breastfeed their children under the labour legislation,
- During the arrival of the insured to a workplace via vehicles provided by the employer,

And leaves the insured physically or mentally disabled immediately or later. According to this, occupational accident can be defined as an event that occurs in certain situations and damages the insured.

On the other hand, art. 3 para. 1/g OHSA defines occupational accident more narrowly than SIGHIA. Accordingly, an occupational accident only includes accidents occurring in the workplace or due to the execution of the work.

13.1.2 Elements of Occupational Accident

13.1.2.1 Accident Victims Being Deemed as Insured in Terms of SIGHIA

Art. 13 SIGHIA has determined the elements and conditions of occupational accident based on the insured concept. Accordingly, it is mandatory that a person who has become physically or mentally disabled due to an accident is an insured person. Accidents occurring to uninsured persons are not considered as occupational accidents.

The concept of the insured covers workers as well as self-employed persons in accordance with art. 3 para. 1/6 SIGHIA. However, self-employed persons may only benefit from occupational accident insurance if they are involved in accidents due to the work they are carrying out.

As those who meet the conditions of insurance will be considered compulsorily insured as of the date of the insurance, the fact that they have not been declared to SSI shall not eliminate their insured qualifications. Accordingly, even if the insured become victims of an accident without being declared to SSI, the accident will still be considered as an occupational accident.[3]

Similarly, for the existence of an occupational accident, it will not be required to have paid premiums for a certain time or to be insured for a certain period of time. Thus, even an accident a few hours after entering work will be considered as an occupational accident.

---

[3] CC, 10th Civ. Div., 18.9.1989, 6374/6203, Çimento İşveren Dergisi, 4/1 (1990), p. 26.

In addition to that the victim of the accident must be insured as a rule, exceptionally, it is seen that some accidents are considered as occupational accidents, although these persons are not considered to be the insured by law. According to this, apprentices, students in vocational training in businesses, intern students in vocational high schools or vocational training, students who are part-time employed in universities and have low earnings, attendees in vocational courses, convicts and detainees in labour and those who work in domestic services for less than 10 days in one month can benefit from the provisions of occupational accident insurance.

13.1.2.2 Insured Suffering an Accident

Occupational accident is in fact a special form of the concept of accident in a particular situation occurring in one of the particular cases. In this respect, there are common points between the elements of the narrow accident concept and the occupational accident concept. Accordingly, for occupational accident to be considered, first of all, the damaging event must originate from an external factor. The external factor must occur suddenly or in a very short period of time.[4] As such, the sudden event must have been unintended for the insured. However, the accident that the insured person will suffer as a result of his/her own fault is also considered as an occupational accident.[5] As a matter of fact, Court of Cassation accepts the suicide of the insured in the workplace as an occupational accident.[6]

13.1.2.3 The Accident Occurring in Certain Situations

For the concept of occupational accident, the accident is required to occur in one of the cases specified in art. 13 para. 1 SIGHIA.

The first one is that the insured suffers an accident in the workplace (art. 13 para. 1/a SIGHIA). The workplace concept here will be determined on the basis of art. 11 paras 1-2 SIGHIA. According to this, the workplace is not only the place where the insured is doing the work, but also the places attached to the workplace and vehicles are also included in the workplace concept. Similarly, an accident to be considered an occupational accident does not necessarily have to take place during working hours, although it occurs in the workplace.

Secondly, in order for an accident to be considered an occupational accident, the insured must be injured by the work carried out by the employer and the work carried out by the insured if he/she works on his/her behalf and account (art. 13 para. 1/b SIGHIA). This possibility targets accidents outside the workplace. Accordingly,

---

[4]See: Mutlay (2014), pp. 184–195.

[5]Güzel et al. (2020), p. 366.

[6]CC, 10th Civ. Div., 29.3.1979, 1978-8413/2759, Yargıtay Kararları Dergisi, 8 (1979), pp. 1167–1169.

even if the accident did not occur in the workplace, for example, the accidents occurring because the employer sends the insured to another location outside the workplace or the insured gets out of the workplace as a requirement of the work are considered as occupational accidents.

Thirdly, the accidents occurring during times when the insured is sent to another location by the employer and cannot perform of his/her actual work are considered occupational accidents (art. 13 para. 1/c SIGHIA). Accordingly, the employer may have obligated the insured with duties out of the workplace. The fact that the said place of work is in the same or another province or in a foreign country is not important in terms of the occupational accident concept.

In this context, Court of Cassation has described the death of the insured as a result of the fall of the plane he/she had boarded while going to another city as an official as an occupational accident.[7] Similarly, regarding a case when the insured, which is sent to a location by the employer, loses his/her life due to the explosion of a bomb while sitting with his/her friends in a park on the road, it has accepted that case as an occupational accident.[8]

Another situation to be accepted, as an occupational accident is the case when a nursing mother has an accident in the time allocated for breastfeeding her child (art. 13 para. 1/d SIGHIA). Female workers are allowed a breastfeeding permit for a total of one and a half hours a day to breastfeed their children under one year of age (art. 74 para. 1 LA). Here, the accident that the insured will suffer during this breastfeeding permit is accepted as an occupational accident. In this regard, Court of Cassation goes one step further and accepts accidents such as the insured being hit by a car while going to work during her breastfeeding permit and losing her life as an occupational accident.[9]

Finally, the accidents occurring during the arrival of the vehicle provided by the employer to the workplace are considered occupational accidents (art. 13 para. 1/e SIGHIA). For this, the workers do not have to be brought together collectively. According to this, accidents that the insured persons will encounter during their transportation to the workplace individually by vehicles provided by the employers will be considered occupational accidents. Again, the accident that the insured person will encounter during his/her travel to the workplace while the vehicle provided by the employer is used by the insured himself/herself will also be considered an occupational accident.

On the other hand, the transfer of the insured by the employer can be caused by the nature of the job, but also by a social purpose. In both cases, the accident that the insured will suffer during transport will be considered an occupational accident.

[7]CC, 9th Civ. Div., 29.12.1981, 11284/15904, IHU, SSK, art. 11 No. 2.

[8]CC, 10th Civ. Div., 13.10.1987, 5024/5139.

[9]CC, General Assembly of Civ. Div., 10.6.1983, 328/652, Çenberci (1985), pp. 120–121.

13.1.2.4 Damage to the Insured Due to Accident

To consider an occupational accident, the insured must be exposed to a physical or mental disability immediately or subsequently due to the accident. Exposure to disability includes all physical and mental disabilities. In this sense, the damage suffered will have to be in a nature and degree that will require the provision of social insurance allowances. According to this, insignificant wounds and abrasions encountered in daily work life will not be sufficient for the existence of an occupational accident.

The incidents that cause a loss of property to the insured other than the physical or mental damages are not considered occupational accidents. On the other hand, it is necessary to deem the damages that occur in the cases where the insured are attached prostheses to serve as organs as occupational accidents. Because, when the artificial organ (for example, prosthetic arm, leg or artificial teeth) that is attached to the body forms an integral part of the insured, it must be considered within the concept of body integrity.[10]

13.1.2.5 Existence of Causal Relation

For the existence of an occupational accident, there should be a relationship between the accident and the physical or mental harm that the insured has suffered, that is, there must be a connection between the cause and the result. According to this, if the damage suffered by the insured is a result that cannot be expected according to the natural flow of events, the causal relation can no longer be considered.[11]

In this context, Court of Cassation has described the death as a result of a cardiac arrest during an argument in the workplace as an occupational accident.[12] However, the Court of Cassation does not consider the case of an insured losing his/her life at a traffic accident going to his/her hometown after being injured at the workplace and being treated at a hospital an occupational accident.[13]

13.2 The Concept of Occupational Disease

The conduct of a professional activity or continuous work in some jobs leads to diseases in the person directly linked to these activities. In this regard, social security systems consider occupational diseases a social risk just like occupational accidents.

---

[10]Güzel et al. (2020), p. 375; Tuncay and Ekmekçi (2019), p. 412; Tunçomağ (1990), p. 264.

[11]Tunçomağ (1990), p. 265.

[12]CC, 10th Civ. Div., 10.12.1976, 4160/8438.

[13]CC, 10th Civ. Div., 25.5.1989, 3064/4630, YKD, 9 (1989), pp. 1271–1273.

13.2.1 Definition of Occupational Disease

Occupational disease is defined in art. 14 para. 1 SIGHIA. According to this, occupational disease is the condition of temporary or permanent illness, physical or mental disability that the insured suffers for a recurrent reason due to the nature of the work done or due to the execution conditions of the work.

In contrast, art. 3 para. 1/l OHSA defines occupational disease as a result of exposure to occupational risks. Thus, the provision in question is based on the concept of "*occupational risk*". However, in the face of the wide meaning and uncertainty of the word "*occupation*", it should be said that the definition of SIGHIA is more accurate.[14]

13.2.2 Elements of Occupational Disease

13.2.2.1 The Insured Suffering from a Disability

The fact that the insured suffering from occupational disease, temporarily or permanently suffers a physical or mental damage as a result of this disease appears to be the basic element of occupational disease. According to this, occupational diseases cannot only cause disability in the physical integrity of the body but also in the mental and nervous system.

13.2.2.2 Disease or Disability as a Result of the Work of the Insured

In order for a disease to be considered an occupational disease, there must be a causal link between said disease (disability or death) and the work of the insured.[15] Accordingly, a recurrent reason due to the nature of the work in which the insured is working or due to the conditions of execution of the work must cause the disease or disability.

Unlike occupational accident, occupational disease has completely professional characteristics. As a matter of fact, it is not necessary for the occupational accident to be found related to the work done, but the occupational disease must arise as a result of the work of the insured.

The identification of the causal relation between the work of the insured and the occupational disease that he/she suffers does not create difficulties in general. Because, which diseases will be considered as occupational diseases is organized into a list in Turkey, as in other countries.

---

[14] *See* also: Akdeniz (2015), pp. 59–60; Güzel et al. (2020), p. 381.

[15] Mutlay (2014), pp. 243–244; Saymen and Ekonomi (1966), p. 88.

13.2.3 *Determination of Occupational Disease*

13.2.3.1 List of Occupational Diseases

It is foreseen that the conditions to be considered as occupational diseases are arranged by a regulation to be issued by SSI (art. 14 para. 6 SIGHIA). This regulation explained the method of determining occupational diseases and gave a list of occupational diseases in its annex.[16] Accordingly, in order for a disease to qualify as an occupational disease, as a rule, its name must be included in the annex list of occupational diseases attached to the regulation in question and should have appeared within the period specified in this list.[17]

The duration of obligation for different diseases in the list of occupational diseases ranges from 3 days to 10 years.

13.2.3.2 Occurrence of Occupational Disease After Leaving Work

Occupational diseases can also occur after the insured has quit work. In this case, benefiting from occupational disease insurance depends on the fact that the time between the date on which the insured has actually quit the job and the occurrence of the disease is no longer than the time specified in the list of occupational diseases for this disease (art. 14 para. 3 SIGHIA).

13.2.3.3 Identification of Occupational Diseases Not Listed

Disputes that may arise from the fact that any disease other than the diseases specified in the regulation to be considered, as occupational disease shall be decided by *social security supreme board of health* (art. 14 para. 6 SIGHIA). Accordingly, if the claims made by the insured or right holders regarding that a disease not included in the list of occupational diseases is SSI does not find an occupational disease appropriate, the social security supreme board of health will solve the dispute. One can apply to the labour court against the decision of this board.

13.2.3.4 Determination of Occupational Disease by the Health Board of SSI

In order for the insured person suffering from the occupational disease to benefit from the social security allowances, it is compulsory for the health board of SSI to

---

[16]OG 11.10.2008, No. 27021.

[17]Akdeniz (2015), pp. 75–76.

determine that the insured has been subject to occupational disease because of the work carried out, as a result of:

- The examination of the health board report and the basis medical reports duly prepared by the health service providers authorized by SSI,
- The examination of the audit reports and other necessary documents, which reveal the working conditions and related medical results in the workplace when deemed necessary by SSI (art. 14 para. 2 SIGHIA). Accordingly, it can be determined whether the disease, which the insured is suffering, is an occupational disease after the completion of a two-stage procedure.

As a matter of fact, in the first stage, it is possible to determine that the insured suffers from the occupational disease due to the work carried out by the relevant health service providers with the health board report and the basis medical reports. In the second stage, the said report and the basis medical reports will have to be determined by the health board of SSI.[18]

It is legally possible to appeal to the social security supreme health board against the decision of SSI and to file a lawsuit against this decision to the labour court. In this case, the labour court shall establish a judgment based on the report to be obtained from *Forensic Medicine Institute*.[19]

13.3 Financial Aids to Be Made to the Insured

13.3.1 Temporary Incapacity Allowance

13.3.1.1 Amount

The amount of temporary incapacity allowance is half of the daily earnings of the insured in inpatient treatments and two-thirds in outpatient treatments (art. 18 para. 3 SIGHIA).

13.3.1.2 Duration and Format of Delivery

Temporary incapacity allowance is given to the insured without a time limitation, depending on the state of health, as long as the treatment and resting continues. This allowance is paid starting from the first day of incapacity to work in the case of occupational accidents and occupational diseases.

The employer is obliged to pay the temporary incapacity allowance of the insured in case the insured suffers from an occupational accident or an occupational disease

[18]*See*: Akdeniz (2015), pp. 68–70.

[19]CC, 21st Civ. Div., 16.11.2009, 5752/14932, Legal İSGHD, 26 (2010), pp. 840–841.

caused by the employer tasking the insured abroad temporarily or permanently or taking him/her abroad, until SSI seizes the work. The employer is responsible for the damages to be incurred on both SSI and the insured due to the delay in fulfilling this obligation. And SSI pays the employer the amount of temporary incapacity allowances paid in accordance with the law and based on documents.

Temporary incapacity allowances are not subject to insurance premium deductions or income tax deductions.[20]

13.3.1.3 Merging of Allowances

If the insured suffers from multiple cases of occupational accident, occupational disease, disease and maternity, the highest amount of temporary incapacity allowance will be given (art. 18 para. 5 SIGHIA).

13.3.1.4 Deduction, Decrease or Withholding of Allowance

SS may deduct the temporary incapacity allowance in cases where the insured is exposed to occupational accidents, occupational diseases, sickness, prolongation of treatment period or increase of the incapacity to work because of the reasons arising from the insured himself/herself (art. 22 para. 1 SIGHIA).

Except for those who have no penal responsibility and those with an acceptable excuse, if the insured fails to comply with the measures and recommendations of the physician regarding occupational accidents and occupational diseases and causes prolongation of the treatment period, increase in the incapacity to work or disability, SSI deducts the incapacity allowance by one quarter of the total, taking the prolonged treatment period or the increase of the incapacity to work as basis (art. 22 para. 1/a SIGHIA).

Again, except for those without penal responsibility, the temporary incapacity allowance of the insured person who has suffered an occupational accident or occupational disease due to a serious defect of himself/herself will be deducted by SSI up to a third of the total allowance, based on the degree of defect (art. 22 para. 1/b SIGHIA).

Finally, the insured, which has suffered an occupational accident or an occupational disease due his/her actions or refuses the treatment offered despite the written notice of SSI, is paid half of the temporary incapacity allowance (art. 22 para. 1/c SIGHIA).

On the other hand, temporary incapacity allowance is not paid to the insured working without receiving a document from the physician stating that the treatment has ended and the insured has the capacity to work (art. 22 para. 1/d SIGHIA).

[20]General Assembly of the Government Accounting Bureau, 21.12.1985, 1985/1, 4487/1.

13.3.2 Permanent Incapacity Allowance

13.3.2.1 Qualification Requirements

As a result of the treatment, the insured will either completely have the capacity to work or he/she will lose no less than 10% of his/her capacity to work. If this situation is determined by the health board of SSI according to the reports issued by the health board of the health service providers authorized by SSI, the allowance to be paid to the insured is called the "*permanent incapacity allowance*" (art. 19 para. 1 SIGHIA).

The main condition for the right to the permanent incapacity allowance is the actualization of permanent incapacity to work. Permanent incapacity to work indicates that the insured has lost no less than 10% of their capacity to work. In this case, if the insured has been determined to lose all of their capacity to work completely (100%), the state of "*permanent and complete incapacity to work*" is in question. If the insured has been determined to lose more than 10% but less than 100% of their capacity to work, the state of "*permanent and partial incapacity to work*" is in question.

13.3.2.2 Calculation of Allowance

The allowance to be given to the insured that is in the state of permanent and complete incapacity to work is 70% of his/her monthly pay. If the insured is in need of constant care from someone else, the rate of the allowance increases to 100% (art. 19 para. 3 SIGHIA).

If the insured has been determined to lose 10–99% of their capacity to work, the amount of permanent and complete incapacity allowance (70% of monthly pay) calculated according to the incapacity ratio will be given. However, if the insured is in need of constant care from someone else, the rate of the allowance increases to 100% (art. 19 para. 3 SIGHIA).

13.4 Allowances to the Right Holders of the Insured

13.4.1 Payment of Funeral Expenses

The right holders of the insured, who has died as a result of occupational accident or occupational disease or while being paid permanent incapacity allowance, are paid the funeral allowance under the tariff. The tariff here is determined by the board of directors of SSI and approved by the Minister of Family, Labour and Social Services (art. 37 para. 3 SIGHIA).

The funeral allowance is given to the spouse, or to the children, or to the parents, or to the siblings of the insured, respectively (art. 37 para. 3 SIGHIA).

13.4.2 *Allowance for the Spouse and Children of the Insured*

13.4.2.1 Calculation of Allowance

Allowance is attributed to the right holders of the insured who has died due to occupational accidents or occupational diseases. For this, it is not mandatory that the insured has worked for a certain period of time and has paid premiums.

70% of the monthly pay of the insured is given to the rights holders as allowance (art. 20 para. 1 SIGHIA).

13.4.2.2 Allowance for the Spouse of the Deceased Insured

The spouse of the insured who died as a result of an occupational accident or occupational disease will be paid 50% of the calculated allowance, while the spouse with no child with allowances will be paid 75% of the allowance, provided that he/she is not employed or is not paid monthly due to his/her own insurance (art. 20 para. 1 and art. 34 para. 1/a SIGHIA).

If the spouse of the deceased insured gets married the allowance is withheld (art. 20 para. 5, art. 34 and art. 35 para. 1 SIGHIA). If the marriage that leads to the withholding of allowance is eliminated, then the allowance is given again (art. 35 para. 3 SIGHIA).

13.4.2.3 Allowance for the Children of the Deceased Insured

Each of the daughters and boys of the insured who has died as a result of occupational accidents or occupational diseases, are given an allowance at 25% of the calculated allowance (art. 34 para. 1/b SIGHIA).

However, each of these children:

- Who are orphaned with the death of the insured or subsequently,
- Parents of whom do not have a marital bond between them,
- Parents of whom had a marital bond on the date of the death of the insured and married later,
- That do not have any other right holders given monthly allowance other than themselves,

Are to be given 50% of the allowance (art. 34 para. 1/c SIGHIA).

The basic legal requirement for children to be given allowance is the fact that the child is not over the age of 18, without any discrimination between boys and girls (art. 34 para. 1/b SIGHIA).

However, of the children, those who are receiving high school or equivalent education will be eligible for allowance until they are 20 years of age and those who are receiving higher education until they are 25 years of age (art. 34 para. 1/b 1 SIGHIA).

In addition, children who lose at least 60% of their capacity to work by the decision of the health board of SSI will be entitled to allowance without seeking any age conditions (art. 34 para. 1/b 2 SIGHIA).

Again, unmarried or married and later divorced or widowed girls, regardless of age, will be entitled to allowance due to the death of the insured (art. 34 para. 1/b 3 SIGHIA).

13.4.3 Marriage Allowance

The two-year period of the allowance is given to the girls, who was given allowance due to the death of the insured, but whose allowance had to be withheld due to marriage, if they wish to marry and make a request, for one time as the "*marriage allowance*" (art. 37 para. 1 SIGHIA).

Marriage allowance consists of giving the two-year allowance to the daughter collectively in case of marriage. The beginning of the two-year period here is the date on which the allowance of the right holder given the marriage allowance has been withheld. Because, if the right holder who receives the marriage allowance is entitled to allowance within two years from the date the allowance was withheld, it is foreseen that the allowance will not be attributed until the end of the two-year period (art. 37 para. 1 SIGHIA).

13.4.4 Allowance for the Mother and Father of the Insured

In the event that the insured dies as a result of an occupational accident or occupational disease, the mother and father of the insured are also given allowance. The main condition for the mother and father to be eligible for allowance is that an extra share remains from the allowance to be attributed to the spouse and children at the time of the death of the insured. According to this, if the insured has a spouse and two children at the time of death, the mother and father will not be given allowance, as there will be no extra share remaining from them.

A second condition is that the income the mother and father obtain from every possible earnings and revenue is less than the net amount of the minimum wage and that they are given no monthly income and/or allowance.

In the event that these two conditions are fulfilled, 25% (12.5% each) of the allowance is given to the mother and father (art. 34 para. 1/d SIGHIA).

13.5 Responsibility of the Employer to SSI

SSI provides the necessary assistance to the insured subject to an occupational accident or occupational disease in relation to the social state characteristic of the State and the persons having the right to social security. However, SSI has the right to ask the employer of the insured for these expenses in the frame of its right of recourse. The responsibility of the employer here depends on whether or not he/she has fulfilled his/her legal obligations.

13.5.1 Responsibility of the Employer That Complies with Legal Obligations

13.5.1.1 Responsibility Conditions

The responsibility of the employer who has previously declared the insured who has suffered from occupational accident or occupational disease to SSI in time was arranged in art. 21 SIGHIA. According to this, the ability of SSI to file recourse against the employer depends on the employer's defective behaviour.

The cases based on the employer's defective behaviour are shown as limited in art. 21 para. 1 SIGHIA. Accordingly, only if the occupational accident and occupational disease occurs as a result of an intention of the employer or actions contrary to the occupational health and safety legislation, the responsibility of the employer against SSI arises (art. 21 para. 1 SIGHIA).

On the other hand, the "*inevitable-accident doctrine*" will be taken into account when determining the employer's responsibility (art. 21 para. 1 SIGHIA). The inevitability here is the occurrence of an occupational accident or occupational disease, despite all the measures to be taken in accordance with the scientific and technical rules applicable at the time of the incident.[21] Accordingly, if the employer has not taken the necessary measures, it is no longer possible to mention the inevitability of the incident.[22]

13.5.1.2 Scope of Responsibility

What SSI can request from the employer in the case of the recourse is shown in art. 21 para. 1 SIGHIA. Accordingly, the sum of the first advance capital value at the date on which the allowance begins and the allowances paid or to be paid to the insured or the right holders by SSI in accordance with SIGHIA are requested by SSI from the employer, limited to the amounts the insured or the right holders may

[21] CC, 10th Civ. Div., 23.3.1995, 2698/2906, Yargıtay Kararları Dergisi, 6 (1995), pp. 901–903.
[22] *See*: CC, 9th Civ. Div., 30.6.1989, 3498/6203, Yargıtay Kararları Dergisi, 3 (1990), p. 382.

request from the employer. The first advance capital value here is determined according to the advance capital value tables that are in effect at the date of payment of the allowance.

On the other hand, the employer may be held responsible in the face of SSI, limited to the amounts the insured or the right holders may request from the employer. Accordingly, the allowance increases to be paid by SSI to the insured or right holders after the first recourse case cannot be requested by a second recourse case from the employer.

The recourse cases filed by SSI are subject to a statutory period of 10 years. The statute of limitation here will be initiated from the date of approval of SSI in terms of allowances to be granted and from the date of payment in respect of allowances such as temporary incapacity allowance and marriage and funeral allowances (art. 93 para. 3 SIGHIA).

13.5.2 Responsibility of the Employer That Does Not Comply with Legal Obligations

13.5.2.1 The Responsibility of the Employer That Does Not Declare the Insured

In the event that the employer does not declare to SSI that the insured is employed with the declaration of employment, SSI shall cover the allowances of the related persons for the occupational accidents or occupational diseases occurring before the date of the late declaration or when SSI determines that the insured is employed. However, if an allowance is granted at the amount of the expenses of all kinds made or to be made by SSI, the employer regardless of whether there is defect pays the first advance capital value at the date of this allowance (art. 23 paras 1 and 2 SIGHIA). Accordingly, in determining the responsibility of the employer in this situation, the employer's intention or action contrary to occupational health and safety legislation will not be important in the incident of occupational accident or occupational disease.

13.5.2.2 The Responsibility of the Employer That Does Not Give the First Health Allowance

The employer is obliged to provide the first health care services required by the health care provider to the insured who is subject to an occupational accident or occupational disease (art. 76 para. 1 SIGHIA). In this context, if the employer's negligence or delay in fulfilling the stated legal obligation causes increase in the treatment period of the insured or causes a disability or increase in the level of disability, the employer is obliged to pay all the health care expenses SSI makes on this regard (art. 76 para. 2 SIGHIA).

13.5.2.3 The Responsibility of the Employer That Does Not Report an Occupational Accident or Disease in Time

If the employer does not report the occupational accident to the Institution within the legal period, the temporary incapacity allowance to be paid to the insured for the period until the date of notification shall be collected by SSI from the employer (art. 21 para. 2 SIGHIA).

Similarly, SSI is entitled to recourse to the employer, who does not fulfil his/her obligation to report the occupational disease to the Institution or who intentionally reports the issues in writing incomplete or false, the expenses covered by SSI on this regard and the temporary incapacity allowances paid to the insured (art. 14 para. 4 SIGHIA).

13.6 Responsibilities of Third Persons Against SSI

If an occupational accident or occupational disease occurs because of the defect of a third person, half of the first advance capital value on the starting date of the allowances paid or to be paid to the insured and the right holders are recourse to third persons causing the damage and, if there is a defect, to those who employ them (art. 21 para. 4 SIGHIA). The third persons here are all persons causing damage other than the injured or sick insured and his/her employer. They do not need to be an assisting the employer.[23]

In order for the third person to be held responsible against SSI, the occupational accident or occupational disease must have occurred due to the defect of the third person. Accordingly, the application of the principles of non-defect responsibility for the third person is not legally possible.

References

Akdeniz AL (2015) Meslek Hastalığı Kavramı Üzerine. Beta Publishing, Istanbul

Çenberci M (1985) Sosyal Sigortalar Kanunu Şerhi. Olgaç Matbaası, Ankara

Gümüş R (2017) Türkiye'de 2015 Yılında Meydana Gelen İş Kazalarının Analizi ve 2014 Yılı Verileri İle Karşılaştırılması. Analysis of occupational accidents in 2015 in Turkey and comparing them with data of 2014. The Journal of Academic Social Science Studies JASSS. Int J Soc Sci 55:277–287. https://www.jasstudies.com/Makaleler/1065365481_20Yrd.%20Doç.%20Dr.%20Rojan%20Gümüş.pdf

Güzel A, Okur AR, Caniklioğlu N (2020) Sosyal Güvenlik Hukuku, 18th edn. Beta Publishing, Istanbul

Mutlay FB (2014) Sosyal Sigorta Yardımlarına Hak Kazanma Koşulları ve Eşitlik İlkesi. Beta Publishing, Istanbul

[23]Saymen and Ekonomi (1966), p. 131.

Saymen FH, Ekonomi M (1966) Sosyal Sigortalar Tatbikatı. Özel İktisadi ve Ticari İlimler Yüksek Okulu, Istanbul. yayınları No. 12
Tuncay AC, Ekmekçi Ö (2019) Sosyal Güvenlik Hukuku Dersleri, 20th edn. Beta Publishing, Istanbul
Tunçomağ (1990) Sosyal Güvenlik Kavramı ve Sosyal Sigortalar, 5th edn. Beta Publishing, Istanbul

Chapter 14
Illness Insurance

14.1 Function of Illness Insurance

Besides affecting the health status of the individual, illnesses also adversely affect the economic situation of the individual. In this sense, the temporary incapacity to work caused by the illness prevents the person from working and therefore making income from the professional activity and causes the person to make expenses such as medicine, doctor and hospital expenses. In this respect, illness insurance aims to eliminate the negativities through health and money aids to provide protection against disease risk.

However, the Turkish legal system deals with the health aids to be made to the insured in case of illness in the framework of the general health insurance for all individuals, and the monetary aids are regulated within the provisions of the SIGHIA related to short-term insurance branches. In this respect, it can be said that the illness insurance in Turkey mainly targets the monetary aids. In order to avoid repetition, health aids to be made in case of illness will not be discussed here, and the explanations will be included in the following general health insurance section (Part 6).

Other than the occupational accidents and occupational diseases of the insured, the illnesses that cause incapacity to work cause the application of illness insurance in terms of SIGHIA. This understanding of illness in SIGHIA has quite a wide range of content. In this sense, all situations that result in deviations in private, social or professional life will be accepted as an illness for the illness insurance provided that they prevent working life. Accordingly, alcohol, drug and nicotine addictions will be considered in the concept of illness.[1]

[1] Sözer (2019), p. 236.

T. Centel, *Turkish Social Law*, https://doi.org/10.1007/978-3-030-64704-9_14

14.2 Temporary Incapacity Allowance

14.2.1 The Purpose of Payment

When the insured patient fails to maintain his/her work in the workplace, he/she loses the income gained from the work. It is foreseen that SSI will pay under the name of "*temporary incapacity allowance*" to the insured patient in order to cover the temporary loss of income. In this respect, the temporary incapacity allowance to be paid to the insured patient means monetary aid for the insured by the illness insurance.

14.2.2 Conditions to Qualify for Payment

14.2.2.1 Having Not Lost the Insured Quality

The first condition for the payment of temporary incapacity allowance is that the person is subject to illness insurance as an insured under the scope of applications of the insured worker (art. para. 1/a SIGHIA) or short-term insurance branches (art. 5 SIGHIA) and has not lost his/her insured quality (art. 9 para. 1/a SIGHIA).

The insured employee maintains his/her insured quality since he/she is obliged to pay premiums during the annual leave (art. 61 LA). According to this, the insured that gets ill during the annual leave can benefit from the temporary incapacity allowance.

14.2.2.2 More Than Two Days of Incapacity to Work

Another important condition of temporary incapacity allowance is that the incapacity of the insured due to illness lasts more than two days (art. 18 para. 1/b SIGHIA). Accordingly, if the resting period of the insured lasts two days or less, temporary incapacity allowance will not be provided by the illness insurance.

The incapacity to work must be documented by a medical report from the physician or health committees authorized by SSI (art. 18 para. 1 SIGHIA).

14.2.2.3 Premium Payment of At Least 90 Days

In order to qualify for the temporary incapacity allowance, a minimum of 90 days of short-term insurance premium must have been paid within one year prior to the date on which the temporary incapacity begins (art. 18 para. 1/b SIGHIA).

The period of military service of the insured enlisted for any reason, the duration of detention not resulting in conviction, the period in which the insured receiving temporary incapacity allowance cannot work due to an illness or the duration of the insured in strike or lockout are not taken into account in the calculation of a year prior to the date of the incapacity to work or prior to the detection of the illness. (art. 24 para. 2 SIGHIA).

14.2.3 Amount of Payment

The daily temporary incapacity allowance to be paid to the insured in case of illness varies according to the manner of treatment of the insured. Accordingly, if the insured receives inpatient treatment, it is half of the daily income, for outpatient (i.e., insured is resting in the house) it is two-thirds of the daily income (art. 18 para. 3 SIGHIA). A higher payment for outpatient treatment is based on the assumption that the insured needs a higher financial support in this case.[2]

14.2.4 Payment Procedure

The payment of temporary incapacity allowance starts from the third day of the illness (art. 18 para. 1/b SIGHIA). Accordingly, for example, an insured patient receiving a 10-day rest with a doctor's medical report will receive an 8-day temporary incapacity allowance.

The temporary incapacity allowance is paid to the insured person or the bank account number of the insured or to the Post (PTT) Bank branches within 7 working days following the transfer of the related documents or information to SSI. Payments for rest periods exceeding 10 days are made at a minimum of 10-day amount.

If the insured falls into multiple cases of occupational accident, occupational disease, illness and maternity, the highest amount of temporary incapacity allowance is paid (art. 18 para. 5 SIGHIA).

14.2.5 Not Making or Deducting the Payment

Except for those who do not have penal responsibility and those who have an acceptable excuse, if the insured does not comply with the measures and recommendations provided by the physician for the illness and causes prolongation of the treatment period, SSI deducts up to a quarter of the temporary incapacity allowance based on the prolonged treatment period (art. 22 para. 1/a SIGHIA).

---

[2] Sözer (2019), p. 240.

Similarly, based on the degree of defect of the insured who is ill due to a severe defect, up to one third of the temporary incapacity allowance is deducted by SSI (art. 22 para. 1/b SIGHIA).

Again, the insured that does not accept the proposed treatment in spite of the written notification of the Institution is paid half of the temporary incapacity allowance (art. 22 para. 1/c SIGHIA).

The temporary incapacity allowance shall not be paid to the insured who starts working without receiving a report indicating that his/her treatment has ended and that he/she is capable to work and the paid ones shall be withdrawn (art. 22 para. 1/d SIGHIA).

14.3 The Responsibility of the Employer Due to the Insured Patient

14.3.1 Operation of the Insured in Works Not Suitable as of Structure

When the insured is employed in a work not suitable as of structure, he/she will probably get ill. In this case, SSI is obliged to provide aid to the insured patient by the illness insurance. However, the employer will be the recourse for the temporary incapacity allowances paid by SSI to the insured who are employed in works that require medical reports in the labour legislation but are employed without any such report or are employed in works not suitable as of structure despite the obtained report for the illnesses detected to have occurred prior to such works or resulting from the works not suitable as of structure (art. 21 para. 3 SIGHIA).

In order to mention the responsibility of the employer, it is not necessary for him/her to be defective. Accordingly, if a report is required to be obtained but is not obtained or if the content of the obtained report is ignored and the employee is employed in a work not suitable as of structure, it is sufficient for the employer to be held responsible.[3]

14.3.2 Failure of the Issuance of the Employment Declaration for the Insured in Time

If the insured is not declared to SSI with the employment declaration within the period of insured employment, SSI pays the temporary incapacity allowance to the concerned person for the illness occurring before the date of the issuance of the late

[3]Güzel et al. (2020), p. 450.

declaration or the date of determination of the employment of the insured. However, in this case, the employer pays any amount of expenses made or to be made by SSI regardless of the presence of a defect (art. 23 para. 1 SIPHIA).

14.4 Responsibility of Third Persons Due to the Insured Patient

It is possible for the insured to get ill as a result of another person's behaviour. SSI is obliged to provide necessary aids from the illness insurance in such cases that are not considered as occupational diseases. In this case, SSI has the right to demand the expenses incurred from the third person causing damages. Accordingly, if the illness occurs due to the defect of a third person, third person is the recourse for the payments made and to be made to the insured (art. 21 para. 4 SIGHIA).

However, if the illness occurs as a result of the actions of public officials, private and public officers or other persons appointed by public offices due to their duties, their institution or the concerned parties will not be the recourse for the payments to the insured, except for those who have a finalized verdict of conviction for such actions (art. 21 para. 5 SIGHIA).

The recourse case of SSI against third person(s) is subject to a 10-year statute of limitation (art. 93 para. 3 SIGHIA).

References

Güzel A, Okur AR, Caniklioğlu N (2020) Sosyal Güvenlik Hukuku, 18th edn. Beta Publishing, Istanbul

Sözer AN (2019) Türk Sosyal Sigortalar Hukuku, 4th edn. Beta Publishing, Istanbul

Chapter 15
Maternity Insurance

15.1 Function of Maternity Insurance

The event of birth brings with it some of the expenses that are not considered as usual before and after birth and also causes loss of income due to the insured mother's inability to work for a certain period of time. As it is difficult for the insured to cover these cost increases and income losses by their own means, maternity insurance aims to eliminate the aforementioned increases and losses through the aids provided.

On the other hand, maternity insurance is not only directed towards the protection of insured women. As a matter of fact, the aids provided by maternity insurance also refer to the uninsured wives of insured men as well as insured women. Similarly, in order for maternity to qualify for insurance aids, the birth does not necessarily have to take place within the unity of marriage. Again, the form of the birth, i.e., premature, normal, caesarean births or the birth of a dead baby is not important.[1]

15.2 Maternity Insurance Aids

Health aids to be made due to maternity are regulated in the Turkish legal system within the framework of the "*general health insurance*" that all individuals benefit from. In this regard, since the general health insurance will be discussed in detail below (Part 6), we will not handle the health aids to be made for maternity in detail here to avoid repetition.

[1]Sözer (2019), p. 244.

T. Centel, *Turkish Social Law*, https://doi.org/10.1007/978-3-030-64704-9_15

15.2.1 Breastfeeding Allowance

From the maternity insurance:

- To insured women or to insured men due to the birth of their uninsured wives,
- To workingwomen with monthly payment from SSI for their work and independent worker women with monthly allowance or to the uninsured wives of men with monthly allowance,

"*Breastfeeding allowance*" is granted, per child, provided that they live, based on the tariff valid at the date of birth and determined by the board of directors of SSI and approved by the Minister of Family, Labour and Social Services (art. 16 para. 2 SIGHIA).

However, in order for a breastfeeding allowance to be given to insured women or to insured men due to the birth of their wives, a minimum of 120 days short-term insurance branches premium must have been paid in the year prior to the birth. For independent workers, it is compulsory to pay at least 120 days short-term insurance premium in the year prior to the birth and to pay any outstanding debts related to the premium, including the general health insurance premium (art. 16 para. 4 SIGHIA).

If the insured, whose insurance is expired and who is entitled to the breastfeeding allowance, delivers a child within 300 days of the expiration date, the insured woman or her husband who will benefit from the rights of maternity insurance can benefit from the breastfeeding allowance if at least 120 days of premium has been paid within the 15 months preceding the date of birth (art. 16 para. 5 SIGHIA).

15.2.2 Temporary Incapacity Allowance

In order to prevent loss of income of insured women during the maternity leave, it is foreseen that SSI grants the temporary incapacity allowance (art. 18 SIGHIA).

15.2.2.1 Qualification Requirements

The prerequisite for benefiting from the temporary incapacity allowance to be paid in the case of maternity is to be insured under the status of worker or self-employed (art. 18 para. 1/c SIGHIA). Temporary incapacity allowance is only granted to the maternity of the insured woman herself.

In order to benefit from temporary incapacity allowance, it is also necessary that at least 90 short-term insurance premiums have been paid within one year prior to the birth (art. 18 para. 1/c SIGHIA).

In addition, in order for the insured independent worker women to benefit from the temporary incapacity allowance, all premiums and debts related to premiums including the general health insurance must have been paid (art. 18 para. 2 SIGHIA).

15.2.2.2 Amount and Duration

The temporary incapacity allowance to be paid in the case of maternity is half of the daily income of the insured in inpatient treatment and two-thirds in outpatient treatment (art. 18 para. 3 SIGHIA).

Temporary incapacity allowance is granted for the unemployed eight-week periods before and after the birth (art. 18 para. 1/c SIGHIA). If the insured woman has a premature birth, the temporary incapacity allowance is also payable for the unused eight-week periods prior to the birth. Similarly, if the insured woman works voluntarily and with the consent of the physician for up to three weeks before the birth, the allowance must be paid for the period of up to three weeks of the eight-week period before the birth and for the periods to be added up to the eight-week period after the birth (art. 18 para. 1/d SIGHIA).

Except for premature birth, the temporary incapacity allowance is given from the first day of the eight-week period to be calculated prior to the birth. The date on which the temporary incapacity allowance will be terminated is the end of the eight-week period after birth. In premature births and working of up to three weeks prior to birth, this date will be extended by the unused periods of the eight weeks before birth.

If the incapacity of the insured woman continues after the eighth week after birth, whether or not the temporary incapacity allowance will continue to be given is not shown in SIGHIA. It may be said that it would be more appropriate to continue paying for these periods to be extended with the doctor's report. Because, art. 74 para. 2 LA regulating maternity leave recognizes the principle of extending maternity resting periods with a doctor's report.[2]

On the other hand, free maternity leave that can be taken for up to six months is not regarded, as incapacity in terms of the insured, and temporary incapacity allowance is not paid for this period.[3]

15.2.2.3 Not Making or Reducing the Payment

Except for those who have no penal responsibility and those who have an acceptable excuse, if the duration of treatment is prolonged or the incapacity rate increases as a result of the insured's failure to comply with the measures and recommendations made by the physician for maternity, SSI reduces the temporary incapacity allowance by up to one quarter based on the prolonged treatment duration or increased incapacity rate (art. 22 para. 1/a SIGHIA).

Again, the temporary incapacity allowance is not paid to the female insured woman that has given birth who starts working without receiving a document

[2]Güzel et al. (2020), pp. 459–460; Sözer (2019), pp. 246–247.

[3]Sözer (2019), p. 246.

from the physician indicating that the treatment is over and she is capable for work, and the paid ones are taken back (art. 22 para. 1/d SIGHIA).

References

Güzel A, Okur AR, Caniklioğlu N (2020) Sosyal Güvenlik Hukuku, 18th edn. Beta Publishing, Istanbul

Sözer AN (2019) Türk Sosyal Sigortalar Hukuku, 4th edn. Beta Publishing, Istanbul

Chapter 16
Disability Insurance

16.1 Function of Disability Insurance

The basis of the idea of monthly allowance due to disability lays in the purpose of financial support to the insured who has lost some or all of the capacity to work and whose economic situation is therefore disrupted.[1] Accordingly, for the insured, which cannot work due to his/her crippling condition and is deprived of his/her income, this lost income is provided from the long-term insurance branch and during the continuation of the disability.

Disability is a social risk that is organized within the long-term insurance branch. In this sense, disability, like old age and death, creates a lasting and permanent effect. However, in order to qualify for disability allowance from disability insurance, the number of insurance days and the number of premium days required are less than those required for pension.

16.2 Disability Allowance

16.2.1 Allowance Conditions

16.2.1.1 Disability

Who are to be considered disabled in terms of disability insurance are organized in art. 25 SIGHIA and those who are considered disabled are separated into two groups. These are, for insured workers and self-employed individuals, the ones who lose at least 60% of their working power or income power in the profession as a result of the occupational accident or occupational disease.

[1] Alper (2015), p. 267; Tunçomağ (1990), p. 330.

T. Centel, *Turkish Social Law*, https://doi.org/10.1007/978-3-030-64704-9_16

The 60% loss of working power here is determined by the Health Board of SSI as a result of the examination of the report of the health boards of the health service providers authorized by SSI and the documents constituting the basis of the report (art. 25 para. 1 SIGHIA).

A different disability status has been determined for insured civil servants. Accordingly, insured public officials must lose at least 60% of their working power or lose their income power in the profession in a way that they cannot perform their duties. In addition, the occurrence of disability after starting to work and the situation being determined by a medical report is possible. For this, the insured must make a request to the health facility to determine the disability and the health board of the healthcare facility must give the disability report. Furthermore, the approval of the disability report by the health board of SSI is also needed. The reports of the health board of SSI are not legally final, and they can be appealed to the supreme health council.[2]

If the insured that started to work for the first time already needs to be considered disabled, he/she will not be entitled to a disability allowance (art. 25 para. 2 SIGHIA). However, if the insured's disability is milder at the time of employment and after being insured the insured reaches 60% loss of working power, 60% loss of income power in the profession or it gets to a condition where he/she cannot perform his/her duties, the insured will be provided disability insurance aids.[3]

16.2.1.2 Being Insured for a Period and Having Paid Premiums

In order to be granted allowance, the insured, except for being considered as disabled, must also be insured for at least 10 years and a total of 1.800 days of long-term insurance premiums must have been paid in the name of the insured. However, if the insured is in need of permanent care of another person, it is sufficient to have paid the 1.800 days of premiums without looking for the insurance period (art. 26 para. 2/b SIGHIA).

The conditions of a certain insurance period and the number of premium days paid for foreseen in the law must take place together. Accordingly, the insured both must be insured for 10 years and at the same time must have paid at least 1.800 days of premium. In this case, for example, a person insured for 8 years and have paid 2.880 days of premium will not be given allowance due to not completing the 10-year insurance period to even though 1.800 days of premium have been paid.

In order for the self-employed persons to be entitled to disability allowance, it is obligatory that all premiums and debts related to premiums, including the general health insurance premium, have been paid (art. 26 para. 2 SIGHIA).

The beginning of the ten-year period of insurance is the first time the insured has started working and the end of this period is the date of granting disability allowance.

---

[2]See: Sözer (2019), pp. 284–285.

[3]Sözer (2019), p. 266.

In this regard, Court of Cassation takes into account the period between the dates the first time the insured has started working and the date of the request for disability allowance as the period of insurance.[4] However, it is not legally necessary to carry out the whole 10-year period by working.[5]

Periods before the age of 18 years are not taken into account in the calculation of the ten years of insurance (art. 38 para. 2 SIGHIA).

16.2.1.3 Leaving Work and Applying to SSI

As long as the insured does not apply, SSI cannot grant the insured allowance by sending the insured to examination by itself.[6] Accordingly, in order for the disability allowance to be granted, the insured must leave the job after the disability is identified by the report or must apply to SSI after closing or transferring the workplace (art. 26 para. 2/c SIGHIA).

Even if the insured has left the job after applying to SSI, the insured will still be granted the disability allowance. However, in this case, the disability allowance will have to be granted according to the date of leaving the job.[7]

16.2.2 Method of Calculating the Allowance

The disability allowance is calculated over 9.000 days for the insured with premium days less than 9.000 days and over the total number of premium payment days for those with 9.000 days and more. This is based on a 2% rate for every 360 days the insured has paid. If the insured is in need of constant care of another person, 10 points increase the rate determined. However, the number of 9.000 premium days is considered as 7.200 days for employees according to the employment contract (art. 27 para. 1 SIGHIA).

If an example is to be given: For an insured who has paid 3.600 days of premiums and has become disabled, 9.000 days of premium payment will be considered as paid, and the insured will be paid allowance at 50% rate ($9.000{:}360 = 25 \times 2 = 50$). For an insured working according to an employment contract: The calculation will be made as if there were 7.200 premium payment days and the insured will be paid allowance at 40% rate ($7.200{:}360 = 20 \times 2 = 40$).

---

[4]CC, 10th Civ. Div., 17.11.1983, 4296/5380, Yargıtay Kararları Dergisi, 2 (1984), pp. 250–253.

[5]Güzel et al. (2020), p. 476; Tunçomağ (1990), p. 333.

[6]Tunçomağ (1990), p. 335.

[7]Güzel et al. (2020), p. 478.

16.2.3 Payment of the Allowance

16.2.3.1 Beginning of the Allowance

The disability pension begins to be paid from the beginning of the month following the written request date, provided the insured has resigned from his/her job, if the date of the report is before the written request date. If the date of the report is after the date of the written request, payment starts from the beginning of the month following the date of the report (art. 27 para. 2 SIGHIA).

SSI is entitled to give advance payment if disability allowances are not paid in time (art. 97 para. 6 SIGHIA).

16.2.3.2 Time of Payment of Allowance

Disability allowance is paid in advance every month. SSI has the authority to determine the payment periods, payment dates, payment methods and payment centres of disability allowances (art. 55 para. 6 SIGHIA).

16.2.3.3 Notice of Allowance

SSI will calculate and determine the allowance to be given to the insured within 3 months at the latest from the date of the completion of the required documents and investigations and report the results in writing (art. 42 SIGHIA).

The insured can file a lawsuit at the labour court against this decision. The subject of the appeal to be filed will be the decision taken by SSI for the calculation of the allowance. In cases where the insurance periods are not calculated correctly or some of the periods are not taken into consideration, the lawsuits to be filed will be different from such an appeal and will not constitute the subject of such appeals.[8]

16.2.4 Increasing the Allowance

Disability allowances are regularly increased twice a year. Accordingly, disability allowances are increased by the rate of change in the general index of consumer prices announced by *Turkish Statistical Institute* compared to the previous six-month period, effective from the January and July payment dates of each year (art. 55 para. 2 SIGHIA).

[8]CC, 10th Civ. Div., 23.2.1984, 1054/1086.

16.2.5 Change of the Allowance

Changes in disability status affect the disability allowance and cause it to change. The change here depends on the decrease or increase of disability. These changes are determined by a control examination.

16.2.5.1 The Right to Undergo a Control Examination

The health status, which causes the insured to be considered as disabled, may change over time. Changes in this status may require the disability allowance to be granted, withheld, increased or decreased. Therefore, the insured may be subject to control examination (art. 94 para. 1 SIGHIA).

The insured or SSI may request the control examination (art. 94 para. 2 SIGHIA). The Court of Cassation considers that it is among the legal duties of SSI to subject the insured to a control examination and considers the exercise of the right to undergo a control examination as compatible with good faith.[9]

16.2.5.2 Effects of Control Examination on the Allowance

If the insured does not undergo a control examination until the payment period after the date specified in the written notification of SSI without an acceptable excuse, the disability allowance is withheld. On the other hand, if the insured undergoes the control examination within three months, the withheld allowance will be granted again starting from the date of the withholding (art. 94 paras 5 and 6 SIGHIA).

The disability allowance of the insured that has undergone the control examination after three months will be granted again from the beginning of the month after the control examination (art. 94 para. 7 SIGHIA). Accordingly, the insured is deprived of the disability allowance for each late month.

As a result of the examinations performed both at the request of SSI or the concerned person, it can be determined that there is no change in the disability status or that the disability increased or decreased. If the disability status has not changed, the insured will continue to be paid the previous disability allowance. If the disability status is increased or decreased, the disability allowance is recalculated, and if the disability status is eliminated, the disability allowance is withheld.

---

[9] *See*: CC, 10th Civ. Div., 19.4.1976, 9479/2868.

16.2.6 Withholding and Restart of Allowance

The disability allowances of those who start working under the legislation of SIGHIA or a foreign country when receiving disability allowance are withheld from the beginning of the payment period following the date of commencement of their employment and receiving of premium is commenced (art. 27 para. 3 SIGHIA).

For those who leave their job and request a restart of disability allowance or those who are retired, the disability allowance is recalculated and restarted.

16.2.7 Combining of Allowances

For the insured, which is entitled to both disability allowance and pension, only the highest of these aids is paid. When the amounts are equal, only the pension is granted (art. 54 para. 1/a 1 SIGHIA).

The insured that is entitled to lump sum pension payment in addition to the disability pension will only receive disability allowance, and the lump sum pension payment will not be made.[10]

If the same insured is entitled to income from the disability allowance and the occupational accident and occupational disease insurance, payment of both aids are foreseen. However, the insured will be given the whole amount of the higher of these and half of the lower. When these are equal, the whole amount of the income to be attributed from occupational accident and occupational disease insurance and half of the disability allowance will be paid (art. 54 para. 1/c 1 SIGHIA).

If those who are receiving duty disability allowance get insured again and are entitled to both the duty disability allowance and the disability allowance, they are given the higher of these allowances. If the allowances are equal, only the duty disability allowance is granted (art. 54 para. 1/a 6 SIGHIA).

16.3 Special Disability Cases for Civil Servants

16.3.1 Duty Disability

16.3.1.1 Conditions Requiring the Consideration of Duty Disability

Duty disability is a qualified type of usual disability for civil servants. Accordingly, the disability for a person with disability insurance resulting from an accident occurring while performing their duties, while doing other tasks of any public office where they are assigned by their offices, while doing a job to protect the interests of

[10] Güzel et al. (2020), p. 490.

these businesses or institutions or while going to or leaving work by a vehicle provided by their offices is called "*duty disability*", and those who suffer from this kind of disability are called "*duty disabled*" (art. 47 para. 1 SIGHIA).

16.3.1.2 Cases Where the Disability Provisions Are Not Applicable

If the duty disability arises from the use of pleasuring drinks and all kinds of substances, acting out of laws and orders, conducting prohibited acts, attempting to commit suicide or purposes of profiting or harming oneself or others, the provisions on the duty disability will not be applied (art. 47 para. 2 SIGHIA).

16.3.1.3 Declaration of Duty Disability to SSI

The public offices are obliged to immediately declare the incident causing the duty disability to the authorities responsible for the area or the competent law enforcement authorities according to their legislation and within 15 working days at the latest to SSI (art. 47 para. 3 SIGHIA).

16.3.1.4 Granting the Duty Disability Allowance

Duty disability allowances are granted at the beginning of the month following the date on which the insured has been dismissed due to disability (art. 47 para. 5 SIGHIA).

The duty disability allowance is given over 10.800 days for those with up to 10.800 days of premium payments and over the number of premium payment days for those with 10.800 days of premium payments. To the allowances that will be calculated by applying a 2% rate for each 360 days on the basis of the most recent premium earnings, 30% increase will be made to those with disability degree 1, 23% to those with 2, 15% to those with 3, 7% to those with 4, 3% to those with 5 and 2% to those with 6 (art. 47 para. 7 SIGHIA).

16.3.1.5 Re-employment of Duty Disabled

The allowance of those starting to work again as civil servants, who already have a duty disability allowance granted, shall be withheld from the beginning of the payment period following the date they started working (art. 47 para. 15/a SIGHIA).

16.3.2 War Disability

16.3.2.1 Conditions Requiring Consideration of War Disabled

Of the officers, staff sergeants, expert gendarmes, expert sergeants, contracted sergeants and privates and insured persons assigned by the Turkish Armed Forces within the scope of public officials, those duty disabled in:

- Under de facto fire in war,
- During war, war operations and services in war zones,
- With the influence of all kinds of enemy weapons in war or in preparation for war,
- During domestic punishment and border movements requiring military action,
- With the causes and effects of flight or diving by pilots and divers, who fly or dive in peace or in extraordinary circumstances on orders or duties,
- In the event that the Turkish Armed Forces are sent to foreign countries, during the stay in the country or in a foreign country or in return to the country,

Are called "*war disabled*" (art. 47 para. 8 SIGHIA).

16.3.2.2 Granting of War Disablement Pension

When calculating the war disablement pension, it is possible to grant a pension on the basis of the premium earnings based on one higher rank of the current rank. In addition, the amounts to be found as a result of multiplying the indicators determined according to the disability status of the war disabled by the monthly wage of civil servants shall be added under the name of "*war disablement increase*" (art. 47 paras 10 and 11 SIGHIA).

On the other hand, of the members of the Turkish Armed Forces and other civil servants, war disabled persons who got disabled during personally providing for the successful completion of an operation and showing courage and sacrifice to be kept exemplary will be given the disablement pensions with a 25% increase (art. 47 para. 12 SIGHIA).

16.4 Other Aids Provided to Disability Allowance Receivers

16.4.1 Healthcare

Those who receive a disability allowance are considered as general health insured without any payment of premium and without registration (art. 60 para. 1/f SIGHIA). Thus, those who receive disability allowance and their dependents benefit from healthcare aids.

16.4.2 Rehabilitation

The insured persons who receive disability allowances are provided with rehabilitation services within the framework of the general health insurance provisions and are thus get accustomed to work (art. 63 para. 1/b SIGHIA).

16.4.3 Social Aid Increase

SIPHIA has terminated the application "*social aid increase*" for those who have previously been receiving disability allowance but has foreseen to continue to pay them for those who previously received disability allowance (prov. art. 1 para. 3 SIGHIA). Those who receive a disability allowance after the entry into force of SIGHIA do not receive a separate payment under the name of social aid increase, and this amount is paid in the pension.

16.4.4 Travel Allowance and Compulsory Expenses

SSI pays the health service expenses made for the purpose of determination and control of the disability status or periodic health examination and travel and daily expenses of those who receive disability allowance (art. 65 para. 4 SIGHIA).

16.4.5 Payment of Retirement Bonus

All military and civil insured persons who are civil servants or public officials, who receive a disability or duty disability allowance and those who are paid lump sum pension payment are paid the amount corresponding to one month of each full year of service under the name of "*retirement bonus*" (art. 89 and add. art. 82 Act No. 5434).

If the insured becomes disabled during going to or returning from the workplace by a vehicle provided by their office or in an accident at the workplace, this disability is called "*duty disability*" and those who suffer from it are called "*duty disabled*" (art. 47 para. 1 SIPHIA).

References

Alper Y (2015) Türk Sosyal Güvenlik Sistemi. Sosyal Sigortalar Hukuku, 7th edn. Dora Publishing, Bursa

Güzel A, Okur AR, Caniklioğlu N (2020) Sosyal Güvenlik Hukuku, 18th edn. Beta Publishing, Istanbul

Sözer AN (2019) Türk Sosyal Sigortalar Hukuku, 3rd edn. Beta Publishing, Istanbul

Tunçomağ K (1990) Sosyal Güvenlik Kavramı ve Sosyal Sigortalar, 5th edn. Beta Publishing, Istanbul

Chapter 17
Old-Age Insurance

17.1 Function of Old-Age Insurance

Old-age insurance is one of the long-term insurance branches, such as disability and death insurances. According to this, old age insurance aims to provide the insured person who loses capacity to work due to reaching a certain age with the opportunity to withdraw from working life and live without having to work and to rest.[1]

Old age appears as a social risk that greatly reduces or completely eliminates the working power of a person due to the biological change that occurs within the physiological structure of the person. In this sense, old age appears as a social risk, which causes the person to become inoperable, causes loss of income and ultimately leads the insured and his/her family to economic difficulties. Accordingly, old age insurance provides social security to remedy said loss of income and grants pension to compensate for the loss of income.[2]

However, the purpose of the old age-insurance should not be limited to meeting the risk related to the decrease in working power related to age alone. According to this, rewarding the many years of working of the insured and ensuring that they spend the rest of their lives resting and dealing with other interests also serves the purpose of old age insurance.

In any case, meeting the loss of income due to the insured not being able to work anymore is provided by the old-age insurance.

[1]Tunçomağ (1990), p. 341.

[2]Alper (2015), p. 280.

T. Centel, *Turkish Social Law*, https://doi.org/10.1007/978-3-030-64704-9_17

17.2 Granting the Old Age Allowance

The basic aid to be made from the old-age insurance is to grant the old age allowance to the insured. However, for those who fail to meet the allowance conditions, long-term insurance premiums that they have previously paid can be returned as a "*lump sum pension payment*", provided that they leave their work under insurance.

As SIGHIA entered into force, the conditions for entitlement to old-age allowance have not been changed. However, for those who start working for the first time after the entry into force of SIGHIA, the conditions for entitlement to old-age allowance have been rearranged. Thus, the insured were collected in two different groups based on the entry into force of SIGHIA.

17.3 Allowance Conditions for Age and Premium in the Period Preceding SIGHIA

17.3.1 For Workers

The age required to receive an old-age allowance was originally estimated to be 60 years in Turkey without discrimination between men and women.

Act No. 506,[3] then issued, originally designed it for 60 years for males and 55 for females. However, this age limit was reduced to 55 years for men and 50 years for women by Act No. 1186.[4] In addition, a third way for pension has been added that does not require an age condition to receive allowance. Thus, those who have been insured for 25 years and have filled 5000 premium days have become entitled to allowance even if they do not meet the 50–55-age condition.

It was later amended by Act No. 2422[5] and the 25-year period of insurance was reduced to 20 years for women and remained 25 years for men. According to this, the possibility for women to be retired at the age of 38 and men to be retired at the age of 43 has been created. In 1999, by the Act No. 4447, it was changed radically with the reason that this situation caused SSI to suffer financially.[6]

The age of entitlement to allowance was, regulated, as a rule, as 58 years for women and 60 years for men by Act No. 4447. However, it was accepted that this amendment be applied to those who will be insured after 8/9/1999, on the date of entry into force of this law. Also, the number of premium payment days has been changed. The number of premium days, which was 5.000 as a rule and 3.600 days for the simplified option, was increased to 7.000 days as a rule and 4.500 days for the

[3]OG 1.8.1964, No. 11766.

[4]OG 3.11.1969, No. 13341.

[5]OG 8.3.1981, No. 17273.

[6]OG 8.9.1999, No. 23810.

simplified option (art. 60 Act No. 506). With the addition of a temporary article, it was foreseen that this increase in both the age and the number of premium days would enter into force gradually (prov. art. 81 Act No. 506).

17.3.2 For Self-Employed Persons

At the beginning, with the condition of having paid insurance premiums by women for 20 years and men for 25 years, as age requirement was not sought, women could be retired at the age of 38 and men at the age of 43.

This principle has been amended by Act No. 4447 and in order for those being insured for the first time after 8/9/1999 to benefit from pensions, the principle for women to complete 58 years of age and men to complete 60 years of age and to pay 25 full years of insurance premiums has been accepted. The issue of rising the premium payment period for women from 20 to 25 years was taken before Constitutional Court, but Constitutional Court had not seen any violation of the law.[7]

17.3.3 For Civil Servants

The ages required by civil servants and other public officials to complete and the numbers of premium days that they had to fill have been changed many times by various laws. SIGHIA has included persons entering civil service for the first time after the entry into force of itself and has not foreseen a transition process for them. Therefore, said changes will not be mentioned here. The situation of those previously insured will be explained below (Chap. 20) when talking about the insured that the provisions of Act No. 5434 will apply for.

17.4 Conditions Required After the Entry into Force of SIGHIA

SIGHIA has again increased both the retirement age and the number of premium days. However, it is foreseen that this increase in age enter into force gradually from 2036 and that the age of retirement be 65 years for both women and men in 2048.

[7]Constitutional Court, 23.2.2001, 1999-42/41, OG 23.11.2001, No. 24592.

17.4.1 For Those Insured for the First Time After 30/4/2008

The general rule is that those who are insured in the status of self-employed individuals and civil servants be granted pensions provided they complete 58 years of age for women and 60 years for men and they pay at least 9.000 days of premium. As a general rule for insured workers, it is foreseen that female workers complete 58 years of age and male workers complete 60 years of age and pay at least 7.200 days (art. 28 para. 2/a SIGHIA).

No change is foreseen in the age requirement for retirement pension until 2036. After this date, the age requirement is gradually increased. Accordingly, the age required for retirement pension will be applied as:

- 59 for women and 61 for men between 1/1/2036 and 31/12/2037,
- 60 for women and 62 for men between 1/1/2038 and 31/12/2039,
- 61 for women and 63 for men between 1/1/2040 and 31/12/2041,
- 62 for women and 64 for men between 1/1/2042 and 31/12/2043,
- 63 for women and 65 for men between 1/1/2044 and 31/12/2045,
- 64 for women and 65 for men between 1/1/2046 and 31/12/2047,
- 65 for both women and men from 1/1/2048 (art. 28 para. 2/b SIGHIA).

It is an indubitable fact that the age of 65 is too high for Turkey. In addition, it should be kept in mind that those who lose their jobs after a certain age have a very low possibility to find new jobs in Turkey.[8]

In addition to the general rule, insured persons may also benefit from the old age allowance as *simplified option*, provided they add three years to their age target and not exceed 65 years of age and pay a premium of at least 5.400 days (art. 28 para. 3 SIGHIA).

17.4.2 For Those Insured for the First Time Between 8/9/1999 and 30/4/2008

A transitional arrangement is envisaged for those insured for the first time between 8/9/1999 and 30/4/2008. Accordingly, those insured for the first time between 8/9/1999 and 30/4/2008 are entitled to old age allowance, provided they:

- Complete 58 years of age for women and 60 for men and pay at least 7.000 days of premium or,
- Complete 58 years of age for women and 60 for men and be insured for 25 years and pay at least 4.500 days of premium (prov. art. 9 para. 1 SIGHIA).

[8]Güzel et al. (2020), p. 511.

Those insured as independent workers for the first time between 8/9/1999 and 30/4/2008 are entitled to partial old age allowance, provided they:

- Complete 58 years of age for women and 60 for men and pay at least 25 years of premium or,
- Complete 60 years of age for women and 62 for men and pay at least 15 years of premium (prov. art. 9 para 2 SIGHIA).

Those insured as civil servants or public officials for the first time between 8/9/1999 and 30/4/2008 are entitled to partial old-age allowance, provided they:

- Complete 58 years of age for women and 60 for men and pay at least 25 years of premium or,
- Complete 61 years of age and pay at least 15 years of premium (prov. art. 9 para. 3 SIGHIA).

17.4.3 Transitional Provisions for Those Insured for the First Time Before 8/9/1999

17.4.3.1 Transition Period for Employees Working on Employment Contract

A transitional period is foreseen for insured workers. Accordingly, the rights of pensioners who had been entitled to retirement on 8/9/1999 according to the former provisions and the women who filled the insurance period of 18 years and the men who filled the insurance period of 23 years were reserved (prov. art. 81 act No. 506).

Constitutional Court found the section of the transitional provisions that reserve the rights to be in conformity with the Constitution but annulled the other parts of the transitional provisions.[9] The new regulation after the cancellation was made by Act No. 4759.[10] According to this, the period of insurance, the date of employment, duration, age and premium requirements for the insured are arranged in detail.[11]

On the other hand, it was accepted that women completing 50 years of age and meeting the requirements of 15 years of insurance and 3.600 days of premium days at:

- 23/5/2002 is entitled to pension whenever they want,
- Those who meet them between 24/5/2002 and 23/5/2005 when they complete 52 years of age,
- Between 24/5/2005 and 23/5/2008 at 54 years of age,
- Between 24/5/2008 and 23/5/2011 at 56 years of age,

[9]Constitutional Court, 23.2.2001, 1999-42/41, OG 23.11.2001, No. 24592.

[10]OG 1.6.2002, No. 24772.

[11]*See* in detail: Güzel et al. (2020), pp. 515–516.

- After 24/5/2011 at 58 years of age (art. 3 Act No. 4759).

Similarly, it was accepted that men completing 55 years of age and meeting the requirements of 15 years of insurance and 3.600 days of premium days at:

- 23/5/2002 is entitled to pension whenever they want,
- Those who meet them between 24/5/2002 and 23/5/2005 when they complete 56 years of age,
- Between 24/5/2005 and 23/5/2008 at 57 years of age,
- Between 24/5/2008 and 23/5/2011 at 58 years of age,
- Between 24/5/2011 and 23/5/2014 at 59 years of age,
- After 24/5/2014 at 60 years of age (art. 3 Act No. 4759).

17.4.3.2 Transition Period for Self-Employed Persons

Transitional arrangements are also included for self-employed individuals. Accordingly, the rights of the pensioner who are entitled to a pension under the former provisions or those who are two years or less to be entitled are reserved (prov. art. 10 para. 1 Act No. 1479).

On the other hand, of those who were insured before 8/9/1999, a nine-stage transition period is foreseen for those who have more than two years remaining to complete the 20 years of premium payment for women and 25 for men as of 1/10/1999, and the required age is gradually increased. However, Constitutional Court abolished this provision.[12] On top of that, the resulting gap was filled with Act No. 4759. According to this, a provision consisting of 16 stages for women and 15 for men was adopted instead of 9 stages.[13]

On the other hand, Constitutional Court approved the transitional provision concerning the ones to receive partial pension of the insured independent workers. Accordingly, of those whom were insured before 8/9/1999, for those who complete 50 years of age for women and 55 for men before 1/10/2001, requesting partial pension whenever they want was accepted. After 1/10/1999, those who meet these requirements between:

- 1/10/2001–1/10/2003 will be entitled to partial pension when they complete 51 years of age for women and 56 for men,
- 2/10/2003–1/10/2005 at 52 for women and 56 for men,
- 2/10/2005–1/10/2007 at 53 for women and 57 for men,
- 2/10/2007–1/10/2009 at 54 for women and 57 for men,
- After 2/10/2009 at 56 for women and 58 for men (prov. art. 10 para. 3 Act No. 1479).

---

[12]Constitutional Court, 23.2.2001, 1999-42/41, OG 23.11.2001, No. 24592.

[13]*See*: Güzel et al. (2020), pp. 518–520.

17.5 Special Pension Regimes

17.5.1 Retirement of Underground Mining Workplace Employees

Due to the fact that they work under heavy and wearing working conditions, special pension conditions were arranged for underground mining workers. On the basis of the regulations on social security law, it is seen that, privileges are recognized only for mineworkers working under the ground, instead of all mineworkers.[14] However, as all the work in the underground is covered, workers who work underground but do not directly contribute to the extraction of ore are also able to benefit from the simplified retirement conditions.[15]

17.5.1.1 Those Insured for the First Time According to SIGHIA

For the insured, who have been working continuously or alternatingly for at least 20 years in underground mining establishments, the age of retirement will be applied as 50 years of age (art. 28 para. 6 SIGHIA). For the insured in this context, as a rule, premium of 7.200 days must be paid.

17.5.1.2 Those Insured for the First Time According to Act No. 506

Of those insured for the first time according to Act No. 506, those who work continuously in underground mining workplaces for at least 20 years and have paid premiums for at least 5000 days in these works, will be given pension without seeking age conditions (prov. art. 9 para. 5/a SIGHIA). Accordingly, these insured persons are provided facilities both in terms of the number of premium days and age. As a matter of fact, the insured in this scope will be entitled to the pension, regardless of age, and by paying 5.000 days of premium instead of 7.200 days.

Again, those who have completed the age of 50 and who have spent at least 1.800 days in the underground mining workplaces will benefit from the old-age allowance (prov. art. 9 para. 5/c SIGHIA).

Finally, if the insured, which started to work in underground mining works before or after SIGHIA, spend at least 1.800 days in underground mining, one-fourth of these works will be added to the total number of premium days (prov. art. 9 para. 6 SIGHIA). Thus, 90 days are earned for each year spent in underground mining.

[14]Mutlay (2014), p. 449.
[15]Baycık (2006), p. 180.

17.5.2 Retirement of Insured Disabled Persons

Insured persons who were disabled enough to be deemed to be disabled before they start insured working for the first time and therefore cannot benefit from the disability allowance will be provided with pension provided they are insured for at least 15 years and have paid a premium of at least 3.960 days (art. 28 para. 4 SIGHIA).

On the other hand, the situation for persons without disabilities at the time of first insurance whose work power loss rate is more than 40% is regulated specially. Accordingly, they will be entitled to pension, provided their ratio of work power loss is:

- Between 50 and 59%, they have been insured for at least 16 years and have paid 4.320 days of premium,
- Between 40 and 49%, they have been insured for at least 18 years and have paid 4.680 days of premium,

Without seeking an age requirement (art. 28 para. 5 SIGHIA).

17.5.3 Early Aging Retirement

The Turkish social security system has mainly adopted the chronological age in retirement. However, strict adherence to calendar age can lead to inequalities. In fact, regardless of age, the health status of the person can vary depending on gender, environmental conditions and the social structure of the country. Accordingly, recognizing the right of retirement at the same age means that inequalities are made to those who are not actually of the same age.[16] In view of the situation, those who age early are allowed to retire at an early age.

According to this, insured persons completing 55 years of age and who are found to have aged early will be able to benefit from pension if they meet other conditions other than age (art. 28 para. 7 SIGHIA).

17.5.4 Retirement of Insured Woman with Severely Disabled Child

Of the insured women requesting pension, for those with a child who is in need of permanent care from someone else, one-fourth of the premium-day numbers are

[16]Mutlay (2014), pp. 429–430.

added to the total number of premium days, and such periods are deducted from the retirement age limits (art. 28 para. 8 SIGHIA).

17.6 Insured Person to Be Retired Leaving the Job

17.6.1 Worker or Civil Servant to Be Retired Leaving the Job

For insured persons working according to an employment contract to request pension, it is imperative that they leave their job and make a written request (art. 28 para. 9 SIGHIA). However, working in a job that is not covered by SIGHIA does not prevent granting of pension.

The insured who wants to retire must apply to SSI before leaving his/her job to receive the pension, find out whether he/she has completed the conditions related to pension and leave only after that. In fact, if the pension conditions are not met, there is the danger that the insured will be deprived of both the pension and the severance pay.

Public servants or those insured in this context should leave their jobs after they have received the approval for retirement from the authorized office upon their request for pension (art. 28 para. 9 SIGHIA).

17.6.2 Pension Request of the Self-Employed Person Without Terminating His/Her Activity

The self-employed individuals do not have to quit their job, i.e. terminate their activities, in order to request pension. Accordingly, it is necessary and sufficient for insured independent workers to make written requests after declaring whether or not they will terminate their activities (art. 28 para. 9 SIGHIA).

However, in order for the self-employed person to be granted pension, the insured should not have any premiums or debts related to premiums due to his/her insurance, including the general health insurance premium as of the date of the request (art. 28 para. 10 SIGHIA). Accordingly, the self-employed person with a premium debt will not be paid pension unless he/she pays the debt. On the other hand, Court of Cassation does not find it fair that pension not be granted to the insured due to a debt, despite the presence of a very small amount of debts, without notifying the insured of this situation.[17]

[17] CC, 10th Civ. Div., 27.3.2007, 2006-16469/4723.

17.7 Application to SSI of the Insured Who Wants to Retire

SSI cannot automatically grant pension to the insured. For this, the insured needs to apply to SSI. However, the situation of civil servants and other public officials in this regard differs. In fact, in mandatory and statutory retirement for civil servants, it is possible that these persons be granted pension without having to apply to SSI.

As there is no mandatory or statutory retirement for insured persons working according to a contract, if the employer terminates the contract of the insured that is entitled to retirement, it does not make it necessary for the insured to automatically be granted pension.[18] Similarly, the fact that the insured independent worker terminates his/her activity and that he/she has fulfilled the conditions of retirement does not require his/her mandatory pension.[19]

As the application date, in applications made by the insured by surface mail or cargo or made directly to SSI in written form, the date on which the request is submitted to SSI records shall be taken as basis, instead of the date on the request.

17.8 Calculation of Pension

The pensions of workers and self-employed persons who start to work for the first time after the entry into force of SIGHIA consist of the amount to be calculated as the average monthly earnings multiplied by the income replacement rate (art. 29 para. 1 SIGHIA).

17.8.1 Average Monthly Earnings

The average monthly income is thirty times the average daily earnings of the insured found by dividing the sum of earnings by years, by the total number of premium days by the update coefficient (art. 29 para. 2 SIGHIA).

17.8.2 Income Replacement Rate

The income replacement rate is applied as 2% for every 360 days of the total number of premium days of the insured. However, the income replacement rate shall not exceed 90% (art. 29 para. 3 SIGHIA).

[18]CC, Plenary Session of Civ. Div., 9.3.1994, 9-5/144.

[19]Güzel et al. (2020), p. 533.

17.9 Pensions of Some Public Officials

17.9.1 Granting Pension to the President of the State, Ministers and Congressmen

President of the State who leave the office for any reason receive a pension of 40% of the monthly allowance paid to the president on their requests (art. 43 para. 1 SIGHIA).

Prime ministers and heads of congress that leave the office for any reason receive a pension of 75% of the pension paid to the president of the State based on the 40% of the monthly allowance paid to the president, on their requests (art. 43 para. 3 SIGHIA).

Ministers outside the parliament or congressmen or those who leave these duties for any reason, provided they are entitled to a pension and have been in these duties for a period of at least two years, receive a pension of 42% of the pension paid to the president of the State based on the 40% of the monthly allowance paid to the president (art. 43 para. 6 SIGHIA).

17.9.2 Granting Pension to Retired Public Servants

17.9.2.1 Statutory Retirement

The age limit that requires the termination of civil servants and other public officials with their duties is, as a rule, the date of their 65th birthday (art. 40 para. 1 Act No. 5434). Statutory retirees are granted pension provided they complete the number of premium days for 5400 days (art. 44 para. 1/a SIGHIA).

17.9.2.2 Retirement Due to Lack of Staff

Those who are civil servants or public officials and are retired due to lack of staff, in accordance with the special laws, are subject to pension provided they completed the number of premium days of 9.000 days, without seeking the age condition (art. 44 para. 3 SIGHIA).

17.9.2.3 Mandatory Retirees Due to Their Discipline or Records

If officers, sergeants, military officers and specialized gendarmes and specialized sergeants retire mandatorily from their institutions due to moral provisions or on grounds of inadequacy or discipline or upon decisions by military courts, they shall be paid pension provided they meet the age and premium conditions for pension.

Similarly, other than those mentioned above, those who retire mandatorily from their institutions on moral or inadequacy grounds shall also be paid pension provided they meet the age and premium conditions for pension (art. 44 para. 2 SIGHIA).

17.10 Payment of Pension

17.10.1 Pension Granting Procedures

In order to be granted pension, the insured needs to apply to SSI with a request prepared by SSI.

17.10.2 Beginning of Pension and Payment Periods

The pension is granted on the date of written request for workers and self-employed persons and at the beginning of the month following the date of termination of duties after retirement approval obtained from the authorized office for civil servants and other public officers (art. 30 para. 1 SIGHIA).

Pensions are paid in cash every month. SSI determines the payment period, payment method and payment centres of pension (art. 55 para. 6 SIGHIA).

17.10.3 Advance Payment

SSI is authorized to advance payments if insured persons cannot be paid the pensions they are entitled to within the period (art. 97 para. 6 SIGHIA).

17.10.4 Increasing of Pensions

The rate of change in the general price index of consumer prices of the previous six-month period announced by *Turkish Statistical Institute* increases pensions, effective from the January and July payment dates of each year (art. 55 para. 2 SIGHIA).

17.10.5 Prohibition of Transfer and Seizure

The pensions of the insured cannot be transferred or assigned. Furthermore, the seizure of pensions is not legally possible except for the premium and alimony debts (art. 93 para. 1 SIGHIA).

17.11 The Situation of Working Retirees

17.11.1 Acceptance of Work by Paying Social Security Support Premium

Paying social security support premium recognizes the possibility of working by paying social security support premium by Act No. 3279[20] for the first time in terms of insured workers. According to this, retirees are given the opportunity to take pensions and to work in a job that is subject to insurance without their pensions being withheld. Retired self-employed persons already had this opportunity. In this case, insured workers and self-employed persons have faced the liability to pay the social security support premium if they wished to work while receiving their pensions.

In the beginning, SIGHIA provided the opportunity to continue working by paying social security support premium to the self-employed persons who are retired while insured, but withheld this opportunity from insured workers and civil servants. This provision in SIGHIA was later amended by Act No. 6663,[21] and retired self-employed individuals are granted the right to continue working without having to pay social security support premium.

17.11.2 Working Again for Workers and Civil Servants

Of the workers and civil servants who are insured for the first time in the period of SIGHIA, the pensions of those who start working under SIGHIA or under the legislation of a foreign land shall be terminated at the beginning of the payment period following the date they start working. From these individuals, premiums of short- and long-term insurance branches and general health insurance are collected over their premium earnings (art. 30 para. 3/a SIGHIA).

Those who were insured prior to the entry into force of SIGHIA are outside the scope of this regulation and they shall be subject to prov. art. 14 SIGHIA. Accordingly, the application prior to SIGHIA will be continued for those who were insured

[20]OG 6.5.1986, No. 19099.

[21]OG 10.2.2016, No. 29620.

workers or civil servants prior to the entry into force of SIGHIA and those who were receiving retirement benefits or retirees who were working and paying social security support premiums at this date (prov. art. 14 para. 1 SIGHIA). Thus, they will either continue to work by paying the social security support premium without having their pensions withheld or they will be able to continue a work subject to all insurance branches by having their pensions withheld. In this regard, the right to choose is recognized by the person concerned.

In return for the social security support premium, only occupational accident and occupational disease insurance provisions are benefited from. The social security support premium rate is 30%, of which one quarter is the share of the insured and three quarters is the share of the employer. In addition to the said rate, a 2% short-term insurance premium is taken, and it is to be paid by the employer (prov. art. 14 para. 1/a SIGHIA).

17.11.3 Working Again for Self-Employed Persons

For self-employed individuals, two situations are arranged. Accordingly, those who start working again when receiving a pension are given the options either to make a written request for withholding of their pensions and to pay premium subject to all insurance branches or to receive pension and continue working without being insured or paying social security support premium (art. 30 para. 3/b SIGHIA).

17.12 Making Lump Sum Pension Payment

Of the insured, those who left their jobs or close their workplaces and do not qualify for a pension even though they have completed the required age condition, the premiums paid up to that date would be returned under the name of "*lump sum pension payment*" (art. 31 para. 1 SIGHIA).

To be entitled to a lump sum pension payment, one must not be entitled to a pension. According to this, the insured person who is entitled to pension cannot be paid a lump sum pension payment.[22]

On the other hand, no lump sum pension payment can be made to the insured unless they want and leave their job. Accordingly, if the insured works in more than one job, he/she must leave all of them.[23]

Multiplying by the update coefficient will increase the premiums paid back to the insured (prov. art. 5 para. 1 SIGHIA).

---

[22]Güzel et al. (2020), p. 607; Oral (2007), p. 123.

[23]Çenberci (1985), p. 393; Oral (2007), p. 120.

SIGHIA does not have an explicit regulation as to the date on which the insured can use the right to request a lump sum pension payment. In this respect, it is generally accepted that the 10-year general statute of limitations period be applied.[24]

If the insured that leaves the job and receives a lump sum pension payment then starts to work in an insured job, he/she does not need to give back the lump sum pension payment. However, in this case, the insurance period begins from the next working date.[25] On the other hand, the insured may pay the updated amount of each year for the years between the payment date of the lump sum pension payment and the written request date and may revitalize these services (art. 31 para. 2 SIGHIA). Thus, the periods that have been liquidated by means of lump sum pension payment must not be taken into account in the calculation of the insurance period.

17.13 Other Aids to Retirees

17.13.1 Healthcare

Those who receive pension are considered as general health insured without any payment of premium and without having to register as general health insured (art. 60 para. 1/f SIGHIA). Accordingly, those who receive pension from SSI and their dependents benefit from the provision of the necessary health services.

17.13.2 Social Aid Increase

The social aid increase for those receiving pension was reduced first and then abolished by SIGHIA. However, those who received this aid in the previous period continue to be paid the amount of the social aid increase in addition to the pensions after SIGHIA (prov. art. 1 para. 3 SIGHIA).

17.13.3 Payment of Retirement Bonus to Retired Civil Servants

For retiree civil servants and other public officials, a monthly amount for each full year of actual service based on the pension is paid as a "*retirement bonus*" (art. 89 para. 1 Act No. 5434).

[24]Çenberci (1985), p. 395; Güzel et al. (2020), p. 607; Tuncay and Ekmekçi (2019), p. 541.

[25]Tuncay and Ekmekçi (2019), p. 541; Tunçomağ (1990), p. 365.

17.14 Pensions of Agricultural Workers

17.14.1 For Those Insured for the First Time After 8/9/1999

A pension is granted to agricultural workers on the condition that they are insured for the first time after 8/9/1999 and are 58 years old for women and 60 for men have been insured for 15 years and have paid at least 3600 days of premium. It is also necessary for the insured to make a request to SSI for his/her pension (art. 20 Act No. 2925).

On the other hand, the pensions of those who started to work in an insured job while receiving pension are withheld from the date they started working (art. 23 para. 1 Act No. 2925).

17.14.2 For Those Insured Before 8/9/1999

Constitutional Court annulled the transitional period foreseen in relation to these persons (prov. art. 2 Act No. 2925) on the grounds that it was incompatible with the social law state.[26] Upon this, the transitional period was rearranged with the Act No. 4759[27] (art. 4).

17.15 Situations Affecting the Age Requirement in Retirement

For those whose year of birth is written but the month and the day of birth is not, the first day of July of the year of birth will be taken as the start. For those whose month of birth is written but the day of birth is not, the first day of that month will be taken as the start (art. 39 para. 2 Act No. 5490).

In the application of the age-related provisions for retirement insurance, the date of birth of the insured persons in the birth record at the date they are subject to insurance and the first written date of birth of their children in the birth record are taken as the basis (art. 57 para. 2 SIGHIA).

As the judicial decisions are final and binding on everyone, the decisions on age corrections must also be complied with and SSI must assess the conditions of pension according to the corrected age. However, in the calculation of income and monthly allowances in occupational accident, occupational disease and disability, old age and death insurances and the advance capital value, the age corrections to be

[26]Constitutional Court, 23.2.2001, 199-42/41, OG 23.11.2001, No. 24592.

[27]OG 1.6.2002, No. 24772.

made after the date the occupational accident occurs or occupational disease is determined by doctor's report or when the insured starts to work for the first time will not be taken into consideration (art. 57 para. 3 SIGHIA).

References

Alper Y (2015) Türk Sosyal Güvenlik Sistemi. Sosyal Sigortalar Hukuku, 7th edn. Dora Publishing, Bursa

Baycık G (2006) İş ve Sosyal Güvenlik Hukuku Açısından Maden İşçileri. Yetkin Publishing, Ankara

Çenberci M (1985) Sosyal Sigortalar Kanunu Şerhi. Olgaç Matbaası, Ankara

Güzel A, Okur AR, Caniklioğlu N (2020) Sosyal Güvenlik Hukuku, 18th edn. Beta Publishing, Istanbul

Mutlay FB (2014) Sosyal Sigorta Yardımlarına Hak Kazanma Koşulları ve Eşitlik İlkesi. Beta Publishing, Istanbul

Oral Aİ (2007) Türk Sosyal Güvenlik Hukuku Açısından Toptan Ödeme. Anadolu Üniversitesi, Eskişehir. yayını No. 1731

Tuncay AC, Ekmekçi Ö (2019) Sosyal Güvenlik Hukuku Dersleri, 19th edn. Beta Publishing, Istanbul

Tunçomağ K (1990) Sosyal Güvenlik Kavramı ve Sosyal Sigortalar, 5th edn. Beta Publishing, Istanbul

Chapter 18
Death Insurance

18.1 Function of Death Insurance

Death insurance is covered in long-term insurance branches. Accordingly, the dependents of the insured are socially secured against the death of the insured.

The death insurance takes the family as basis in social protection as the protection unit. In this respect, death insurance is the guarantee of family members who survive against the risk of death.

In terms of the Turkish legal system, the concept of death is closely related to two different branches of insurance. One of them is occupational accident and occupational disease insurance covered in short-term insurance branches and the other is death insurance, which is considered to be within long-term insurance branches. According to this, losing one's life as a result of an occupational accident or occupational disease concerns the occupational accident and occupational disease insurance provisions, and allowance is granted to the relatives of the deceased insured. In the death insurance, those who lost their lives for any reason are protected. In this respect, the determination of whether the death occurred for any reason or as a result of an occupational accident or occupational disease is important for the provisions regarding the insurance branch to be applied in terms of the Turkish legal system.

18.2 Those to Benefit from Death Insurance Aids

Those to benefit from death insurance aids and especially are to be granted allowance are the deceased's spouse and children and his/her mother and father.

In order to be considered as the spouse of the insured, it is necessary to have a marriage bond between the insured and his/her spouse as determined by the

T. Centel, *Turkish Social Law*, https://doi.org/10.1007/978-3-030-64704-9_18

legislation.[1] According to this, living as husband and wife is not sufficient for the existence of official marriage bonds.[2]

The children of the insured also benefit from the death insurance aids as right holders. Children born from the insured women are right holders by their mother as of their birth. Being right holders of the children by their fathers depends on the fact that they were born in a marriage bond.

In addition, children who are recognized and bound to their fathers by a court order and children whose bloodlines are corrected and adopted in accordance with the law are also right holders. However, stepchildren cannot be right holders.

Finally, it is not legally possible for stepmother and stepfather to benefit from death insurance aids. Similarly, the adopter cannot be a right holder.[3]

On the other hand, the death allowance is not granted to persons who have been confirmed to commit the murder of the insured to be paid monthly with the final order of the court (art. 56 para. 1/a SIGHIA). Likewise, the death allowance is not granted to those who are removed from being heir through a death-related saving by the final order of the court (art. 56 para. 1/b SIGHIA).

On the other hand, there is no legal regulation about the renunciation of inheritance. In this case, the renunciation of inheritance of the deceased will not affect the right to claim a death allowance.[4]

18.3 Conditions of Death Allowance

18.3.1 Conditions for the Deceased Insured

18.3.1.1 Death of the Insured

The first requirement for the right holders to receive allowance is the death of the insured. Death is the complete and definite termination of life, in other words, the vital functions.[5] According to this, vegetative state will not be considered as death, and the rights holders of the insured in this state will not be provided with the death insurance aids.[6]

---

[1]Çenberci (1985), pp. 162–163.

[2]Güzel et al. (2020), p. 615.

[3]Tuncay (2010), p. 1233.

[4]Güzel et al. (2020), p. 617; Tuncay and Ekmekçi (2019), p. 574.

[5]Çenberci (1985), p. 399.

[6]Güzel et al. (2020), p. 618.

18.3.1.2 Being in a Certain Relation with SSI

The insured must either die while receiving monthly allowance or income from SSI, or have paid the amount of premiums foreseen in the law. Accordingly, if the insured dies while entitled to or receiving a disability or duty disability allowance or retirement pension or dies while already entitled to these but before the procedures are completed or after these are withheld because of starting to work as insured, the survivors are granted death allowance (art. 32 para. 2/b-c SIGHIA).

On the other hand, if the insured dies while working, the amount of the premium foreseen in the law must be declared in order for the death allowance to be granted. The amount of this premium differs depending on whether the insured is a worker, a self-employed person or a public officer.

Accordingly, if the deceased insured is insured as a self-employed person or public officer, a minimum of 1.800 days of long-term insurance premiums must be declared for the right holders to be granted the death allowance (art. 32 para. 2/a SIGHIA).

For deceased insured workers, a simplified option is foreseen. According to this, if the insured worker dies after having been insured for at least 5 years and declared a premium for a total of 900 days, a death allowance may be granted to the right holders (art. 32 para. 2/a SIGHIA).

18.3.1.3 Completion of the Relation by the Right Holders

The right holders through borrowing or the recovery of services can complete the relation between SSI and the insured. Accordingly, the right holders can complete the number of missing premium days by making military borrowing (art. 41 para. 1/b SIGHIA) in the name of the deceased insured or by making foreign borrowing in accordance with Act No. 3201. As such, the number of missing premium days liquidated by taking a lump sum pension payment can be completed by returning the lump sum pension payment collected by the right holders to SSI with the interest and reviving the old services of the deceased (art. 31 para. 2 SIGHIA).

18.3.2 Requirements for Right Holders

18.3.2.1 For the Widow Spouse

In order for the spouse who is widowed by the death of the insured to be granted the death allowance, a legal marriage must exist between them. It is not enough to be married only by religious marriage ceremony.[7]

[7]CC, 10th Civ. Div., 1.3.2010, 2008-18155/2758, Sicil, 22 (2011), pp. 180–182.

In order for the widow to be paid a death allowance, it is mandatory and sufficient for her to not remarry. Accordingly, whether the widow is working in an insured or uninsured job or receiving an income or monthly allowance does not prevent her from being granted death allowance but will only affect the rate of the allowance.

Thus, if the widow is remarried, the death allowance is withheld. On the other hand, if the marriage that causes the death allowance to be withheld is terminated, the death allowance must be granted again. However, in the event that the marriage ends in death, the spouse entitled to death also from the next spouse will be granted one of the allowances of her choosing (art. 54 para. 1/a 7 SIGHIA).

18.3.2.2 For the Children

Children adopted by the insured, recognized or whose bloodline is corrected, or the paternity has been sentenced and children born after the death of the insured benefit from the death allowance (art. 34 para. 2 SIPHIA).

The first condition for children is that they are under 18 years of age. However, this age requirement increases to 20 if they are in secondary education and 25 for higher education. With the completion of these ages, the death allowance is withheld (art. 34 para. 1/b 2 SIGHIA). In addition, in order for the children to be entitled to a death allowance, they must not be employed in accordance with the provisions of SIGHIA or a foreign country or have been granted no income or allowance due to their own insurance (art. 34 para. 1/b SIGHIA).

On the other hand, girls after the ages of 18 to 20 and 25, can be entitled to the death allowance provided they are unmarried and not working or not receiving income or monthly allowance from SSI (art. 34 para. 1/b 3 SIGHIA).

Finally, the children of the deceased insured who have lost their working capacity by at least 60% by the decision of the health board of SSI and determined to be disabled and who are not employed or receiving income or monthly allowance will benefit from the death allowance, regardless of age (art. 31 para. 1/b 2 SIGHIA).

18.3.2.3 For the Mother and Father

The mother and father to receive a death allowance is based on whether a share is left of the spouse and children who are the right holders and that their income is less than the net amount of the minimum wage and/or that they are not granted an allowance (art. 34 para. 1/d SIGHIA).

18.4 The Monthly Amount to Be Taken as Basis for the Death Allowance

18.4.1 Death of the Insured While Receiving Allowance

If the insured dies while receiving allowance from SSI, the allowance to be distributed to the right holders is the disability or duty disability allowance or the retirement pension that the insured was receiving or entitled to.

18.4.2 Death of the Insured Who Starts Working While Receiving Allowance

If the insured that is given a disability allowance or pension starts to work again, his/her allowance/pension will be withheld. In this case, the allowance/pension of the insured who dies while working again is recalculated by taking into account the premiums paid by the insured during the reemployment period and the last calculated allowance/pension is distributed to the right holders.

18.4.3 Death of the Insured Paying Social Security Support Premium

Workers and civil servants who have been insured for the first time before SIGHIA comes into force have the possibility to work again without having their pensions withheld, provided that they have paid social security support premium. The right holders of the insured who died while in this situation will be allocated the allowance/pension he/she was receiving, and the periods the social security support premium has been paid will not change the monthly allowance/pension to be distributed.

18.4.4 Death of the Insured While Working

The death allowance to be paid to the right holders of the insured who dies without being granted disability allowance or pension or without having made a request on this regard will be calculated over 9.000 days if the number of the premium days of the insured is less than 9.000 days and over the total premium days if the number of days is 9.000 and more (art. 33 para. 1/c SIGHIA). However, 9.000 premium days will be applied as 7.200 days for insured workers (art. 33 para. 1/c SIGHIA).

18.5 Distribution of the Death Allowance Among the Right Holders

18.5.1 The Spouse Being a Right Holder Alone or Along with the Mother and Father

If the spouse does not work or does not receive income or allowance due to his/her own insurance and does not have a child to receive allowance, he/she will receive 75% of the allowance (art. 34 para. 1/a SIGHIA).

It is not important that the spouse works under SIGHIA or a foreign legislation. In both cases, the rate of the allowance of the spouse is 50%, in other words, half of the allowance (art. 34 para. 1/a SIGHIA).

The entitlement of the insured's parents to the allowance does not affect the monthly rate of the spouse.

18.5.2 The Spouse Being a Right Holder Along with the Children

If the spouse becomes a right holder along with children, he/she receives 50% of the allowance.

18.5.3 Children Being Right Holders by Themselves

The entitled children share the allowance, each with a share of 25% at most.

However, children who are orphaned due to the death of the insured or who have subsequently become so, children whose parents have no marital bond or do have at the date of the death of the insured but remarry later and the children who are the only right holders receiving allowance will each receive allowance at a 50% rate (art. 34 para. 1/c SIGHIA).

18.5.4 The Mother and Father Being Right Holders by Themselves

In order for the mother and father to be granted death allowance, the spouse and children must not have been given the full allowance, except for the condition of being over 65 years old. Accordingly, the mother and father have equal rights over the extra amount left from the spouse and children. However, the share of each of them cannot exceed 25% of the allowance of the insured (art. 34 para. 1/d SIGHIA).

18.5.5 The Spouse Being a Right Holder Along with the Mother and Father

If the deceased insured only has his/her spouse and mother and father, who do not work and do not receive allowance or income from SSI, in other words, if he/she does not have a child, 75% of the allowance and the remaining 25% of the allowance is given to the mother and father, each receiving half. If only the mother or the father of the insured is alive with the spouse, he/she will receive 25% of the allowance.

18.5.6 The Spouse, the Children and the Mother and Father All Being Right Holders

In this case, the allowance rate of the spouse is 50% and of the single child is 25%, and the remaining 25% is divided into half to the parents.

18.5.7 Exceeding the Allowance

The sum of the allowances to be granted to the right holders cannot exceed the sum of the allowance of the insured. In order not to exceed this limit, discounts are made proportionally to the allowance of the right holders, if needed (art. 34 para. 3 SIGHIA).

18.6 Rights Holders Applying to SSI

Rights holders are required to apply to SSI within *five years* following the birth of the right. SSI will not grant allowance when there is no application. Accordingly, if the right holders apply within a five-year period, the allowance is granted from the beginning of the month following the date of death. Thus, if the death allowance is not requested within five years of the date of the entitlement, it will be dropped due to prescription (art. 97 para. 1 SIGHIA).

18.7 Payment of Death Allowance

The death allowance is initiated from the beginning of the month following the date of death of the insured (art. 35 para. 1/a, b SIGHIA).

The death allowance granted to the right holders is paid in cash every month. SSI determines payment period, payment method and payment centres of death allowance (art. 55 para. 6 SIGHIA).

The amount based on the calculation of the death allowance cannot be less than 35% of the average monthly earnings as of January of the year of request or death. The allowances of the right holders cannot be less than 80% of the lower limit salary if the right holder is one person and less than 90% if the right holders are two persons.

Death allowances are regularly increased twice a year. Accordingly, effective from the January and July payment dates of each year, payments are increased by the rate of change in the latest consumer prices general index announced by the Turkish Statistical Institute compared to the previous six-month period (art. 55 para. 2 SIGHIA).

18.8 Withholding of Death Allowances

18.8.1 Withholding of Allowance of the Spouse

If the spouse of the insured gets married, the death allowance is withheld. When the marriage causing the withholding of the allowance is terminated, the withheld allowance is granted again from the beginning of the month following the application date (art. 35 para. 3 SIGHIA).

18.8.2 Withholding of Allowance of the Male Child

The male child's allowance is withheld when he is 18 years old, 20 if he is in middle school and 25 if he is in higher education (art. 35 para. 1 SIGHIA). However, the marriage of a male child within the specified age limits does not require the withholding of his allowance.[8]

On the other hand, in the event that the male child starts working under SIGHIA or under the legislation of a foreign country, his allowance will be withheld.

[8]Tunçomağ (1990), p. 373.

18.8.3 Withholding of Allowance of the Female Child

The death allowance granted to female children is withheld in the event she marries or starts working or is granted an income or allowance due to her own insurance. However, if the female child is also disabled, getting married does not lead to the withholding of the death allowance.

The death allowances of the female children who are determined to be living with their divorced husbands will be withheld. The amounts paid to these individuals are withdrawn as groundless payment (art. 56 para. 2 SIGHIA). Constitutional Court did not approve the claim that this was contrary to the Constitution.[9]

If the female child receiving a death allowance actually lives with someone else, the death allowance is not withheld.[10]

18.8.4 Withholding of Allowance of the Mother and Father

If the income of the mother and father exceeds the net amount of the minimum wage, or if they are paid an allowance or income, the death allowance granted to them will have to be withheld (art. 34 para. 1/d SIGHIA).

18.9 Combination of the Death Allowance with Other Allowances

18.9.1 Combination of the Death Allowance with Allowance Entitled from Occupational Accident and Occupational Disease Insurance

If the death allowance is combined with the allowance entitled from occupational accident and occupational disease insurance, the right holder is granted the complete amount of the higher of these allowances and half of the lower of these allowances. If they are equal, the complete amount of the allowance and half of the death allowance will be granted (art. 54 para. 1/c SIGHIA).

[9]Constitutional Court, 28.4.2011, 2009-86/70, OG 15.12.2011, No. 28143.

[10]Centel (2012), p. 191.

18.9.2 Being Entitled to Allowance from Two Separate Persons

18.9.2.1 Being Entitled to Allowance from Parents and Spouse

Children who are entitled to separate allowances from their mother and father are granted the complete amount of the higher of these allowances and half of the lower of these allowances (art. 54 para. 1/a 3 SIGHIA). The parents who are entitled to allowances from more than one child are paid the complete amount of the higher of these allowances and half of the lower of these allowances of the first two files that allow for the maximum payment (art. 54 para. 1/a 4 SIGHIA).

The procedure will proceed for those entitled to death allowance from their spouse and the mother and/or father according to their preference (art. 54 para. 1/a 5 SIGHIA). Similarly, if the new spouse of the spouse of the deceased insured also dies and he/she is entitled to death allowance from both, he/she will be entitled to the allowance of his/her choice (art. 54 para. 1 a 7 SIGHIA).

18.9.2.2 Being Entitled to More Than Two Allowances

If a person is entitled to more than two allowances, they are granted allowance over the two files that allow the maximum payment of these allowances, and the rights to the other files are foreclosed (art 54 para. 2 SIGHIA).

18.10 Advance Payment and Prohibition of Seizure

In case the allowances of the right holders are not paid within the period, SSI is authorized to pay an advance payment (art. 97 para. 6 SIGHIA).

Death allowances cannot be transferred or assigned. In addition, death allowance cannot be seized except for premium debts and alimony debts (art. 93 para. 1 SIGHIA).

18.11 Other Death Insurance Aids

18.11.1 Healthcare

Those who receive a death allowance from SSI are considered as general health insured without any premium payment obligation and without registration (art. 60 para. 1/f SIGHIA). Accordingly, those who receive a death allowance have the opportunity to benefit from health service.

18.11.2 Making Lump Sum Payment

If none of the right holders of the deceased insured can be granted a death allowance, all long-term insurance premiums paid by the deceased insured are distributed to the right holders as "*lump sum payments*" at the monthly rate (art. 36 para. 1 SIGHIA).

What matters in death insurance is that death allowance is granted to the surviving right holders of the insured. However, in the event that the allowance granting conditions are not met, making lump sum payments to the right holders is required.[11]

18.11.3 Granting of Marriage Allowance

If the daughters granted death allowance due to the death of the insured get married, the two-year amount of their allowance is paid to them as a "*marriage allowance*" for one time (art. 37 para. 1 SIGHIA).

If the daughter given the marriage allowance divorce her husband or her husband dies within two years, she is not paid allowance until two years are completed (art. 37 para. 1 SIGHIA).

The beginning of the two-year period is the date on which the allowance of the right holder receiving marriage allowance is withheld.

18.11.4 Granting of Funeral Allowance

In the event of the death of the insured, a certain amount of money, as determined by the Board of Directors of SSI and approved by the Minister of Family, Labour and Social Services, is paid to the right holders as "*funeral allowance*" (art. 37 para. 3 SIGHIA).

In order to be granted a funeral allowance, the deceased must have died while receiving incapacity, disability or duty disability allowance or pension, or 360-day long-term insurance premium must have been declared for the deceased (art. 37 para. 3 SIGHIA).

The funeral allowance is given in order to the spouse, children, parents or siblings (art. 37 para. 3 SIGHIA). However, if natural or legal persons have performed the funeral of the insured, the costs shall be paid to those persons without exceeding the amount determined for the relevant year (art. 37 para. 4 SIGHIA).

[11] Oral (2007), p. 126.

18.11.5 Payment of Social Aid Increase

The application of social aid increase was terminated with SIGHIA, but the payment of the social aid increase amounts paid in the previous period are continued (prov. art. 1 para. 3 SIGHIA).

18.11.6 Payment of Retirement Bonus

All of the retirement bonus that will be calculated for those who die without receiving disability or duty disability allowances or pensions monthly or in lump sum payments shall be paid to the spouse and children who shall be entitled to a death allowance or lump sum payment in proportion to their shares (art. 89 para. 7 Act No. 5434).

The retirement bonuses of the public officials who die without receiving the accrued or to be accrued retirement bonuses and the public officials who die without leaving a right holder spouse or children behind at the date of death are paid to their legal heirs (art. 89 para. 10 Act No. 5434).

Similarly, for those who enter the civil service for the first time after the entry into force of SIGHIA, the right holders of these persons who are granted death allowance or are to be paid lump sum payments shall be paid retirement bonuses by SSI (prov. art. 82 para. 1/e-f Act No. 5434).

18.12 The Right of Recourse of SSI of the Death Allowance to Third Persons

If the death of the insured occurs due to the intent of a third person, half of the first advance capital value at the date of the beginning of the death allowance to be granted to the right holders shall be recourse to third persons who have caused the damage by SSI (art. 39 para. 1 SIGHIA).

References

Çenberci M (1985) Sosyal Sigortalar Kanunu Şerhi. Olgaç Matbaası, Ankara

Centel T (2012) Boşandığı Eşiyle Birlikte Yaşayanın Aylığının Kesilmesi – Anayasa Karşısında Bir Ülke Gerçeği. Sicil İş Hukuku Dergisi 25:190–196

Güzel A, Okur AR, Caniklioğlu N (2020) Sosyal Güvenlik Hukuku, 18th edn. Beta Publishing, Istanbul

Oral Aİ (2007) Türk Sosyal Güvenlik Hukuku Açısından Toptan Ödeme. Anadolu Üniversitesi, Eskişehir. yayını No. 1731

Tuncay AC (2010) 5510 Sayılı Kanun Açısından Ölüm Sigortası. In: Prof.Dr. Ali Güzel'e Armağan, vol 2. Beta Publishing, Istanbul, pp 1231–1244
Tuncay AC, Ekmekçi Ö (2019) Sosyal Güvenlik Hukuku Dersleri, 20th edn. Beta Publishing, Istanbul
Tunçomağ K (1990) Sosyal Güvenlik Kavramı ve Sosyal Sigortalar, 5th edn. Beta publishing, Istanbul

Chapter 19
Unemployment Insurance

19.1 Unemployment in the Scope of Social Security

Establishing assurance against the risk of unemployment is included in the social security system. In fact, art. 25 para. 1 Universal Declaration of Human Rights - the United Nations (1948) states that *everyone has the right to security in the event of unemployment*. Similarly, the European Social Charter (Revised) - Council of Europe to which Turkey is also a party, states that *all employees have the right to protection in the event of termination of the employment contract* (art. 24).

In Turkey, unemployment insurance, effective since 1/6/2000 has been accepted as a short-term separate insurance branch under *Unemployment Insurance Act* No. 4447.[1] The adoption of unemployment insurance in Turkey is of great importance in terms of approaching international standards.[2] In this regard, the Turkish legislator was cautious about establishing unemployment insurance, taking into account the negative experiences of Western countries and has considered the financing risks that might arise.[3]

UIA emerged as a separate law from SIGHIA. However, it contains regulations related to SIGHIA in areas such as application and collection and registration of premiums.

[1]OG 8.9.1999, No. 23810.

[2]*See*: Haenlein (2001), p. 287; Keser (2000), p. 81.

[3]Haenlein (2001), p. 285.

T. Centel, *Turkish Social Law*, https://doi.org/10.1007/978-3-030-64704-9_19

19.2 Features of Unemployment Insurance

Unemployment insurance refers to the "*compulsory insurance that operates in an insurance technique that meets the loss of income of insured persons due to being unemployed upon losing their jobs while working in a workplace, despite their willingness to work, talent, health and competence, in a certain amount and for a certain period of time*" (art. 47 para. 1/c UIA). Accordingly, unemployment insurance primarily aims to provide financial assistance under the name of "*unemployment allowance*" to the insured that is temporarily unemployed. However, the functions of unemployment insurance that enable the unemployed to acquire a new job and provide them with vocational training are also important today.[4]

UIA, though in part, reflects the basic objectives and characteristics of unemployment insurance. As a matter of fact, the aim of unemployment insurance is defined as "*to regulate the rules and application principles of unemployment insurance and to provide the services foreseen in this Law*" (art. 46 para. 1 UIA) by the UIA. In this respect, the most important assistance provided in UIA is the provision of unemployment allowance if the insured are unemployed. In addition, UIA accepts the services of professional development, obtaining a new occupation and training for insured persons to find a new job among the aims of unemployment insurance.

Another fundamental feature of unemployment insurance is that it includes the principle of mandatory. This principle establishes a legal relation between the insured and the employer and the Institution with mandatory provisions. According to this, unemployment insurance is mandatory and insurance rights and obligations for insured persons and employers begin with the commencement of insurance (art. 48 para. 3 UIA).

19.3 Unemployment Insurance Coverage

19.3.1 Insured Persons

UIA defines the term "*insured*" as an employee who works on the basis of an employment contract within its scope and pays the unemployment insurance premium during his/her employment (art. 47 para. 1/d UIA). Art. 46 para. 2 UIA regulates in more detail that will be covered by unemployment insurance. Accordingly, employees under the scope SIGHIA who work under an employment contract are also insured in terms of unemployment insurance.

Thus, those who work under the employment laws (LA No. 4857, Press LA and Maritime LA) and TCO according to an employment contract are covered by the unemployment insurance. In addition, those subject to special funds of banks,

[4]Başterzi (1996), p. 201.

insurance companies, chambers of commerce and industry, and stock exchanges are also covered by unemployment insurance.

On the other hand, special arrangements have been introduced for part-time workers. According to this, employees who work under the scope of a part-time labour contract subject to LA No. 4857 and are under the scope of voluntary insurance and pay unemployment insurance premium benefit from unemployment insurance. In addition, part-time workers in commercial taxi and similar urban public transportations and in fine art branches to be determined by the Ministry of Culture and Tourism in less than 10 days in one month can benefit from unemployment insurance provided that they pay the unemployment insurance premiums themselves.

Finally, foreigners working under employment contracts in Turkey have the right to benefit from unemployment insurance without seeking a bilateral social security agreement.[5]

19.3.2 Uninsured Persons

UIA has dealt with those who cannot benefit from unemployment insurance in connection with the scope of SIGHIA. Accordingly, self-employed persons (art. 4 para. 1/b SIGHIA), public officials (art. 4 para. 1/c SIGHIA), partially insured (art. 5 SIGHIA) and uninsured (art. 6 SIGHIA) under the scope of SIGHIA are not considered as unemployment insured.

19.3.3 Registration of Insured Persons

Persons covered by UIA shall be insured as of the date of commencement of employment (art. 48 para. 1 UIA). However, they must be registered.

In this respect, SSI shall inform TLI of the insured persons who are registered under SIGHIA and covered by the unemployment insurance, the *Unemployment Insurance Department* established under TLI shall keep the record of the insured persons (art. 46 para. 4 UIA).

[5]Güzel et al. (2020), p. 715; Tuncay and Ekmekçi (2019), p. 672.

19.4 Execution and Financing of Unemployment Insurance

19.4.1 Management of Unemployment Insurance

The administrative management of the unemployment insurance has been granted to the General Directorate of TLI. In this respect, the close relation of unemployment insurance with labour markets, professional training and job placement has been taken into consideration. The *Unemployment Insurance Department* was established under the General Directorate of TLI for the stated purpose (art. 46 para. 4 UIA).

The duties of the Unemployment Insurance Department are stated as:

- To carry out transactions related to the evaluation of workers, employers and state contributions transferred to the UIF,
- To make all kinds of transactions related to the payment of unemployment allowances by keeping a record of the premiums on an individual basis,
- To ensure that the insurance premiums are submitted to SSI,
- To carry out the procedures related to professional training measures for the unemployed,
- To carry out other duties assigned to it regarding the implementation of UIA (art. 46 para. 4 UIA and art 9 para. f Act No. 4904).

19.4.2 Unemployment Insurance Premiums

The unemployment insurance premium needs to be paid to cover the payments and service and management costs required by the unemployment insurance. The insured persons and employers and the State pay this premium. In addition, it is foreseen that the State will contribute if the unemployment insurance fund has a deficit (art. 53 para. 3/A-c UIA).

19.4.2.1 Rate and Calculation of Premiums

Unemployment insurance premium rates were determined separately and differently for the insured, employer and the State. Accordingly, the insured pays 1% unemployment insurance premium, the employer 2% and the State 1% (art. 49 para. 1 UIA).

From those who would like to pay the unemployment insurance premium with voluntary insurance, the insurance premium at a total of 3%, of which 1% is the share of the insured and 2% is of the employer, is collected.

Unemployment insurance premiums are calculated based on the monthly gross earnings of the insured (art 49 para. 1 UIA; arts 80 and 82 SIGHIA).

Employers cannot deduct or reduce from the wages of the insured due to their premium obligations related to unemployment insurance (art. 49 para. 2 UIA).

19.4.2.2 Collection of Premiums and Transfer to Fund

UIA has appointed SSI to collect the unemployment insurance premium shares of the insured and employer. SSI shall transfer the premiums, late fees and delay fines collected within one month to UIF until the 15th of the month following the month of collection (art. 49 para. 7 UIA).

In addition, TLI shall request the state share from the Ministry of Family, Labour and Social Services, taking into account the share of the insured and employer transferred to UIF. The Ministry of Family, Labour and Social Services will transfer the requested amount to UIF within 15 days following the request date (art. 49 para. 8 UIA).

19.4.2.3 Applied Financing Method

UIA has adopted capitalization as the method of financing. Accordingly, *"Unemployment Insurance Fund"* has been established to provide financial resources to unemployment insurance, to evaluate these resources in market conditions and to make payments (art. 53 para. 1 UIA). UIF, which is under the guarantee of the State, shall be operated and managed within the framework of the decisions of the board of directors of TLI (art. 47 para. 1/g UIA).

UIF is out of the budget coverage and its revenues cannot be deducted or registered as revenues to the general budget, except for tax deductions (art. 53 para. 4 UIA).

On the other hand, in the event that the employer is incapable of making payments, a separate *"Wage Guarantee Fund"* is foreseen under UIF to cover the last three months' wages of the workers (add. art. 1 para. 1 UIA). The Wage Guarantee Fund is one percent of the annual total of payments made by employers as unemployment insurance contributions (add. art. 1 para. 2 UIA). These payments will be transferred to the Wage Guarantee Fund.

19.5 Unemployment Insurance Aids

19.5.1 Unemployment Allowance

19.5.1.1 Conditions for Entitlement to Unemployment Allowance

In order to benefit from the unemployment allowance, first of all, the employment contract must have been terminated for one of the reasons listed in UIA. In this respect, it is seen that UIA has recognized superiority to the concept of *"unemployment out of will"*. As a matter of fact, since the termination of the employment contract through the agreement of the parties is not a termination, the insured shall not be entitled to unemployment allowance.[6]

Accordingly, the insured will be entitled to unemployment allowance when:

- The employer in accordance with the priorities of declaration terminates the employment contract,
- The employment contract is terminated by the insured for a justified reason,
- The employment contract is terminated by the employer before the expiry of the period or before the notice of termination,
- The insured becomes unemployed due to the expiration of the employment contract or when the seamen is unemployed at the end of the voyage,
- The employee is dismissed from work due to changing hands, transferring or closing of the workplace or changing of the nature of the work or workplace,
- The insured is unemployed as a result of privatization practices (art. 51 para. 1 UIA).

On the other hand, if the employment contract is suspended due to lockout or strike or a performance of a duty arising from the law, the insured will not be paid unemployment allowance (art. 51 para. 2 UIA).

Similarly, if the insured goes to long-term military service or goes on an unpaid leave by agreeing with the employer, the unemployment allowance will not be paid.[7]

Unemployment insurance is intended to provide economic security.[8] For this reason, it is not possible to pay the unemployment allowance to the insured that are granted pension from social security institutions (art. 52 para. 1/b UIA). On the other hand, income or allowance from social security institutions other than the pension shall not prevent the right to unemployment allowance.

In order to qualify for unemployment allowance, it is necessary to work by paying a premium of 600 days (20 months) in the last three years and paying a premium in the last 120 days (four months) before the termination of the employment contract (art. 50 para. 2 and art. 51 para. 1 UIA).

The employer is obliged to issue a *"termination declaration"* about the insured persons whose employment contracts are terminated in a way to create entitlement for unemployment allowance and give a copy of it to the insured and keep a copy in the workplace (art. 48 para. 4 UIA).

In order to benefit from unemployment allowance, the insured must apply directly or electronically to the nearest unit of TLI within 30 days following the termination of the employment contract with the termination declaration (art. 48 para. 5 UIA).

The delayed period in application does not constitute an obstacle to receiving unemployment allowance. However, the delayed time is reduced from the total period for which unemployment allowance is granted (art. 48 para. 5 UIA).

[6]Güzel et al. (2020), p. 723.

[7]Tuncay and Ekmekçi (2019), p. 686.

[8]Keser (2000), p. 75.

In past practices, the insured had to apply in person, and the applications made through a lawyer were not considered as an application in person.[9]

19.5.1.2 Amount and Duration of Unemployment Allowance

The daily unemployment allowance is 40% percent of the daily average gross earnings calculated by taking into consideration the premium earnings of the insured for the last four months. However, the amount of unemployment allowance to be calculated in this way cannot exceed 80% of the gross amount of the monthly minimum wage (art. 50 para. 1 UIA).

Unemployment allowance will be paid for:

- 180 days (6 months) to insured unemployed workers who have been insured for 600 days and have paid unemployment insurance premiums,
- 240 days (8 months) to insured unemployed workers who have been insured for 900 days and have paid unemployment insurance premiums,
- 300 days (10 months) to insured unemployed workers who have been insured for 1.080 days and have paid unemployment insurance premiums (art. 50 para. 2 UIA).

19.5.1.3 Payment and Prohibition of Seizure of Unemployment Allowance

Unemployment allowance is paid monthly to the unemployed starting at the end of the month following entitlement and at the end of each month (art. 50 para. 3 UIA).

If the insured is reemployed without filling out the unemployment allowance period and becomes unemployed again without fulfilling the conditions set by UIA in order to benefit from the unemployment insurance allowance, the insured continues to enjoy this right until he/she completes the previous unemployment allowance period. In the case of being unemployed again by fulfilling the conditions foreseen by UIA, unemployment allowance is granted only for the duration of this new entitlement (art. 50 para. 4 UIA).

Unemployment allowance is not subject to any tax. Similarly, unemployment allowance cannot be seized or transferred to another person, except for alimony (art. 50 para. 3 UIA).

[9] CC, 10th Civ. Div., 3.5.2005, 2910/4925, CC, General Assembly of Civ. Div., 6.5.2006, 10-243/271.

19.5.1.4 Withholding and Refund of Unemployment Allowance

Art. 52 UIA has elaborated on the reasons for foreclosure of the entitlement to unemployment allowance and has specified each case in which the unemployment allowance will be withheld. According to this, the unemployment allowances of the insured who:

- Refuse a job that is recommended by TLI, is appropriate for their profession, is within the municipality area of the place of their residence, is close to the wages and working conditions of their last job without a reasonable cause,
- Are found to be working in a job that produces income or receiving a pension from any social security institution during the period they receive unemployment allowance,
- Refuse or accept but do not continue the professional and vocational education and training recommended by TLI,
- Do not answer the calls made by TLI in the required period of time or who do not provide the required information and documents within the foreseen period without a reasonable cause, will be withheld (art. 52 para. 1 UIA).

19.5.2 Part-Time Working Allowance

"Part-time working allowance" is paid to the insured that gives birth or adopts, for the period of free leave (art. 74 para. 2 LA) that is half of the weekly working time (generally 45 hours). Part-time working allowance is paid monthly from UIF.

The amount of part-time working allowance after birth and adoption is the gross amount of the daily minimum wage (add. art. 5 para. 1 UIA).

In order for the insured to benefit from the part-time working allowance:

- At least 600 days of unemployment insurance premium must have been declared in the name of the insured in the last three years prior to the date of birth or adoption,
- The insured must have worked for half of the weekly working time, i.e. 22,5 hours in general,
- An application must be made to TLI after the birth or adoption, within a period of 30 days from the end of maternity leave, along with a part-time working document (add. art. 5 para. 1 UIA).

19.5.3 Short Time Working Allowance

19.5.3.1 Conditions for Entitlement to Short Time Working Allowance

In the case of a temporary reduction of the working hours in the workplace due to a general economic, sectorial or regional crisis or due to compelling reasons, or if the activity in the workplace is temporarily halted in whole or in part, short-time working may be carried out in the workplace for a period not exceeding three months.[10]

In the case of short-time working, short-time working allowance is granted from the UIF. For this, the insured must fulfil the conditions for entitlement to unemployment allowance,[11] except for the termination of the employment contract. Accordingly, short time working allowance will be given to those who have worked as an insured for at least 600 days in the last three years and paid unemployment insurance premium of those who have worked consistently by paying premiums for the last 120 days before the termination of the employment contract (art. 50 para. 2 and add. art. 2 para. 3 UIA). However, the duration of 120 days has been reduced to 60 days and 600 days to 450 days exceptionally for the covid-19 period (prov. art. 23 para. 1 UIA).

19.5.3.2 Amount and Duration of Short Time Working Allowance

The amount of the short time working allowance is 60% of the daily average gross earnings calculated by taking into consideration the earnings of the insured based on the premiums of last 12 months. The short time working allowance to be calculated in this way shall not exceed 150% of the gross amount of the monthly minimum wage (add. art. 2 para. 4 UIA).

The duration of the short time working allowance is three months, provided that it does not exceed the short term of working. However, the President of the State is authorized to extend this period up to six months (add. art. 2 paras 1 and 6 UIA).

In this sense, short-time work practice under covid-19 measures was designed for three months, (from the beginning of March 2020 to the end of June) but with three Presidency Decrees, it has been extended first until the end of July and then until the end of August and then until the end of October 2020. Between April-July 2020, app. 11 million employees have benefited from short-time benefits with a total payment of app. 2 million Euros.

[10]*See* in detail: Caniklioğlu (2005), pp. 501–518; Ekmekçi (2009), pp. 47–48.

[11]*See* above Sect. 19.5.1.1.

19.5.4 Unpaid Leave Scheme

In order to protect employment and wages and keep the businesses alive, within the scope of combat against the pandemic in Turkey, some amendments were made in the UIA and the LA with the laws No. 7226 and 7244.

In this sense, as a means to protect employment during Covid-19 pandemic, the termination of employment contracts is temporarily banned for three months (it has been extended for another two months later), apart from termination for just cause and some other exceptions like the ending of a fixed-term contract, the closure of workplaces etc. In this regard, the government introduced an unpaid leave scheme, where the employer can send employees who are not entitled to short-time work benefits to unpaid leave without taking their consent and employees can get an *"unpaid leave allowance"* from UIF.

We must say this option is not commonly used, because mainly short-time work is practiced in the companies. Just like short-time work practice unpaid leave scheme was designed for three months, (from mid April 2020 to the mid July) but with two Presidency Decrees, it has been extended for two months. Between April-July 2020, app. 4 million employees have benefited from short-time benefits with a total payment of app. 500.000 Euros.

19.5.5 Payment from Wage Guarantee Fund

A separate *Wage Guarantee Fund* has been established under UIF in order to cover the unpaid wages of the workers for three months, provided that the employer has difficulty in paying due to a concordat, insolvency, bankruptcy or delay of bankruptcy (add. art. 1 para. 1 UIA).[12]

The Wage Guarantee Fund covers 1% of the annual total of payments to be made by employers as unemployment insurance premiums (add. art. 1 para. 2 UIA).

In the wage payments to be made from the Wage Guarantee Fund, the fact that the employee has worked in the same workplace in the last year before the employer had difficulty in paying is taken as basis and the payment is made over the basic wage. Wage payments will not exceed the upper limit on earnings based on the premium account (add. art. 1 para. 1 UIA).

[12] *See* in detail: Kıymaz (2007), pp. 38–41.

19.5.6 Payment of Insurance Premiums

Persons benefiting from unemployment allowance and short time working allowance are considered to be general health insured (art. 60 para. 1/e SIGHIA). General health insurance premiums of these persons are covered by UIF (art. 50 para. 5 UIA).

Similarly, the insured and employer shares of the premiums of the insured persons receiving part-time working allowance equal to the days this allowance is received is covered by UIF with a total rate of 32.5% on the lower limit of earnings (add. art. 5 para. 2 UIA).

19.5.7 Employment and Vocational Training Aid

It is also among the duties of TLI to find a new job for those who are unemployed. Because activities of finding a new job and vocational training cannot be carried out quickly, when unemployment insurance processes difficult.[13]

Employment and vocational training aids are carried out by the *"Department of Employment"* which is one of the main service units of TLI.

In fact, art. 48 UIA counts *"finding a new job"* and *"courses and programs within the scope of active labour services"* among the aids to be made to the unemployed insured (art. 48 para. 6/c-d UIA). Accordingly, 30% of the previous year's premium income of UIF could be used to carry out works on increasing and protecting employment. The President of the State is authorized to increase this rate of 30% up to 50%. However, this limitation will not be taken into account for services for those who benefit from unemployment allowances (art. 48 para. 7 UIA).

19.6 Unemployment Insurance for Independent Employees

Additional Article 6, which was added to the Unemployment Insurance Act in 2017 by Act No. 6824, established a compulsory insurance system for independent employees (self-employed), by foreseeing the establishment of the *Tradesmen's Fund*. However, naming the aforementioned fund in as resembling the *ahi-order* system is not considered as accurate, since the regulation in question covers a large number of independent workers instead of only tradesmen.[14]

On the other hand, add. art. 6 UIA is not yet in force. Hence, although the aforementioned regulation was accepted in 2017, it was determined to enter into force on 1/1/2018, then, the effective date was postponed firstly to 1/1/2020 and then to 1/1/2021.

---

[13]Keser (2000), p. 80.

[14]Akpulat (2019), p. 173; Güzel et al. (2020), pp. 742–743.

19.6.1 Fund Management and Financing

The fund shall be operated and managed as per the decisions of the Board of Directors of the TLI. In this context, the Fund will be evaluated within the framework of the same procedures and principles as the resources of the Unemployment Insurance Fund and will be audited by the Court of Accounts.

The income and expenses that will form the basis for the financing of the fund are clearly shown in the law. Accordingly, Fund revenues consist of premiums and earnings and revenues to be obtained as a result of their evaluation, State contributions to be provided in case of deficit of the Fund, penalties, delay increases and interests to be received from the insured, and other revenues and earnings and donations. On the other hand, Fund allowances, insurance premiums to be paid as per SSI, expenses related to the services listed under art. 48 para. 7 UIA, and the expenses that are made by the TLI for performing the Fund services and the lease of service building, purchase of services, computer, computer software, and hardware purchase expenses will be placed within the expenses of the Fund.

19.6.2 Coverage of the Fund Per Person

19.6.2.1 Those Who Are Considered as Insured by the Fund

Within the scope of art. 4 para. 1/b SIGHIA, those who work on their own behalf and account, without being bound by an employment contract, are considered to be insured by the Fund. According to this, those who are:

- real or simple income taxpayer due to commercial or self-employment incomes,
- exempt from income tax and registered in the register of tradesmen and craftsmen,
- shareholders of joint-stock companies who are members of the board of directors, the active partners of the partnerships in commended whose capital is divided into shares, and all the partners of other partnerships and equipping subsidiaries are deemed to be insured by the fund.[15]

19.6.2.2 Those Who Are Not Considered as Insured by the Fund

Voluntary insurance holders, jockeys and trainers, village and neighbourhood chief, and those engaged in agricultural activities are excluded from the Fund insurance coverage.

[15] Akpulat (2019), p. 174.

On the other hand, there is no clarity in the law as to whether individuals who work independently of individuals who are specified not to be deemed to be insured as per art. 6 SIPHIA will be considered as insured by the Fund. However, in accordance with art. 4 para. 1/b SIPHIA, despite their independent work, the persons in question, who are not considered to be insured, should not be able to be insured by the Fund.[16]

19.6.3 Fund Benefits

19.6.3.1 Fund Allowance

The fund allowance aims to compensate for the loss of income of the insured in the period when he/she loses his/her job.

Amount of Allowance

The amount of the fund allowance is 40% of the daily average earning of the insured, which is calculated by taking into account the earnings subject to the last four months premium. However, the fund allowance cannot exceed 80% of the gross amount of the monthly minimum wage.

Duration of Payment

To those who worked continuously for the last 120 days before the termination of insurance for fund insurance holders, the following allowance shall be given if they meet the following within the last three years:

- 180 days for those who worked for 600 days and have paid Fund premium,
- 240 days for those who worked for 900 days and paid Fund premium,
- 300 days for those who worked for 1080 days and have paid their Fund premium.

Conditions for Benefiting

The first condition for benefiting from the allowance is the termination of the Fund insurance under certain circumstances and the insured being unemployed. Accordingly, among the insured, those who have applied to the court with a request for bankruptcy or whose insurance will terminate by closing their workplace although not subject to bankruptcy will be able to benefit from the allowance. In this context,

[16] Akpulat (2019), p. 176.

it does not matter whether the insured or his creditors filed for bankruptcy. Because, in the absence of any clarity in the law, the issue of who will have to apply to the court for bankruptcy does not matter.[17]

In order for the insured to benefit from the allowance, it must also be insured for a certain period of time and have paid a premium. Accordingly, within the last three years, it should at least work for 600 days within the last three years and paid the premium and continuously worked for 120 days before the termination of the insurance.

The premiums here will be collected from the daily earnings subject to premium as 2% insured and 1% State share. However, the daily premium amount to be collected cannot be more than the amount to be calculated over twice the daily earning limit for premium. If the fund insurance is terminated for any reason, neither the insured nor the State premium share amounts will be refunded. On the other hand, premiums paid to the Fund by the insured are considered as an expense in determining the earnings.

Apart from this, in order for the insured to benefit from the allowance, there should be no Fund premium and any debt related to the said premium.

Finally, the insured's application is sought in order to benefit from the allowance. It is stipulated that the said application will be made directly or electronically and within 30 days from the day following the expiration of the insurance. However, failure to comply with the specified period will not eliminate the right to benefit from the allowance, and the delayed period will be deducted from the total period entitled to receive the allowance unless there is a compelling reason. In addition, the insured must register at the time of application that they are ready to take up a new job.

Discontinuation of the Allowance

Regarding discontinuation of the payment, it is stipulated that art. 52 UIA will be applied by analogy to the insurance holders of the Fund. Accordingly, the payment of the Fund insurance holder who refuses the offered job without any just cause, who are determined to be working at an income-generating work or receiving retired pay, who refuse to receive the offered occupational training without just cause, or who does not continue the training or does not timely respond to the calls without just cause or who does not provide the requested information and documents within the stipulated period during the allowance payment shall be discontinued.

Withdrawal of Payment

Payments made to the insured who have made fraudulent bankruptcy or who transferred their workplace to descendants or kin or to third parties in collusion,

[17] Akpulat (2019), p. 177.

and the overpayments determined to be caused by the fault of the insured shall be taken back from the insured together with the legal interest. However, excess and improper payments made to the deceased insured will not be refunded.

19.6.3.2 Other Aids

Regarding other aids to be made within the scope of the fund, insurance premiums payable pursuant to the SIGHIA were mentioned; however, which insurance branches these will be related to were not specified in art. 6 para. 9/b UIA. However, it is observed that the premiums in question primarily concern the general health insurance. Because, while listing those who are deemed to be universal health insurance holders, among them, people benefiting from Fund allowance were also counted.

Furthermore, since the occupational disease and general health insurance premiums of those who participate in occupational training, development, and modification will be paid by the TLI, Fund insurance holders may be able to benefit from the said opportunity.

Finally, Fund insurance holders have the opportunity to find a new job and to benefit from courses and programs within the scope of active labour services.

References

Akpulat AK (2019) Bağımsız Çalışanların İşsizlik Sigortası: Esnaf Ahilik Sandığı Sigortası. Sicil İş Hukuku Dergisi. 41:166–182

Başterzi S (1996) İşsizlik Sigortası. Ankara Üniversitesi Hukuk Fakültesi, Ankara

Caniklioğlu N (2005) 4857 Sayılı İş Kanununa Göre Kısa Çalışma ve Kısa Çalışma Ödeneği. In: A. Can Tuncay'a Armağan. Legal Publishing, Istanbul, pp 499–547

Ekmekçi Ö (2009) Kısa Çalışma ve Kısa Çalışma Ödeneği Uygulamasına İlişkin Sorunlar. Sicil İş Hukuku Dergisi 14:47–59

Güzel A, Okur AR, Caniklioğlu N (2020) Sosyal Güvenlik Hukuku, 18th edn. Beta Publishing, Istanbul

Haenlein A (2001) Neue Arbeitslosenversicherung in der Türkei – oder: Experimentelle Gesetzgebung als Aufgabe für die Praxis. Recht der Internationalen Wirtschaft 4:284–287

Keser H (2000) İşsizlik Sigortası ve Getirdikleri. İzmir Barosu Dergisi 65(4):69–81

Kıymaz T (2007) Ücretin Korunmasına Dair Hükümler Bağlamında "Ücret Garanti Fonu". Sicil İş Hukuku Dergisi 7:36–41

Tuncay AC, Ekmekçi Ö (2019) Sosyal Güvenlik Hukuku Dersleri, 20th edn. Beta Publishing, Istanbul

Chapter 20
Aids for Civil Servants of Pre-SIGHIA

20.1 Aids from Retirement Fund Act

20.1.1 Status of Civil Servants Before the Transitional Period

In the period preceding SIGHIA, the social security of civil servants and other public officials was provided primarily through *Retirement Fund Act* No. 5434[1] and *Retirement Fund*. After SIGHIA came into force, a painful process was experienced in relation to Act No. 5434.

In fact, Constitutional Court annulled the provisions of SIGHIA by finding it contrary to the Constitution in terms of public officials. In the legal regulations made upon this, public officials were excluded from the short-term insurance provisions of SIGHIA. In the case of long-term insurance branches, the principle of continuing the implementation of Act No. 5434 on civil servants and other public officials subject to Act No. 5434 prior to the entry into force of SIGHIA has been adopted.

Thus, in terms of civil servants and other public officials, two different groups were formed in Turkish social law. One group of these is those who were civil servants before SIGHIA and subject to Act No. 5434. In the other group are civil servants and other public officials who started civil service for the first time in the SIGHIA period and subject to the provisions of SIGHIA. Accordingly, it has been necessary to deal with the provisions related to that subject to the Act No. 5434 separately.

[1]OG 17.6.1949, No. 7235.

T. Centel, *Turkish Social Law*, https://doi.org/10.1007/978-3-030-64704-9_20

20.1.2 Entitlement to Pension for Participants of Retirement Fund

Act No. 5434 regulates three types of retirement. These are voluntary retirement, mandatory retirement and statutory retirement.

20.1.2.1 Entitlement to Pension in Voluntary Retirement

Entitlement to voluntary pension occurs when:

- The President of the State leaves the office, if he/she wishes,
- Women complete the age of 58 and men the age of 60, of the participants of those who complete 25 years of active service, if they wish,
- They reach the statutory age (or mandatory retirement by their institution), if they wish,
- They complete the age of 61, of those whose pension deductions are not refunded, if they wish,
- Disabled persons assigned under the relevant legislation complete 15 years of actual service, if they wish (art. 39 Act No. 5434).

20.1.2.2 Entitlement to Pension in Mandatory Retirement

Entitlement to pension in mandatory retirement occurs when:

- If the institutions of those who completed 30 years of service deem necessary,
- If the institutions of officers, military officers, warrant officers and privates deem necessary due to them being convicted of morality, inadequacy or lack of discipline, or in case of registry irregularities related to lack of discipline or military court orders,
- If the institutions of other officials deem necessary for registry irregularities related to lack of discipline or inadequacy, and mandatory retirement procedures are carried out (art. 39 Act No. 5434).

20.1.2.3 Entitlement to Pension in Statutory Retirement

The entitlement of participants to pension for statutory retirement comes from the fact that they reach a certain age foreseen by Act No. 5434 or by some other special laws. Accordingly, the age limit requiring the termination of the participants' duties is generally the date when they have reached the age of 65 years (art. 40 para. 1 Act No. 5434).

In contrast, the age limit for university lecturers is the date when the age of 67 is completed. Similarly, for officers and military officers, limits have been determined varying between 41 and 68 years according to their rank and duties. Again, for the members of the police, limits have been determined varying between 55 and 60 years according to their duties. The age limit is 50 years for customs protection officers and 55 years for section chiefs. For mail, telegraph and telephone line careers and distributors, the age limit is 55 years. For the employees of the National Intelligence Agency, there are limits varying between the ages of 52 and 60 according to their duties (art. 40 Act No. 5434).

20.1.3 Transitional Provisions for Civil Servants Before 8/9/1999

A special transition process is foreseen for those working as civil servants prior to 8/9/1999. According to this, female participants who complete 20 years of actual service and male participants who complete 25 years of actual service as of 8/9/1999 will be granted pension upon their request. Of other participants, those with less than two years to complete their retirement service period as of 8/9/1999 will be entitled to a pension provided they complete 38 years of age for women and 43 for men. Thus, no change has occurred for the officers in these groups.

On the other hand, the age limit of those with less than three years to fill their retirement service periods is increased gradually (prov. art. 205 Act No. 5434). Constitutional Court annulled this very arrangement.[2] The resulting gap was filled out by a new regulation made with Act No. 4759.[3,4]

20.1.4 Period of Service to Be Taken as Basis for Pension

20.1.4.1 Actual Service Period

The actual service period is the period of time starting from the beginning of the month when premiums are deducted from the insured and goes on with paying premiums (art. 31 Act No. 5434).

20.1.4.2 Actual Service Period Increase

Actual service period increase is the increasing of the actual service periods of those who work in some heavy and debilitating tasks by a predetermined period of time.

[2] Constitutional Court, 23.2.2001, 1999-42/41, OG 23.11.2001, No. 24592.

[3] OG 1.6.2002, No. 24772.

[4] *See* in detail: Güzel et al. (2020), pp. 662–664.

Accordingly, the actual service period increase is taken into account in the calculation of both the length of time required to be entitled to the pension and of the pensions.

The conditions in which the actual service period increase is recognized are shown in the list at art. 32 Act No. 5434. These periods are 2, 3 or 6 months. These periods to be added will be considered as actual services in retirement procedures, but their sum will not exceed 8 years (art. 33 Act No. 5434).

20.1.4.3 Nominal Service Period

Nominal service periods to be included in the actual service periods of retirement pension, premium refund and lump sum payments are accepted (art. 35 Act No. 5434). Accordingly, the periods worked in certain special cases are added to the actual service period of the insured as nominal service period (art. 36 Act No. 5434).

These periods cannot be less than three months each or more than 5 years in total. The actual service period increase can be taken into consideration in terms of pension and retirement bonus, but the nominal service period is only taken into account in the granting of pension. The nominal service period is foreseen for pilots and divers depending on war and conflict (art. 37 Act No. 5434).

20.1.5 Calculation of Pension

In calculating pension, the dashboard based on the granting of salary of Civil Servants Act (art. 43 Act No. 657) is used. Thus, the indicator used for the calculation of the salary of the civil servant during his/her service will be used in the calculation of his/her pension.

To the number of indicators, the number of additional indicators and the base pension, if any, and the seniority allowance are added. Language allowance and housing allowance are not taken into account in the calculation of pension. The monthly rate is 75% (art. 41 para. b Act No. 5434).

In the calculation of the monthly rate, 25-year service period is taken as basis. The monthly rate of those with a service period of more than 25 years is increased by 1% for each full year and deducted by 1% is for each full year less than 25 years (art. 41 para. b Act No. 5434).

20.1.6 Entitlement of Retirement Fund Participant to Disability Allowance

The disability determination of the Retirement Fund participant is not attributed to a working capacity expressed in numerical value, and the participants who are unable to perform their duties are considered to be disabled (art. 44 Act No. 5434).

20.1.6.1 Permanent Disability

The participant who is unable to perform his/her duty due to a malfunction in his/her body or an impossible to treat illness, for whatever reason, is deemed as permanently disabled (art. 44 para. 1 Act No. 5434). However, if the person so wishes in writing, the disability provisions shall not be applied, and he/she shall be assigned to another position compatible with his/her injury and shall be deemed to have resigned from his/her first position (art. 44 para. 2 Act No. 5434).

All kinds of disabilities and illnesses of participants are determined by the health committee reports of full-fledged hospitals. Where these hospitals are not available, reports may be given by local hospitals with at least three physicians. If these are not present as well, the disability status is determined by a report to be given by at least three physicians, provided one is an expert on the subject (art. 50 paras 1 and 2 Act No. 5434).

Persons who fall victim to an impossible to treat illness after working for a minimum of 5 years in a duty to be taken as basis for retirement and are unable to survive without the help of others are entitled to disability allowance as if they had actual services for 15 years (art. 53 para. 4 Act No. 5434). However, these allowances do not pass onto widows and orphans (art. 53 para. 5 Act No. 5434).

Permanent disability allowance is calculated on the same basis and rates of pension, according to the total number of years of service of the participant who has completed at least 10 years of actual service, on the basis of the allowance or wage they receive during the termination of their job (arts 41 and 53 Act No. 5434).

20.1.6.2 Duty Disability

If the disability results from:

- Duties of the participants during the period of their duties,
- Activities out of their duties but related to other institutions and given by their institutions,
- Duties with the purpose of protecting the benefit of their institutions,
- Accidents that occur at the workplace before the start of work, at work or at the end of work, or arising from the nature of the workplace or work,

This is called "*duty disability*" and these persons are called "*duty disabled*" (art. 45 Act No. 5434).

If the duty disability occurs due to the use of pleasure-inducing substances, acts contradictory to legislation, prohibited acts or suicide attempts, the provisions of permanent disability will be applied instead of those of duty of disability (art. 48 Act No. 5434).

The duty disability should be reported to the Retirement Fund in writing within a maximum of one year after the occurrence. The participant himself/herself or his/her mother, father, spouse, children, siblings and the institution can make this statement. If notification is not made within the said period, the provisions of permanent disability are to be applied. The said notification period is one and a half years for private officers (art. 49 para 1 and 2 Act No. 5434).

The calculation of the duty disability allowance is done over 30 years for those with actual and nominal service periods up to 30 years and over the total period for those with more than 30 years (art. 55 para. 1 Act No. 5434).

Persons with a duty disability allowance will be examined twice at the end of each third year (art. 61 Act No. 5434). At the end of these examinations, if it is understood that the disability level will not change, no further examinations are done, and the situation is recorded. On the other hand, if there is an increase in the level of disability, a re-examination may be requested for one time only within three years after the last report (art. 61 para. 3 Act No. 5434).

If it is determined the disability level is changed or completely disappeared, the allowance is recalculated and paid from the beginning of the month following the report or completely withheld (art. 62 para. 1 Act No. 5434). If those whose allowances are withheld are not assigned to a new duty and if their actual service periods are between 5 and 10 years, their deductions will be returned upon their request and their relationship with Retirement Fund will be terminated. If they do not want their relation to be terminated or their service period is 10 years or more, they will be granted pension when they reach the age of 61, and if their service period is less than 10 years, they will be paid in lump sum payment. Those whose services are more than 30 years may always ask for a pension (art. 62 para. a Act No. 5434).

20.1.6.3 War Disability

If the duty disability occurs:

- Under fire in battle,
- During operations and services in war zones,
- During preparation for war,
- Under enemy weapons,
- During military discipline or border movements
- During the duty in a flight,
- With the effect of flight in the air and on the ground,
- During the duty in a dive,

- During the duty on a submarine or in a diving team,

During the presence of personnel of the Turkish Armed Forces in the country or abroad in accordance with the decision of the Turkish parliament or international treaties,

"*War disability*" will be in question (art. 64 Act No. 5434).

If the war disabled is a soldier, war disability allowance is granted over one higher rank; if he/she is a civilian, it is granted over one higher rank of what the rank of the civilian is or may be (art. 64 para. 2 Act No. 5434).

War disabled are also paid for a war disability increase. War disability increase is calculated as a result of multiplying the indicator regulated by disability with the coefficient and added to the allowance (art. 64 para. 6 Act No. 5434).

The war disability increase is provided at 25% to those who get disabled while they are showing exemplary courage and sacrifice, with the approval of the General Staff and the Minister of National Defence (art. 64 para. 7 Act No. 5434).

20.1.7 Granting Allowance and Other Aids to the Right Holders of Deceased Participant

20.1.7.1 Right Holders of Deceased Participant

As the right holders of the deceased participant, his/her spouse, children and parents are shown (art. 67 Act No. 5434).

The spouse is the person who has contracted a marriage with the deceased participant in accordance with the provisions of the Turkish Civil Code. The fact that the spouse works under Retirement Fund or other social security institutions or receives allowance or income from these institutions does not prevent him/her from being deemed a right holder.[5]

In accordance with the provisions of Turkish Civil Code, the child, whose bloodline is correct or corrected, who is adopted, whose bloodline is not correct in case of granting allowance from the mother, who is recognized or whose father is determined by a court order will be entitled to an orphan pension (art. 73 Act No. 5434).

In addition, according to the gender of the child, some additional conditions are sought. Accordingly, in order to grant an orphan pension to boys, they must be less than 18 years old at the date of death, 20 years if they are in the middle education and 25 years if they are in higher education, and they must have not married. In order for girls to be granted an orphan pension, it is sufficient for them to not be married at the time of the death of the participant, and no further conditions for age and education are required. However, if girls later get married, their pensions will be withheld. In

[5] Güzel et al. (2020), p. 687.

the event of divorce or widowhood, orphan pension is granted again (art. 75 paras 1 and 2 act No. 5434).

Finally, their mothers who are not associated with the Retirement Fund and their fathers who are not associated with Retirement Fund and who have reached the age of 65 are granted the pension as right holders (art. 72 para. 1 Act No. 5434).

20.1.7.2 Conditions to Grant Pension

In order for widow and orphan pension to be granted to right holders, it is obligatory that the death of the participant be within the conditions specified in the law. According to this, for participants who:

- Die when they were presidents of the State or after they leave office,
- Die after at least 10 years of actual service,
- Die while receiving pension, permanent disability or duty disability allowance, or after being granted these,
- Die during treatment or surgery on accident or injury due to reasons arising from duties,
- Die before the refunding of their deductions even though their actual service periods are at least 10 years and before completing the age of 61,
- Die while their allowance is withheld due to the termination of their disability and before given new posts and after having completed 10 actual years of service,

Pension can be granted to their right holders. Similarly, the right holders of private soldiers who have died due to reasons arising from their duties or during treatment or surgery related to them or those who have died while receiving a duty disability allowance or while granted the allowance must also be granted pension (art. 66 Act No. 5434).

20.1.7.3 Calculation of the Pension

In calculating widow and orphan pensions, the pension, the permanent disability or duty disability allowance granted or to be granted to the deceased shall be taken as basis, and this pension/allowance is distributed at certain rates among the survivors (art. 68 Act No. 5434). Accordingly, spouses are granted 50% of the pension/allowance, and the spouses without children receiving allowances are granted 75%. For each child and mother or father, 25% of the pension/allowance is granted (art. 68 para. 1 Act No. 5434).

If the deceased has a spouse and an orphan entitled to pension/allowance, 60% is applied to the spouse and 30% to the orphan (art. 68 para. 2 Act No. 5434).

The widow pension shall be paid at the rate of 50% to the widow who receives pension/allowance from Retirement Fund or is a participant (art. 68 para. 4 Act No. 5434).

If the deceased participant does not leave a widow behind or the widow is not entitled to pension/allowance, the share is added equally to the pensions of children and parents. However, the sum of these pensions/allowances after the additions will not exceed 50% of the pension is there is one orphan, 80% if two and 100% if three (art. 68 para. 6 Act No. 5434).

On the other hand, if the participant is at least 30 years older than his/her spouse, the spouse is granted half of the pension. However, if the marriage contract has been made at least 10 years ago or they had children, this deduction is not applied. These provisions also apply to those who marry after retirement (art. 71 Act No. 5434). With such an arrangement, the aim was to prevent marriages to be made solely to get pensions/allowances, but it is not possible to legally justify such a limitation of a subjective nature to protect the benefit of Retirement Fund.[6]

20.1.7.4 Death Allowance

In the event of death of those receiving pension or permanent disability or duty disability allowance, those they have declared in their health, or their families if they did not declare anyone, are paid a certain amount of the pension as "*death allowance*" by Retirement Fund without waiting for a payment order. War disability increase is not taken into account in the calculation of death pension. Death pension cannot be seized or assigned (add. art. 4 paras 1 and 4 Act No. 5434).

It is stated that the death pension will be made to the family of the deceased unless the declaration is given, but it is not stated who will be deemed as part of the family. In this case, it would be appropriate to accept that, according to the provisions of art. 208 para. 2 act No. 657, the family concept would include the spouse, children, parents and siblings, respectively.[7]

20.1.7.5 Marriage Bonus

Marriage bonus is an aid recognized only to widow wives, daughters and mothers who are receiving a widow or orphan pension. Accordingly, boys are not paid a marriage bonus. The amount of the marriage bonus is the 12 months amount of the widow or orphan pension (art. 90 para. 1 Act No. 5434).

If a wife or daughter gets divorced before 12 months of marriage or decides to the annulment or termination of the marriage, they will be granted pension again. However, the amount of the bonus paid in advance for the remainder of the 12-month period is refunded, and no pension is paid until the amount for this period is collected. If the marriage is terminated after 12 months, the widow or orphan

[6]Centel (2012), p. 55; Güzel et al. (2020), p. 693.

[7]Güzel et al. (2020), p. 694.

pension will be granted again, starting from the following month (art. 90 para. 2 Act No. 5434).

20.1.8 Lump Sum Payment to Participants

Lump sum payment refers to the amount found by multiplying each full year of the total periods corresponding to the money the participants pay for the actual and nominal service periods and the period of service owed with twice the amount of the retirement allowance at the date their duties are terminated (art. 83 Act No. 5434).

Conditions for lump sum payments are shown one by one in art. 82 Act No. 5434. The conditions in question consist of four cases of inability to qualify for a pension due to age or length of service.

20.1.9 Refund of the Deductions of the Participant

Those who have left their jobs due to certain reasons and who do not work in a job subject to another social security institution are refunded the deductions collected from their pensions/allowances without interest. Accordingly, refunds are specifically for cases such as resignation, transfer to a staff not entitled to the right to retirement, dismissal for administrative or criminal penalties, conviction and termination of the right to retirement (art. 87 para. 1 Act No. 5434).

However, those with the actual service periods and actual service period increase less than 5 years cannot benefit from the deduction refund (art. 87 para. 2 Act No. 5434).

The deduction refund rights of those who do not use them within 5 years are dropped due to statute of limitation (art. 117 Act No. 5434).

20.2 Aids Born of Civil Servants Act

20.2.1 Sick Leave

Civil servants, in case of illness, on the need to be shown in the reports to be given, without affecting the wages and personal rights, a "*sick leave*" is granted up to 6 months for those with 10 years of service (including 10 years), up to 12 months for those with more than 10 years of service and up to 18 months for those with a disease requiring long-term treatment such as cancer, tuberculosis or a mental illness (art. 105 para. 1 Act No. 657).

The duration of treatment of civil servants is taken into account in the calculation of the duration of sick leave. The leaves of the officers whose illnesses are determined by report to be continuing at the end of the leave period are extended up to one time the original period. The retirement provisions are applied to civil servants who do not recover at the end of these periods. If those who are determined to have regained the necessary health conditions want to work again, they are appointed to tasks that are appropriate to their former levels and qualifications (art. 105 paras 2 and 3 Act No. 657).

Civil servants, who are attacked because of their duties, suffer an accident or occupational disease during their duties and due to their duties are deemed to be on sick leave until they recover (art. 105 para. 4 Act No. 657).

20.2.2 Family Benefit

Married civil servants are granted the "*family benefit*". This benefit is foreseen for the unemployed spouse and children of the civil servant. If the civil servant has more than two children, the benefit is only made for two children (art. 202 Act No. 657).

The family benefit is paid to the civil servant together with each month's salary. If both the husband and wife are civil servants, the family benefit is granted only to the husband. The family benefit is paid without any tax or deduction and cannot be seized (art. 203 Act No. 657).

In addition, a 16-week "*maternity leave*" is given to the civil servant for 8 weeks before birth and 8 weeks after birth (art. 104 Act No. 657). After the expiry of these periods, the civil servant may be allowed up to 18 months of leave without pay (art. 108 para. A Act No. 657).

20.2.3 Death Benefit

Of civil servants, those whose spouse that is not a civil servant and children entitled to family benefit die, a "*death benefit*" shall be given at the highest amount of civil servant monthly salary; if the civil servant dies, it shall be given to the person they declared in their health, and if none, to the spouse and children, parents or siblings, in order, at twice the highest amount of civil servant monthly salary (art. 208 Act No. 657).

In the event of death of civil servants, the funeral expenses, including the transfer of the funeral to another place, shall be paid to their institutions. All necessary expenses of the spouses of deceased civil servants and those who are in permanent posts abroad for bringing the bodies of the mother, father and children they are obliged to take care of to Turkey are covered by their institutions (art. 210 Act No. 657).

References

Centel T (2012) Ölen Eşinden 30 Yaş Küçüğe Yarım Aylık. Ne Ölçüde Adil ? Güncel Hukuk 99:53–55

Güzel A, Okur AR, Caniklioğlu N (2020) Sosyal Güvenlik Hukuku, 18th edn. Beta Publishing, Istanbul

Part VI
General Health Insurance

Chapter 21
General Health Insurance Coverage

21.1 Transitional Period to General Health Insurance System

21.1.1 Structure of Health Services

The determination and management of health policies in Turkey has a fragmented appearance. Accordingly, different institutions have undertaken different tasks in the field of health. As a matter of fact, although the basic task is convened in the Ministry of Health, it is seen that various public institutions and private organizations are active in health services.

On the other hand, in the past, social security institutions have provided health benefits to the insured as well as various social insurance benefits. These institutions were the Social Insurance Institution (initially known as Labour Insurance Institution), Civil Servants' Retirement Fund, Social Insurance Institution of the Self-Employed Persons (Bag-Kur) and charity funds of some banks and insurance companies. As a matter of fact, in addition to providing financial benefits to the insured against the risks of occupational accident, occupational disease, disease, maternity, disability, old age and death, these institutions also undertook health benefits. In this sense, the Retirement Fund has been involved in health benefits since 1949, the Social Insurance Institution since 1965 and Bag-Kur since 1985.

However, social security reform activities, which were especially intensified in 2004, aimed at gathering the mentioned three institutions under one roof and collecting health benefits from them and gathering them in a single law and system. In these works, the general health insurance was requested to have three main functions. These are:

- Everyone who lives in Turkey is mandatory to have general health insurance,
- To make the system work over premiums and to receive premiums from everyone according to their income, earnings and payment power, and

T. Centel, *Turkish Social Law*, https://doi.org/10.1007/978-3-030-64704-9_21

- Providing health services through health service providers through purchase without any distinction between public and private sectors.

In 2006, *Social Security Institution Act* No. 5502[1] and *Social Insurance and General Health Insurance Act* No. 5510 [SIGHIA][2] were adopted, the social security institutions until then were gathered under a single roof, general health insurance was accepted, and the provision of health benefits was taken from these institutions.

21.1.2 Acceptance of General Health Insurance

Legislation draft and design works on general health insurance appeared in Turkey in 1967 for the first time.[3] These preparatory works on different dates have led to the general health insurance being discussed in Turkey for years, and the issue has created a continuous agenda in development plans and government programs.[4] However, these works have not been able to be enacted until 2006.

Of the drafts prepared within the framework of the social security reform, the Draft Retirement Law and the Draft General Health Insurance Law were merged and submitted to the Turkish parliament. As a result of the discussions, the Social Security Institution Act first and the Social Security and General Health Insurance Act second were adopted. However, the State's president of the time sent both texts back to the Turkish parliament for reconsideration. Upon this, the texts prepared were re-discussed and accepted by the parliament. However, the President applied to Constitutional Court for both laws with the intention of cancellation of certain provisions.

On the other hand, in order to facilitate the implementation of general health insurance, two important laws were passed before SIGHIA was adopted. One of them is *Family Medicine Act*[5] and the other is *Act on the Transfer of Health Units of Some Public Institutions and Organizations to the Ministry of Health*'.[6] The second of these has foreseen the seizure of social insurance hospitals established by the contributions of insured workers by the Ministry of Health. However, the sale of a portion of the social insurance hospitals seized and the transfer of a part of the income to the treasury and another part to the provincial special administrations was allowed by Act No. 5227 (prov. art. 1). It is clear that this situation will adversely affect the efforts for the implementation of the general health insurance.[7]

---

[1]OG 20.5.2006, No. 26173.

[2]OG 16.6.2006, No. 26200.

[3]*See*: Güzel et al. (2020), pp. 764–766.

[4]*See*: Sözer (2018), pp. 4–5.

[5]OG 9.12.2004, No. 25665.

[6]Rep. OG 19.1.2005, No. 25705.

[7]Güzel et al. (2020), p. 770.

Art. 60 SIGHIA, which regulates the scope of the general health insurance for individuals, has had new additions over time, and the scope of those who are considered as general health insured has been considerably expanded. Finally, the general health insurance application is made mandatory in all of Turkey as of 1/1/2012.

In this context, the general health insurance is the health system that ensures that all members of the community are protected against the risk of possible and emerging diseases, regardless of their income level.[8]

21.2 Scope of General Health Insurance for Individuals

21.2.1 Those Considered as General Health Insured

Persons whose residences are in Turkey and who are covered by the general health insurance can be listed according to art. 60 para. 1 SIGHIA as follows:

- Employees based on employment contract,
- Permanent or contracted employees in public administrations and those deputed,
- Village and neighbourhood headmen and self-employed persons,
- Optional insured,
- Citizens whose income in the family is less than one third of the minimum wage,
- Stateless persons and asylum seekers,
- Turkish citizens over 65 years old and in need and are receiving pension,
- Those with a Medal of Independence and who receive an honorary pension,
- Those who receive service pension,
- Those who receive monetary compensation or allowance,
- Children, disabled, elderly and women under protection,
- Those who receive war disability allowance or terrorism victim allowance,
- Temporary village guards,
- State athletes and their families,
- Persons uninsured from foreign legislations who have obtained residence permit,
- Those who receive unemployment and short-time working allowances,
- Those who receive income or allowance from SSI or from their affiliated funds,
- Of the insured persons employed in public administration workplaces, those whose employment contracts are suspended,
- Turkish workers who are taken abroad by employers who undertake works in countries that have no social security agreement with Turkey,
- Of Turkish citizens without general health insurance or any dependents without a determination of income, children who are not over 18 years of age,

[8]Sözer (2018), p. 3.

- Daughters who have received marriage allowance and are not dependent by their husbands and have divorced from their husbands within a two-year period,
- Public officials on leave without pay,
- Those dismissed from work or arrested or detained for any offense, whether related to the duty or not, those dismissed and returned to duty,
- Apprentices without dependents status and vocational training students, interns in vocational high schools and in higher education, scholarship students for publicly funded projects and part-time students in higher education institutions,
- TLI trainees,
- Foreign university students,
- Lawyer interns without general health insured or dependent status,
- Those who complete their education and are not general health insured,
- Those who work temporarily in agriculture and forestry services with an employment contract,
- Workers in commercial taxi and similar urban public transport establishments and part-time workers in works to be determined by the Ministry of Culture and Tourism,
- The spouses and children of self-employed persons,
- Those out of Turkish citizenship,
- Turkish citizens working in countries without social security agreements with Turkey,
- Soldiers and officers to be employed in the Turkish Armed Forces with a contract,
- Beneficiaries of work programs for the benefit of society organized by TLI,
- Among those who will be staff of prisons and detention centres, those taken to training prior to service,
- Turkish citizens who do not have the right to benefit from health insurance in another country.

On the other hand, in some cases it will first be checked whether the person concerned is a dependent. Those who are essentially dependents do not need to be registered as general health insured, but if they are not, they will be covered by the general health insurance. The persons in question are shown as follows:

- The unpaid working spouse of the employer,
- Among relatives living in the same residence, those working in housing works,
- Those who work with the same employer for less than 10 days a month and are domestic workers,
- Students working in practical construction and production works in formal vocational or art schools and in high schools, in normal education terms,
- Patients or disabled rehabilitated by health care providers,
- Those under the age of 18 of village or neighbourhood headmen, self-employed persons, employees in public administrations or those deputed,
- Agriculture and forestry workers with low annual income and discontinuous jobs, farmers and agriculture workers with a low annual income and over 65 years of age,
- Self-employed tradesmen and craftsmen with low income.

If these persons are not dependents, they will be able to benefit from general health insurance (art. 60 para. 2 SIGHIA).

21.2.2 Beneficiaries as Dependents

Besides the general health insured, their dependents also benefit from health services and other rights (art. 62 para. 2 SIGHIA).

The dependents of the general health insured are those who are not paying any premiums but who will receive health services due to the active insured they are dependent on. These are spouses, children and parents. However, these persons are not absolutely considered to be dependents, and some additional conditions are also sought.

21.2.2.1 The Person Depended on Being General Health Insured

In order for the person to be deemed to be a dependent, firstly, the person, which he/she depends on, must be a general health insured in terms of SIGHIA.

However, it is impossible for some people with general health insurance to benefit from the health insurance of their dependents. These are:

- Candidate apprentices, apprentices, students attending vocational training at businesses, students subjected to internship during their vocational high school education or higher education, scholarship students employed in publicly funded projects and part-time university students,
- Citizens with income per person less than one third of the minimum wage,
- International protection applicants and stateless persons,
- Persons with free access to care and rehabilitation services,
- Turkish citizens whose parents are not Turkish and who are not over the age of 18,
- Foreign students in higher education in Turkey,
- Lawyer interns.

21.2.2.2 Being the Spouse, Child or Parent of the General Health Insured

The spouses of the general health insured people who are not voluntary or compulsory insured and those who are not granted income or allowance due to their insurances should be considered as the "*dependents*" of the insured.

However, those who work on part-time or on-call and who work at some hours of the day and who receive wages at an hourly rate and who work for 10 or more but less than 30 days in household services are considered to be dependents (art. 3 para. 3 SIGHIA).

In addition, for foreign citizens with residence permits in Turkey and who are not insured from foreign legislation and married persons not entitled to benefit from health insurance in another country, it is left to the preferences of the persons to determine which of the spouse is to be deemed as dependent (art. 60 para. 4 SIGHIA).

The male children of the general health insured who do not have mandatory or voluntary insurance, who are not granted income or allowance due to their own insurance, who have not completed 18 years of age (20 if in secondary education or vocational training or apprenticeship in a business, 25 if in higher education) and who are not married and the children who are not married and who are found to be disabled without regard to their age will be able to benefit from the general health insurance as dependents.

Finally, the mother and father who live by the general health insured, who are found to be in need or poor as a result of the income test and who do not receive health care from their other children will be able to benefit from health aids as dependents.

21.2.2.3 Those Who Are Not Dependents

Art. 60 para. 3 SIGHIA shows that which people cannot be considered as dependents. These are:

- Those who are given continuous health aids by their schools,
- Those who are doing military service as soldiers and officers and the students of officer cadet schools,
- Those who are transferred to Turkey on behalf of a company abroad and are insured in the country they are sent from and who work independently in their own name and account and who live abroad and are subject to the social legislation of that country,
- Contracted personnel of Turkish origin working in the external representations of public administrations with permanent residence permits in the country where the representative office is located or with the citizenship of that country, who certify that they are insured in the social security institution of that country and the contracted personnel working in the external representations of public administrations and who are made insured by their employers in that country,
- Convicts and detainees in prisons and detention houses,
- Foreigners residing in Turkey for less than one year,
- Those who do not reside in Turkey and receive allowance/pension by foreign borrowing,
- The spouses, children and parents of those receiving income and allowance from SSI, except for those who receive them due to their own works,
- The spouses, children and parents of dependents,

- The spouses, children and parents of persons who are granted income and allowance as rightful owners,
- Except for those studying abroad, those who are dependents of the general health insured and are residing abroad.

21.2.3 Income Test Application

The income test application is considered as a financing instrument in terms of general health insurance. Accordingly, it is aimed that the general health insurance will be financed with premiums determined according to the ability to pay of the concerned persons. Thus, everyone will pay premiums in person or someone else, namely the State, will pay premiums in their name.

21.2.3.1 Application for the Determination of Income Through a Direct Registration

Those not deemed as general health insured or dependents and those whose general health insurance or dependent status is terminated are registered directly by SSI. For these, a thirty-day amount of the daily minimum wage based on premiums shall be taken as basis until the income tests are concluded. In addition, SSI notifies them that they must apply to social assistance and solidarity foundations within one month to undertake the income test.

The income of those who do not want an income test and those who do not approve the income test within one month despite the notification is accepted as double the minimum wage.

21.2.3.2 Application Place

The application is made to the foundation in the province or district where the residence of the person concerned is located, along with the application form that includes information essential for the income test.

21.2.3.3 Authorization for Income Determination

The authorization for the determination of income was given to the board of trustees established in accordance with Act No. 3294 and not to SSI.

21.2.3.4 Persons to Be Subject to Income Test

The income test will be applied to those who are not employed but who will pay full or partial premiums due to their income, those who do not work and those who do not have the ability to pay. We can sort these groups as:

- Those who have lost their conditions as dependents,
- Insured workers whose term of compulsory insurance and the period to benefit from general health insurance are terminated,
- Part-time employees who are not dependents and whose working periods are less than 30 days a month,
- Allowance rights holders, who have lost this right.

21.2.3.5 Premium to Be Paid

The purpose of the income test is to determine the income per person of the household living in the same residence. The status of this income to be determined against the minimum wage is used as a measure in determining the premium to be paid by the person concerned.

Accordingly, if the income tester's income in the family is less than one-third of the minimum wage, the general health insurance premium will be paid by the State. On the other hand, if the person's income is between one third of the minimum wage and the minimum wage, the person will pay premium at 12% of one third of the minimum wage; if it is between the minimum wage and double the minimum wage, or more than double the minimum wage, the person will pay premium at 12% of double the minimum wage (art. 80 para. 4 and art. 81 para. 1/f SIGHIA).

Foreigners who have a residence period of more than one year in Turkey are considered as general health insured and they are obliged to pay a premium over double the minimum wage (art. 80 para. 4 SIGHIA). Accordingly, foreigners have to pay the premium over the upper limit without entering the income test.

21.3 Those Not Considered as General Health Insured

We can sort the individuals that are not considered as general health insured as:

- Those who are doing military service as soldiers and officers and the students of officer cadet schools,
- Those who are transferred to Turkey on behalf of an organization abroad and certify their insurance in the country they are sent from and those who work independently in their own name and account and who live abroad and are subject to the social legislation of that country,

- Contracted personnel of Turkish origin working in the external representations of public administrations with permanent residence permits in the country where the representative office is located who certify that they are insured in the social security institution of that country,
- Foreign citizens who have obtained a residence permit, are not insured under the legislation of a foreign country and are residing in Turkey for a period of less than one year,
- Prisoners and detainees in prisons and detention centres,
- Those receiving allowances by making overseas borrowing and not residing in Turkey,
- Foreign citizens who are voluntarily insured and are residing for less than a year in Turkey.

21.4 Registration of the General Health Insured

21.4.1 Registration Without Notification

Registration without notification may also be referred to as "*direct registration*". Because here, the general health insured is registered to the general health insurance by SSI without any notification.

Those who are registered as insured and who are considered as registered in terms of general health insurance without any notification can be sorted as:

- Employees working under employment contracts,
- Permanent and contracted employees in public administrations and deputed civil servants,
- Village and neighbourhood headmen and self-employed persons,
- Voluntarily insured.

21.4.2 Registration with Notification

For some groups, benefiting from the general health insurance is subject to their application to SSI within a certain period of time (*one month*) from the date they entered a certain status. According to this, persons need to apply to SSI along with the "*general health insurance declaration*" within one month can be sorted as:

- Those whose monthly income in the family are less than one third of the minimum wage, from the date of determination of this situation,
- Those receiving allowances under social assistance or social indemnity and those under war disability pension or the Anti-Terror Act, from the date they entitled to these allowances/pensions,

- Internationally protected persons, from the date on which they have applied for protection, have received internationally protected status or are considered as stateless persons,
- Beneficiaries of care and rehabilitation services, from the date when they start benefiting from these services,
- Foreigners who are not insured in their own country and whose residence exceeds one year, from the date they make a request,
- Beneficiaries of unemployment or short-time working allowances, from the date on which they start benefiting from such allowances,
- Foreign students studying at the university, from the date when they make a request,
- Lawyer interns, from the date on which they begin their internship by the Turkish Bar Association.

References

Güzel A, Okur AR, Caniklioğlu N (2020) Sosyal Güvenlik Hukuku, 18th edn. Beta Publishing, Istanbul
Sözer AN (2018) Türk Genel Sağlık Sigortası, 2nd edn. Beta Publishing, Istanbul

Chapter 22
Health Services Provided by General Health Insurance

22.1 Content of Health Services

The content of health services is determined depending on the purpose desired to be provided by these services. The purpose of health services is to ensure that the general health insured and the dependents remain healthy, regain their health if they become ill, to provide the necessary health allowances in case of occupational accident, occupational disease, disease and maternity, to eliminate or to reduce their inability to work and help them start working again (art. 63 para. 1 SIGHIA).

22.1.1 Preventive Health Services

Preventive health services constitute the most important element of general health insurance. Because preventing the patient from getting ill is the important point. In this regard, the provision and spreading of preventive health services to prevent disease are among the main objectives of the general health insurance.

Preventive health services are the services offered regardless of the persons' health, and prevention of substance addiction that is harmful to human health is also within the scope of preventive health services.[1]

Any kind of health service that will prevent illness is covered by preventive health services. Accordingly, preventive health services include all measures to prevent illnesses and to diagnose diseases at an early stage.

---

[1] *See*: Sözer (2018), p. 224.

T. Centel, *Turkish Social Law*, https://doi.org/10.1007/978-3-030-64704-9_22

22.1.2 Health Assistance in Case of Illness

If the insured gets ill despite preventive health care, the treatment process of general health insurance starts. The treatment process in this scope includes:

- Clinical examination by the doctor,
- Conducting laboratory examinations and tests if physicians deem necessary,
- Use of other diagnostic methods such as X-ray, ultrasound or tomography,
- Medical interventions and treatments required for diagnosis,
- Monitoring during the treatment and rehabilitation services if necessary,
- Organ, tissue or cell transplantation procedures,
- Cell therapy,
- Emergency medical services and
- Medical care and treatments such as physical therapy or massage by healthcare professionals upon doctor's decision (art. 63 para. 1/b SIGHIA).

These treatments may be performed on an outpatient basis but may also be performed by inpatient care by hospitalization in inpatient treatment institutions.[2]

22.1.3 Health Assistance in Maternity

Health assistances provided by the general health insurance in maternity are determined as:

- Clinical examination by the doctor,
- Conducting laboratory examinations and tests if physicians deem necessary,
- Use of other diagnostic methods such as X-ray, ultrasound or tomography for diagnosis,
- Medical interventions and treatments required for diagnosis,
- Monitoring during the treatment,
- Providing birth,
- Emergency health services,
- Medical care and treatments such as physical therapy and massage by healthcare professionals upon the doctor's decision (art. 63 para. 1/c SIGHIA). These treatments may be performed on an outpatient basis but may also be performed by inpatient care by hospitalization in inpatient treatment institutions.[3]

On the other hand, among the maternity health assistances, there is also the possibility to have children through artificial reproductive techniques. Those who can benefit from these assistances are the women with general health insurance who are married and cannot have children or the wives of general health insured men. In

[2]Sözer (2018), p. 226.

[3]*See*: Sözer (2018), pp. 229–230.

addition, some other conditions are sought, such as the fact that the future mother is older than 23 years of age and younger than 40 years, is a general health insured or a dependent for at least five years, has paid 900 days of general health insurance premiums and tries the assisted reproductive method up to three times (art. 63 para. 1/e SIGHIA).

22.1.4 *Oral and Dental Treatment*

Orthodontic dental treatments and dental prostheses have been restricted to age and quantity in the oral and dental treatment of general health insurance. In fact, those older than 18 years will not benefit from orthodontic treatment. In addition, the cost of precious metals in dental treatments, substances with precious metals and osseous dental implants are not covered.[4]

In this sense, it is seen that unforeseen limitations and restrictions in oral and dental treatment assistances and most of the other health assistances have been imposed for orthodontics and prosthetic assistances. Compliance of such limitations with the right to health (art. 56 Const.) seems to be extremely difficult.[5]

Apart from this, oral and dental treatments that the insured can benefit from in inpatient and outpatient services are shown separately. It is possible to sort them as follows:

- Oral and dental examination,
- Clinical examination necessary for the diagnosis of oral and dental diseases, if required by the physician,
- Conducting laboratory examinations and tests if the physician deems necessary,
- Application of other diagnostic methods such as x-ray or ultrasound,
- Medical interventions and treatments depending on the diagnosis,
- Tooth extraction,
- Conservative dental treatment and canal treatment,
- Monitoring the patient during and after the treatment,
- Trauma and oncological treatment-related prosthesis applications,
- Emergency health services for oral and dental diseases,
- Orthodontic dental treatment of those under 18 years of age (art. 63 para. 1/d SIGHIA).

[4] *See*: Sözer (2018), p. 234.

[5] Güzel et al. (2020), p. 802.

22.1.5 *Other Health Assistances*

Other health assistances include aids to support health assistances. These are aids for blood and blood products, bone marrow, vaccines, medicines, orthotics, prostheses, medical devices and equipment, medical devices and medical supplies for personal use to be required for diagnosis and treatment and instalment, repair, maintenance and renewal of these devices after the warranty period (art. 63 para. 1/f SIGHIA).

22.2 Treatment Abroad

The basic rule in the provision of health services is the fulfilment of these by domestic health service providers. However, in some cases and conditions, art. 66 SIGHIA enables health services to be provided from abroad as well.

22.2.1 *Those Who May Benefit from Treatment Abroad*

First of all, workers sent abroad by their employers for temporary duties and public servants sent abroad by their public administrations for temporary duties will be able to benefit from treatment abroad in case of emergencies (art. 66 para. 1/a SIGHIA).

Then, workers sent abroad by their employers for continuous duties and public servants sent abroad by their public administrations for continuous duties and those residing together with these workers and civil servants and their dependents will be able to benefit from treatment abroad (art. 66 para. 1/b SIGHIA).

The term "*continuous duty*" hereby refers to the assignment abroad for more than six months (art. 66 para. 9 SIGHIA).

Finally, the general health insured, which are found to be unable to be treated in the country on the appropriate opinion of the Ministry of Health, will be able to benefit from treatment abroad (art. 66 para. 1/c SIPHIA). Similarly, it is possible to carry out examinations abroad, which cannot be done in the country (art. 66 para. 2 SIPHIA).

22.2.2 *The Amount to Be Paid by SSI for Treatment Abroad*

The cost to be borne by SSI shall not exceed the amount paid to the health service providers for the same health service in the country, in the case of temporary or continuous overseas assignments. The employer will pat the amount exceeding this cost (art. 66 para. 3 SIGHIA).

In the treatment of those who cannot be treated in the country, SSI will cover all expenses made abroad. However, this amount shall not exceed the amount paid to the contracted healthcare providers of SSI abroad, if any (art. 66 para. 6 SIGHIA).

22.3 Other Health-Related Aids

22.3.1 *Travel Expenses and Daily Expenses*

If the treatment of the general health insured or dependent is not possible where they are located, they are referred to the nearest relevant health unit. In this case, SSI shall cover the travel expenses and daily expenses of the insured person and his/her dependents. SSI is authorized to provide the transportation services of the persons in question by procedures such as purchase and lease of services, if deemed necessary (art. 65 para. 1 SIGHIA).

22.3.2 *Companion Expense*

If a companion is appointed during the transfer of insured persons and dependents, the companion's travel expenses and daily expenses shall be borne by SSI. However, the number of companions is limited to one (art. 65 para. 1 SIGHIA).

In addition, if the doctor or dentist in the inpatient treatment considers the medical companion as necessary, the bed and food expenses are covered by SSI, limited to one person (art. 65 para. 2 SIGHIA).

22.3.3 *Determination of Travel, Bed and Food Expenses*

The travel, bed, food and daily expenses to be paid due to the referrals made in the country or abroad are determined by the "*health services cost review commission*" (art. 65 para. 3 and art. 72 SIGHIA).

22.4 Health Services Outside the Scope

22.4.1 *Aesthetic Health Services*

All kinds of health services and orthodontic dental treatments for aesthetic purposes are excluded from the scope of health services to be provided by SSI. However, aesthetic interventions to be carried out in order to ensure the integrity of the body and occurring due to occupational accident, occupational disease, accidents, diseases or congenital causes are included in the scope of health services to be provided (art. 64 para. 1/a SIGHIA).

As a criterion here, the existence of non-functional and only aesthetic interventions for external appearance should be taken as basis. On the other hand, situations which constitute a mental problem or which require the aesthetic intervention in terms of the work of the insured should be covered.[6]

22.4.2 *Unauthorized or Unlicensed Health Services*

Traditional, complementary, alternative medicine practices, health services not authorized or licensed by the Ministry of Health and health services that are not considered to be medical services by the Ministry of Health are excluded (art. 64 para. 1/b SIGHIA). In this context, services such as treatment with Botox, laser, animals such as leech and fish or with electromagnetic field in beauty centres are excluded.[7]

22.4.3 *Chronic Diseases of Foreigners*

Chronic diseases of foreign citizens that existed before the date on which they are deemed general health insured or deemed to be dependents are excluded (art. 64 para. 1/c SIGHIA).

References

Güzel A, Okur AR, Caniklioğlu N (2020) Sosyal Güvenlik Hukuku, 18th edn. Beta Publishing, Istanbul

Sözer AN (2018) Türk Genel Sağlık Sigortası, 2nd edn. Beta Publishing, Istanbul

[6]Sözer (2018), pp. 240–241.

[7]Sözer (2018), p. 242.

Chapter 23
Benefiting from Health Services

23.1 Paying a Certain Amount of Premiums

The rate of premium to be paid to benefit from the general health insurance is 12.5% of the premium earnings for insured workers, independent workers, public officials and insured taken to countries where there is no social security contract with Turkey for employment. 5% of this is paid by the insured and 7.5% by the employer (art. 81 para. 1/f SIGHIA).

This rate is 5% for apprentices and students in vocational training in businesses and 4.5% for trainees (art. 81 para. 1/d SIGHIA).

The rate of general health insurance premiums is 12% for those with optional insurance and those who receive unemployment allowance, short time working allowance or compensation job loss (art. 81 para. 1/f SIGHIA).

For lawyer interns, this rate is 6%, and the Turkish Bar Association pays the premiums (art. 60 para. 8 SIGHIA).

It is also foreseen that the State will contribute in terms of premiums. Accordingly, the State shall make contributions to SSI by one fourth of the general health insurance premium collected by SSI per month. The amount to be calculated as the Treasury shall pay State contribution to SSI within 15 days following the request date (art. 81 para. 3 SIGHIA).

23.2 Premium Payment of a Certain Amount

23.2.1 Those Where Premium Conditions Are Not Sought

Health aids provided by SSI are made to:

- Those under 18 years of age,
- Those medically in need of someone else's care,

T. Centel, *Turkish Social Law*, https://doi.org/10.1007/978-3-030-64704-9_23

- In traffic accidents,
- In emergencies,
- In cases of occupational accidents and diseases,
- In cases of contagious diseases mandatory to be notified,
- In preventive health services,
- In maternity health services,
- In cases of general disasters,
- In cases of mobilization and war,
- In cases of strikes and lockouts,

Where premium conditions are not sought. However, health care expenses incurred by SSI in cases of disaster or war are transferred to SSI within one year from the general budget (art. 75 SIGHIA).

23.2.2 Those Where 30-Day Premium Is Sought

In order to benefit from general health insurance, as a rule, the insured must have paid a total of 30 days of general health insurance premiums within one year prior to the date of application to health care providers. However, exceptionally, it is seen that this condition is not sought in those receiving income or allowance from SSI and those with low earnings, wages and incomes (art. 67 para. 1/a SIGHIA).

23.2.3 Those Who Should Not Have More Than 60 Days of Premium Debt

In order for the headmen and self-employed individuals to benefit from the general health insurance, they should not have more than 60 days of general health insurance premium debts to SSI (art. 67 para. 1/b SIGHIA).

23.2.4 Those Who Should Not Have Any Premium Debt

In order for optional insured persons, foreigners with residence permits and residing in Turkey for a year and foreign university students to benefit from the universal health insurance, they should not have any premium debts or debts related to premiums at the time they apply to health service providers (art. 67 para. 1/c SIGHIA).

23.3 Identification Declaration

General health insured persons and their dependents are obliged to declare their identity when they apply to health care providers, except for emergencies (art. 6 para. 3 SIGHIA).

The reason for the identity declaration is to prevent the general health insured or their dependents from receiving unfair health aids from SSI.[1] Accordingly, health care providers are obliged to obtain documents from the concerned person during the delivery of health services to the general health insured and their dependents or after the end of the emergency situation in emergency cases and to check whether these documents belong to the applicant (art. 71 para. 1 SIGHIA).

It is forbidden for someone else to obtain health services instead of the general health insured and his/her dependent or to obtain unfair benefits from SSI. Otherwise, the damage suffered by SSI shall be compensated to the persons by twice the amount plus the legal interest, and penal provisions shall be applied for the concerned persons (art. 71 para. 2 SIGHIA).

23.4 Duration of Health Aids

Health aids begin with the acquisition of the title of the health insured directly or by registration and ends with the loss of this title. However, in some cases, it has been agreed that health aids will continue for a longer period. Accordingly, employees with employment contracts benefit from general health insurance for a period of 10 days after the date of the termination of their compulsory insurance (art. 67 para. 4 SIGHIA).

If the employees with employment contracts have 90 prior days of compulsory insurance within one year from the date of loss of insurance, they can benefit from health services, including their dependents, for 90 days from the date of loss of insurance (art. 67 para. 4 SIGHIA).

In addition, these persons will continue to be deemed as general health insured for periods not exceeding one month within a calendar year and free leave periods certified by their employers, in addition to the period of free leave within the annual leave, free maternity leave and other free leave periods (art. 67 para. 5 SIGHIA).

Finally, those who have graduated from high school or equivalent education, provided they are not over 20 years of age, and those who have graduated from higher education, provided they are not over 25 years of age, can benefit from health services for a period of two years from the day of graduation. Similarly, those who do military service as soldiers and officers may benefit from general health insurance for 30 days from the date of discharge (art. 67 para. 4 SIGHIA).

[1] Güzel et al. (2020), p. 816.

23.5 Health Care Costs

The determination of the costs to be paid for health services is left to a central system in the Turkish legal system. According to this, the method of determining these costs by themselves, instead of the institutions that provide services for service costs, is accepted. The task is carried out by the "*health services cost review commission*" (art. 72 SIGHIA).

23.6 Provision of Health Services

23.6.1 Health Care Providers

Private or public institutions in or out of the country, which SSI has a contract with, carry out health services. Apart from that, in case of emergencies, services can be purchased from non-contracted health institutions.[2] Accordingly, the function of SSI is to provide the payment of health care costs for the general health insured person or his/her dependents in accordance with the law (art. 73 para. 1 SIGHIA).

23.6.2 Changes in Health Care Service Costs According to the Providers

23.6.2.1 In Terms of Private Health Care Providers

For contracted private health care providers (including foundation universities) other than public health care providers, the President of the State has been authorized to determine the additional cost upper limit up to one time the amount, in addition to costs and subsidies and the costs determined by the cost review commission. SSI will determine the additional costs to be received within the said upper limit (art. 73 para. 2 SIGHIA).

23.6.2.2 In Terms of Public Health Care Providers

Public health care providers charging additional costs are essentially not accepted. However, exceptionally, charging additional costs in hotel services, namely in inpatient treatment, for bed, food and cleaning and similar services provided for the patient and his/her companion above the standards determined by SSI is accepted. Again, extras can be charged for health services offered to faculty

[2] Sözer (2018), pp. 108–109.

members in public administration and foundation university health care providers. On the other hand, SSI may determine an upper limit for the additional costs to be charged for the faculty members (art. 73 para. 3 SIGHIA).

23.6.2.3 In Terms of Exceptional Health Services

A group that gives importance to the quality of the service has been formed under the name of "*exceptional health services*" in the cost changes in health services. According to this, contracted health care providers may receive additional costs not exceeding three times the specified costs for normal services, taking into account vitality and the availability of alternative treatments, for services that meet the requirements above the standards determined by SSI, such as hotel services (art. 73 para. 4 SIGHIA).

23.6.2.4 In Terms of Non-contracted Health Care Providers

Except for emergencies, SSI shall not pay the health care services purchased by persons from non-contracted health care providers (art. 73 para. 6 SIGHIA). The health service costs in case of emergencies will be paid in turn for invoice. In addition, non-contracted health care providers will not be able to request additional costs in emergencies (art. 73 para. 7 SIGHIA).

23.6.2.5 In Terms of Purchase of Health Care Services with Lump Sum Price

SSI may provide health services to be provided in public administrations through a service purchase contract over a lump sum price. If such a contract is made, public health service providers have to provide all kinds of health services to the concerned persons in exchange for the agreed lump sum. Except for this price, only additional costs and patient shares may be charged. In this case, no further invoice or document is required from the concerned person (art. 73 para. 8 SIGHIA).

23.7 Patient Share

23.7.1 Health Services Where Patient Share Will Be Charged

Health services where patient shares will be charged are foreseen as:

- Examination of doctors and dentists in outpatient treatment,
- Limb prostheses and orthotics

- Drugs provided in outpatient treatment,
- Health services financed in inpatient treatment according to the disease groups determined by SSI (art. 68 para. 1 SIGHIA).

The patient share was determined as 2 TL for the examination of the doctor and dentist in the outpatient treatment.

SSI will determine the patient share, between 10% and 20% for limb prostheses and orthotics and drugs provided for outpatient treatment. The Minister of Family, Labour and Social Services, is authorized to reduce the participation rate down to 1% on the offer of SSI (art. 68 para. 2 SIGHIA).

Finally, the patient share in artificial reproductive treatment will be applied as 30% for the first attempt, 25% for the second and 20% for the third (art. 68 para. 5 SIGHIA).

On the other hand, the patient share in limb prostheses and orthotics may not exceed 75% of the minimum wage. Likewise, the amount of patient share in inpatient treatment cannot exceed one-fourth of the minimum wage for each inpatient treatment, provided that it does not exceed the minimum wage amount in a calendar year (art. 68 para. 4 SIGHIA).

SSI is authorized to deduct the patient shares from the incomes or allowances of those receiving them and to deduct the wages or salaries of employees, or to collect them through pharmacies and other institutions and organizations and to determine the payment method of the patient shares. In this respect, the remaining amount after deducting the amount of patient share collected is paid to the contracted health service providers (art. 68 para. 6 SIGHIA).

23.7.2 *Not Charging Patient Share*

23.7.2.1 Conditions Where Patient Shares Will Not Be Charged

Occupational accident, occupational disease, military drills and manoeuvres and disaster and war situation are determined as cases where patient share will not be charged (art. 69 para. 1/a-b SIGHIA).

23.7.2.2 Health Care Services Where Patient Shares Will Not Be Charged

Health care services where patient shares will not be charged are listed as:

- Personal preventive health services,
- Family doctor examinations,
- Organ, tissue and stem cell transplantation,
- Vital orthotics, prosthesis and healing tools and equipment,
- Chronic diseases determined by SSI and based on report,

- Control examinations (art. 69 para. 1/c-d-e SIGHIA).

23.7.2.3 Persons from Whom Patient Shares Will Not Be Charged

Persons from whom patient shares will not be charged are sorted as:

- Those receiving honorary pensions and their spouses,
- Those receiving national service pensions,
- Those receiving cash compensation and allowances and their dependents,
- Those who benefit freely from protection, care and rehabilitation services,
- Those receiving a duty disability allowance,
- Those receiving a war disability pension and their dependents,
- Those receiving pensions in accordance with the Anti-Terror Act and their dependents,
- Military students and those in basic military training as non-commissioned officers,
- Students studying under the General Directorate of Security,
- Those injured in the fight against terrorism and who are under treatment until their treatment is completed or the injuries are finalized.

23.7.3 Return of Patient Share

Those with low incomes, those with an application or status for international protection, stateless persons, those who are over 65 and are paid allowances due to their in need status and their dependents will pay the patient shares at first, but if they so wish later, they will be able to withdraw their patient share (art. 68 para. 5 SIGHIA).

This regulation on the return of the patient share is not practical or logical. Because, these persons are already in need and have a limited income. Charging these people and then returning their payment does not go beyond making them go through unnecessary procedures.[3]

23.8 Service Grading and Referral Chain

It is foreseen that the Ministry of Health as first, second and third grades will grade health service providers. SSI determines the referral chain between these grades and the health service providers with the opinion of the Ministry of Health. In this

[3]Güzel et al. (2020), p. 825.

context, family physicians are included in the first-grade care providers (art. 70 para. 1 SIGHIA).

General health insured and dependents are obliged to act in accordance with the referral chain (art. 70 para. 2 SIGHIA). In case of non-compliance with the referral chain, the costs of health services, SSI does not cover travel expenses, daily expenses and companion expenses.[4]

23.8.1 Official Health Care Institutions

23.8.1.1 First Grade Official Health Care Institutions

These are the first-grade health institutions affiliated to the Ministry of Health, institutional hospitals within public administrations, emergency health service unit (112), medico-social units of universities, first grade health care units of Turkish Armed Forces and polyclinics belonging to municipalities.

23.8.1.2 Second Grade Official Health Care Institutions

Public hospitals and branch hospitals without education and research hospitals, district polyclinics affiliated to these hospitals, integrated district state hospitals, oral and dental health centres affiliated to the Ministry of Health, hospitals of the Turkish Armed Forces without education and research hospitals, hospitals belonging to municipalities, medical centres and branch centres of public institutions and *Istanbul Darülaceze Hospital*[5] are among the second grade official health care institutions.

23.8.1.3 Third Grade Official Health Care Institutions

These are education and research hospitals affiliated to the Ministry of Health and private education and research hospitals, district polyclinics, university hospitals and health practice and research centres connected to these hospitals, institutes, dentistry faculties of universities, medical school hospital and education and research hospitals of Turkish Armed Forces.

[4]Sözer (2018), p. 275.

[5]"*Darülaceze*" is a home for poor, homeless, handicapped people and homeless children located in Istanbul.

23.8.2 Private Health Care Institutions

Inpatient and outpatient treatment institutions established by natural or legal persons and mineral springs and hot springs for treating patients that are given permission by the Ministry of Health are considered as private health institutions.[6]

23.8.2.1 First Grade Private Health Care Institutions

Workplace hospitals, centres and units that offer home care services, private poly-clinics and private health institutions that provide oral and dental health services are among the first- grade private health care institutions.

23.8.2.2 Second Grade Private Health Care Institutions

Private hospitals and private medical centres are between the second-grade private health care institutions.

23.8.3 Non-gradable Health Care Institutions

Dialysis centres, imaging centres, laboratories, optician institutions, suppliers of medical devices and supplies and hot springs are within the scope of non-gradable health care institutions.

23.9 Provision of Health Care Services

23.9.1 Additional Costs in Health Care Facilities

23.9.1.1 Additional Costs in Non-public Health Care Institutions

For non-public health care institutions, charging additional costs is granted and the authority to determine the upper limit for these costs was left to the President of the State. He/she will carry out this determination by taking into account the expenses of health care providers, the cost of health services and the subsidies made (art. 73 para. 2 SIGHIA).

[6]*See*: Sözer (2018), pp. 102–105.

23.9.1.2 Additional Costs in Public Health Service Providers

As a rule, public health service providers cannot charge additional costs. However, it is seen that there are three basic exceptions, namely hotel service, faculty member cost and exceptional health service (art. 73 para. 3 SIGHIA).

23.9.2 Determination of Additional Costs

Contracted health service providers are obliged to inform SSI of the health services prices determined within the upper limits determined for the additional costs within 30 days after the publication of the determined health service costs. Changes to these prices will be notified to the Institution within five working days. These prices, even if they are in accordance with the upper limit, cannot be increased before the period determined by SSI (art. 73 para. 4 SIGHIA).

23.9.3 Conditions Where Additional Costs Will Not Be Charged

23.9.3.1 Persons from Whom Additional Costs Will Not Be Charged

No additional costs will be charged from persons receiving honorary pensions and some public officials receiving compensation for injury, disability or death during their duty, and those receiving war disability allowance, and those receiving compensation under the fight against terrorism and their dependents.

23.9.3.2 Services for Which Additional Costs Will Not Be Charged

Services for which additional costs will not be charged are shown as:

- Emergency health services provided due to emergencies,
- Intensive care services,
- Burn treatment services,
- Treatment of cancer within the scope of radiotherapy, chemotherapy and radioisotope treatments,
- Health services to new-borns,
- Organ, tissue and stem cell transplantations,
- Health services for surgical procedures for birth-related anomalies,
- Dialysis treatments,
- Cardiovascular surgical procedures.

23.9.4 *Health Service Providers*

23.9.4.1 Announcement of Health Service Providers

The titles, names and addresses of contracted health service providers who are to be applied by the general health insured and their dependents to benefit from the health services shall be announced by SSI in electronic environment or by other means (art. 77 para. 1 SIGHIA).

General health insured persons and their dependents have the right to choose among these announced contracted health service providers (art. 77 para. 2 SIGHIA).

23.9.4.2 Obligations of Health Service Providers

Health service providers that have contracted with SSI shall send the information about the persons they serve to SSI within a certain period of time by following the determined methods. Which information will be requested and which method will be used to send which ones will be shown in the contract to be made between SSI and the service provider. The health service costs to be requested without sending this information will not be paid until the information is sent (art. 78 para. 1 SIGHIA).

On the other hand, confidentiality is essential during the provisions and execution of health services. Everyone who will work in health services must follow this basis, which is the basis of medical ethics. As a matter of fact, it is foreseen that the health information of the general health insured and the dependents will be kept confidential (art. 78 para. 2 SIGHIA).

References

Güzel A, Okur AR, Caniklioğlu N (2020) Sosyal Güvenlik Hukuku, 18th edn. Beta Publishing, Istanbul

Sözer AN (2018) Türk Genel Sağlık Sigortası, 2nd edn. Beta Publishing, Istanbul

Part VII
Complementary Social Security Institutions

Chapter 24
Charity Funds

24.1 Eregli Coal Workers' Fund

24.1.1 Establishment of "Labour Union"

24.1.1.1 Acceptance of Act No. 151

Act No. 151[1] dated 10/9/1921, adopted before the proclamation of the Republic and one of the two major laws regarding labour in this period, addressed the working conditions of mine workers in the *Zonguldak Eregli* coal basin. Art. 4 Act No. 151 has foreseen that the accumulated and charity funds to be established by the workers would provide cash aids not less than one percent of all salaries of the workers employed by the mine employers.

Following the adoption of this law, a "*labour union*" was established in the coal basin and the establishment of a workers' charity fund was provided in each coal basin in accordance with the regulation put into effect by the decree dated 4/8/1923.[2] Afterwards, these charity funds were gathered under the roof of *Eregli Coal Basin Union Accumulated and Charity Fund*, and this fund was later included in the organizations of the Ministry of Labour and Social Security (art. 30 para. 1/b Act No. 3146).

The fund is still in the form of a fund that is established to provide economic and social aids to its members; it still possesses its administrative and financial self-regulation and legal entity and is an affiliate of the Ministry of Family, Labour and Social Services (art 1 and art. 4 para. 1 Eregli Fund Bylaw).

[1] http://www.mevzuat.gov.tr/Metin1.Aspx?MevzuatKod=1.3.151&MevzuatIliski=0&sourceXmlSearch=&Tur=1&Tertip=3&No=151.

[2] Şen (2007), p. 79; Yurtoğlu (2016), p. 218.

T. Centel, *Turkish Social Law*, https://doi.org/10.1007/978-3-030-64704-9_24

24.1.1.2 Making of the Regulation Regarding Health Needs

Art. 6 Act No. 151 have obliged all miners to have a hospital, pharmacy and physician in the vicinity of the mine basin to ensure that all workers and patients injured by accident receive free treatment. In accordance with the provisions of the aforementioned law, a regulation has been enacted to meet the hygienic needs of the workers working in the mines in Eregli coal basin.[3]

Prov. art. 16 Act No. 506, which was later adopted in 1965, accepted that the illness insurance provisions would be implemented starting from the date to be determined by the Council of Ministers for the places where Act No. 151 was applied.

In addition, art. 113 Act No. 506 has foreseen that the provisions of art. 6 Act No. 151 would not be applied to the treatment of the insured persons who work and get ill in the places where the provisions regarding the illness insurance are applied.

In this context, the Council of Ministers decided to apply the provisions regarding the illness insurance from 15/10/1975 in the places where Act No. 151 is applied.[4] Thus, the provisions of Act No. 151 and the provisions made based on it, which had previously provided the health care needs of approximately 40.000 mine workers and their spouses and their children, have continued to exist as an organization which, after this date, provides additional rights to the coal workers in the Eregli coal basin.[5]

24.1.1.3 Making of the Fund Bylaw

Today, a new fund regulation has been adopted (art. 4 Act No. 151), which replaces the previous regulations and regulates the management, operation and aids of the Fund.[6] Many issues not detailed in Act No. 151 have been addressed in this latest regulation, issued after the three previous regulations.

24.1.2 Members of the Fund

24.1.2.1 Compulsory Members

All workers employed in workplaces within the boundaries of the coal basin of the General Directorate of the Turkish Hard Coal Institution and the 5th Regional Directorate of the General Directorate of Turkish Electricity Transmission

[3] OG 25.8.1942, No. 5193.

[4] OG 10.9.1975, No. 15352.

[5] Şen (2007), p. 83; Tunçomağ (1990), pp. 51–52.

[6] OG 21.3.2000, No. 23996.

Corporation, workers assigned elsewhere for any reason while working in these workplaces and workers whose employment contracts are temporarily suspended due to their involvement in the management bodies of workers' organizations all must be members of the Fund (art. 6 para. 1/a Eregli Fund Bylaw).

24.1.2.2 Optional Members

Persons who leave compulsory membership for any reason and without receiving their last aids may become optional members. They cannot leave the membership unless six months have passed since the date of membership and may not be a member of the fund again if they leave (art. 6 para. 1/b Eregli Fund Bylaw).

24.1.3 Structuring of the Fund

The structure of the fund consists of an advisory board, central board, branch boards and a supervisory board (art. 7 Eregli Fund Bylaw). Of these, the central board is the decision-making body of the fund and carries the highest authority and responsibility for the management of the fund. As a matter of fact, all procedures of the fund shall be carried out by the central board, which shall consist of a chairman appointed by the Ministry of Family, Labour and Social Services for a period of three years, a member appointed by the same ministry within the ministry and one employee representative and one employer representative for each branches (art. 15 Eregli Fund Bylaw).

24.1.4 Incomes of the Fund

Incomes of the fund consist of:

- Membership fees,
- Incomes from movable and immovable properties,
- Incomes from investments, partnerships and management,
- Aids made by the State,
- Donations and aids by natural and legal persons,
- Incomes to be passed to the fund as a result of the absence of legal heirs of deceased members,
- And other incomes (art. 28 Eregli Fund Bylaw).

24.1.5 *Membership Fees*

24.1.5.1 Amount of Membership Fees

The membership fee is 3% of the gross wage of the member. The worker and 1% by the employer cover 2% of it. The fees of optional members are the amount to be found by adding the employer's fee to the average employee fee determined in the account of the fees income in the fund budget (art. 29 Eregli Fund Bylaw).

24.1.5.2 Payment of Membership Fees

The workplaces of compulsory members are obliged to deduct the fees to be calculated over the monthly gross wages of the members they employ within one month and add the employer's share to this amount and pay it to the fund until the end of the seventh day following the deduction (art. 30 para. 1 Eregli Fund Bylaw). A legal interest shall be applied to the collection of unpaid fees within time (art. 30 para. 3 Eregli Fund Bylaw).

Optional members pay their fees by the end of the current month. The membership of the optional member who does not pay fees for three consecutive months will be terminated, except for cases of force majeure (art. 30 para. 4 Eregli Fund Bylaw).

24.1.6 *Aids by the Fund*

24.1.6.1 Temporary Incapacity Allowance

Members given a rest report due to a disease and members who are not entitled to legal temporary incapacity allowance, although they do not have the capacity to work, and receive no payment from their institutions are given "*temporary incapacity allowance*". However, the duration of such aid may not exceed six months, albeit intermittently (art. 39 para. 1/a Eregli Fund Bylaw).

The amount of temporary incapacity allowance is the amount to be calculated by multiplying the duration of temporary incapacity by the allowance coefficient and the allowance indicator (30 if the member is married, 15 if single) (art. 39 para. 1/b Eregli Fund Bylaw). The allowance coefficient here is found by dividing the fund in the balance sheet of the most recent year by the total number of days of the total premium payment of all members of the fund (art. 5 para. 1/d Eregli Fund Bylaw).

The temporary incapacity allowances up to one month shall be paid in cash and in one payment, and the temporary incapacity allowance over a month shall be paid by the presidency of the fund by dividing into parts for each month (art. 39 para. 1/c Eregli Fund Bylaw).

24.1.6.2 Support to Health Services

The fund may provide support by providing medical equipment, patient clothing, bedstead and bed aids and arranging and laying of patient room to the official health institutions within the boundaries of the coal basin and by establishing martyrdom, memorial and museum related to mining or participating in the maintenance and repair of existing ones. For these aids, up to 1.5% of the fund revenues are allocated as allowances (art. 40 Eregli Fund Bylaw).

24.1.6.3 Final Pay

If the membership of the fund member is terminated for any reason, a "*final pay*" is made by the amount found by multiplying the total number of fees paid by the member with the allowance coefficient. The final pay to be calculated in the event of death of the fund member is paid to the legal heirs of the member (art. 41 paras 1 and 2 Eregli Fund Bylaw).

In case of the member who received their final pay starts working again, the final pay received by the fund is returned with the legal interest within one year from the date of recruitment, and the previous membership rights are restored. Otherwise, one will need to make procedures as a new member (art. 41 para. 4 Eregli Fund Bylaw).

24.1.6.4 Educational Allowance

Members of the fund, members whose employment contract is terminated due to a disability at a rate of 80% or above and the children in higher education of deceased members shall receive monthly and unpaid "*educational allowance*" at an amount found by multiplying the educational allowance indicator (22 in open education, 75 in others), with the allowance coefficient (art. 42 Eregli Fund Bylaw).

24.1.6.5 Burial Allowance

A "*burial allowance*" is made to the member, if a family member or mother or father of the member of the fund dies and to the legal heirs if the member dies. Burial allowance is the amount to be found by multiplying the allowance coefficient with the allowance indicator (1.200 in the death of the member and 181 in the death of the family member) (art. 43 Eregli Fund Bylaw.).

24.1.6.6 Occupational Accident Allowance

If a member of the fund or a staff of the fund is disabled beyond capacity to work in the event of an occupational accident in the course of their duties, an "*occupational accident allowance*" is paid on the basis of the amount found by multiplying the allowance coefficient with the indicator number (4.500), to the member in case of disability and to the legal heirs in case of death (art. 44 Eregli Fund Bylaw).

24.2 Charity Fund of Primary School Teachers

"*Primary School Teachers Health and Social Assistance Fund*", "*ILKSAN*" in short, is a complementary institution established in 1943 by Act No. 4357[7] aiming to provide additional social security assurance for primary school teachers. Membership to the aforementioned fund, which has a legal entity but is affiliated with the Ministry of National Education, was initially compulsory but was made optional on 1/6/2012.

24.2.1 Income Sources of the Fund

Incomes of the fund are composed of the monthly membership fees, donations and state aids, incomes from the management of the fund and the rent and operating incomes of the fund institutions (art. 11 para. 4 Act No. 4357).

24.2.2 Bodies of the Fund

24.2.2.1 Board of Representatives

The board of representatives consists of representatives to be elected from among them by considering the number of members in the provinces. The board is renewed every four years and has duties such as selecting the members of the board of directors and reviewing and releasing the study reports.

[7] OG 19.1.1943, No. 5308.

24.2.2.2 Board of Directors

The board of directors of the fund consists of seven members, three elected by the board of representatives, one member of the Ministry of National Education and the other three members are selected from persons with expertise in fields such as banking, law and finance. The term of office of the members of the board of directors is two years and they are responsible for the management of the fund in line with its purposes and duties.

24.2.2.3 Supervisory Board

It consists of three persons elected for a two-year term from the board of representatives.

24.2.2.4 General Manager

The general manager of the fund is elected from among the members of the board of directors of the fund.

24.2.3 Aids for the Members

24.2.3.1 Retirement Allowance

Retirement allowance is a one-off assistance for those retiring who have paid fees for at least 120 months. The amount is calculated by taking into account the total fees paid by the member.

24.2.3.2 Disability Allowance

Disability allowance is an aid provided to those who are disabled when they are members of the fund, regardless of their membership period, based on the incapacity report. The amount of this allowance is determined according to the principles of retirement allowance calculation.

24.2.3.3 Death Allowance

The death allowance is an aid that is paid to the heirs of the deceased who is a member of the fund and is determined according to the principles of the retirement allowance calculation, regardless of the membership period.

24.3 The Law Enforcement Fund

24.3.1 Establishment of the Police Care and Assistance Fund

The past of the "*Police Care and Assistance Fund*", "*POLSAN*" in short, is based on the 2nd Constitutional period. The fund was officially established in 1913 with the "*Police and Police Officers' Savings Fund Regulation*", which included issues such as the establishment, organs, lending principles, the assistance to be made, and the supervision of transactions, the partnership fees and revenues of the fund. Then, with the "*Regulation on Police Care and Assistance Fund*" dated 5/9/1951, based on art. 90 Law Enforcement Act No. 3201, the previous regulation in 1913 was abolished and the previous Police and Police Officers' Savings Fund was transferred to a new fund with its assets and liabilities. Finally, the 1951 Regulation, which was unable to respond to the economic conditions and the common needs of today, was abolished by the Regulation dated 4/8/1998 and a new structuring process was initiated, and modern organization was enabled.[8]

24.3.2 Social Security Aids of the Fund

24.3.2.1 Retirement Allowance

Retirement allowance can be obtained after a minimum of three years of fund partnership.

24.3.2.2 Disability Allowance

In case of any loss of income that may arise due to disability or death that may be incurred in or outside of their duties, the partners shall have the opportunity for allowances to compensate the loss of income for themselves and/or their families. Accordingly, disability allowance is made for those who have at least one year of partnership (in case of disability due to accident, the one year is not required).

24.3.2.3 Death Allowance

Death allowance is paid to the legal heirs of the deceased partner and to the partner himself/herself whose spouse or dependent child is deceased.

[8]https://www.polsan.com.tr/index.php/kurumsal/tarihce.

24.4 Additional Funds

Special funds called "additional funds" are in the state of "*charity funds*" providing additional social security. However, some of these are legally established pension funds, and another part is considered to be in the "*foundation*" status. In this respect, although both are called additional funds, they must be distinguished from each other.

24.4.1 Funds of Banks and Insurance Companies

24.4.1.1 Obtaining the Qualification for a Pension Fund Established by Law

In the past, some banks, insurance and reinsurance companies, chambers of commerce and industry and the associations have established special funds in the form of foundations to provide assistance in cases of disability, old age and death of the personnel working there. These funds provided social security to the employees working there until 1964, when *Social Insurance Act* No. 506 was adopted. The majority of the people covered by these funds are white-collar workers who were excluded from the scope of LA No. 3008 which was effective at that time.

Prov. art. 20 Social Insurance Act, adopted in 1964, allowed these funds to maintain their existence and to remain outside the scope of the Social Insurance Act, taking into account some of the characteristics of these funds, provided they meet certain conditions. According to this, provided that banks, insurance and reinsurance companies, chambers of commerce, chambers of industry, stock exchanges or the associations they established provide assistance in the event of disability, old age and death, and funds established as foundations or associations before the date of publication of the Social Insurance Act (29/7/1964) submit to the Ministry of Labour and Social Security, in the following six months from the date of publication of the Social Insurance Act, that they have become foundations that will:

- Include all personnel of the bank, insurance company, reinsurance company, chamber of commerce, chamber of industry, stock exchange or their association,
- Provided the assistance specified in the Social Insurance Act to the personnel in the case of work accidents, occupational diseases, illness, maternity, disability, old age and death and maternity of spouses, diseases of spouses and children,
- Transfer the acquired rights to the other fund if the personnel subject to the status of the fund are transferred to another fund,

Along with a certification documenting this, it is foreseen that the personnel of these funds shall not be insured in the implementation of the Social Insurance Act, so the provisions in the status of the funds shall be applied to these personnel (prov. art. 20 para. 1 Act No. 506).

The status and status changes of these funds, in practice referred to as "*fund subject to the Provisional Article 20*" in short, have been subject to the approval of the Ministry of Labour and Social Security. The financial statuses of these funds are also under the joint control and inspection of the ministry of family, labour and social services and the ministries of finance and trade. These funds and their organizations are obliged to fulfil the necessary measures to be taken at the end of the control and inspection of their financial conditions (prov. art. 20 para. 2 Act No. 506).

24.4.1.2 Developments Related to the Transfer of Funds

The status of the funds of banks and insurance companies is considered to be incompatible with the principle of "*collecting social security institutions under a single roof*".[9]

On top of that, firstly, an additional article has been added to Social Insurance Act with Act No. 1992, and it is foreseen that these funds will be transferred to the Social Insurance Institution. However, Constitutional Court annulled this amendment.[10]

Then, Banking Act[11] decided to transfer fund members receiving disability, old age or death allowances and their right holders to SSI within three years with their assets and liabilities (prov. art. 23). Note that this regulation did not affect the legal entities of the existing funds and required the transfer of only the participants.

SIGHIA, replacing Social Insurance Act after the social security reform activities, was added a new provisional article by Act No. 5754[12] in 2008, and it was foreseen that the funds of banks and insurance companies would be transferred to SSI within three years, and the previous prov. art. 23 Banking Act has been abolished (art. 106 and prov. art. 20 para. 1 SIGHIA). The three-year period here was extended in 2011, 2013 and 2014, by 2, 1 and again 1 years, respectively, with the decisions of the Council of Ministers. Finally, with the amendment made to prov. art. 20 para. 1 SIGHIA by the Act No. 6645 in 2015, it was stated that the Council of Ministers (currently, President of the State) was authorized to determine the date of the transfer, and the transfer of the funds of banks and insurance companies to SSI was postponed to an uncertain date.

Considering the significant financial burden that the funds of banks and insurance companies will bring to SSI, it can be said that the political will and intentions related to the transfer of these funds are not seen at the moment. Essentially, the transfer of some of the economically difficult situated funds to SSI was carried out on different dates before. In particular, along with the operations to rescue some of the bankrupt banks, some of the funds belonging to their personnel have been transferred over to SSI over time.

---

[9]*See* also: Tuncay and Ekmekçi (2019), pp. 137–139.

[10]Constitutional Court, 25.1.1977, 1976-36/2, OG 9.5.1977, No. 15932.

[11]OG 1.11.2005, No. 25983.

[12]OG 8.5.2008, No. 26870.

24.4.1.3 Current Status of Funds

Their status has been adjusted to comply with prov. art. 20 Act No. 506, and the number of active private funds are still 17. Of these funds, banks, 6 by insurance companies and 1 by members of the Union of Chambers and Commodity Exchanges of Turkey owns 10. As of June 2020, the number of people affiliated with the funds in question reached 425.326 persons, including 140.736 insured, 94.624 pensioners and 189.966 dependents (spouses, children, parents).[13]

24.4.1.4 Legal Status of Funds

In the past, it has been controversial whether people who have received pensions from funds subject to prov. art. 20 Act No. 506 will receive pensions by benefiting from the Social Insurance Act. The unified decision of Court of Cassation on this issue resulted negatively, and it was decided that these persons could not receive extra pensions.[14] While Court of Cassation made the unified decision, it accepted that the funds subject to prov. art. 20 Act No. 506 were legally in the nature of "*retirement funds established by law*".

24.4.2 Charity Funds in the Status of Foundation

In practice, in the case of workers in banking and insurance sectors, some charity funds in the status of foundation, called "*additional funds*", are not subject to prov. art. 20 Act No. 506 and provide additional assistance to their members. However, there is no social security relationship between them and their members. Therefore, it has been accepted that the legal disputes between these funds and their members should be discussed in general courts rather than in labour courts.[15]

These charity funds, which are not established by the law and which are in the status of a foundation, first emerged as the funds of the banks and insurance companies established after the six-month period. In addition, it is seen that charity funds have been established in the status of foundations, with the concern that private funds will be transferred to the State or that they will not be able to perform their duties due to financial difficulties. The legal basis for all these charity funds in the status of foundations is constituted in Article 110 Turkish Civil Code and Article 522 TCC.

Accordingly, the executives of the charity foundations for workers and employees are obliged to provide the beneficiaries with the necessary information

[13]http://www.sgk.gov.tr/wps/portal/sgk/tr/kurumsal/istatistik/aylik_istatistik_bilgileri.

[14]CC, Plenary Session of Civ. Div., 23.6.1983, 1/1, OG 23.6.1983, No. 18086.

[15]CC, 10th Civ. Div., 24.3.2009, 11459/4800, Yargıtay Kararları Dergisi, 36/1 (2010), p. 57.

about the organization, operation and financial situation of the foundation (art. 110 para. 1 Turkish Civil Code). For beneficiaries to request the fulfilment of the performances of the foundation by means of litigation is bound to them paying fees or having recognized these rights by the provisions regulating the foundation (art. 110 para. 4 Turkish Civil Code).

On the other hand, art. 522 para. 1 TCC allows reserve funds to be separated in the company's master contract for the purpose of establishing aid organizations for the executives, employees and workers of the company or maintaining these or allocating them to the public legal entities carrying this purpose. Establishment of a foundation becomes mandatory by the leaving of these reserve funds specific to the purpose of aid (art. 522 para. 2 TCC).

In addition, if fees are received from executives, employees and workers, except for the reserve fund that the company is aiming for this purpose, then, if they cannot benefit from the distinction made according to the foundation voucher at the end of the employment relationship, at the least the amounts paid by the employees and workers will be returned to them with the statutory interest as of the payment date (art. 522 para. 3 TCC).

As a successful and powerful example of charity funds in the status of foundation in Turkey, it is possible to show the fund of the members of Turkey İş Bank. Accordingly, *"Turkey İş Bank Inc. Members Additional Social Security and Charity Fund Foundation"*, in short, the *"Additional Fund Foundation"*, is an additional social security foundation established in accordance with the provisions of the Turkish Civil Code to provide beneficiaries with social security and charity rights in addition to compulsory social security aids.[16]

Apart from this, although there are not sufficient and reliable data on their qualifications and capacities, there are many foundations of public institutions and organizations and private industries, which are complementary to social security in Turkey.[17] However, they cannot be said to be very powerful and effective.

24.5 Army Assistance Agency

"Army Assistance Agency", in short "*OYAK*", is a successful example of complementary vocational retirement funds in Turkey. As a matter of fact, the previous examples of civil servants' assistance institution (MEYAK) aimed to be established for civil servants, workers' assistance institution (IYAK) aimed to be established for workers and "*compulsory savings*" application[18] based on Act No. 3417, were not

[16]https://www.tibasvakfi.org.tr/TR/Sayfalar/hakkimizda.aspx.

[17]*See*: Alper et al. (2015), pp. 113–119 and 127–130.

[18]*See*: Alper et al. (2015), pp. 108–113.

successful in Turkey. The foundations of OYAK, in fact, date back to the *Military Loan Fund Regulation* dated 12/4/1911.[19]

On the other hand, in addition to the assistance and services it provides to its members, OYAK has substantially contributed to Turkey's economy with its participants in various sectors and continues to do so.

In addition, OYAK has been an institutional supportive member of *Pensions Europe*, which has been working to ensure that pension funds in Europe offer sustainable and safer retirement benefits since 2003.[20]

24.5.1 Establishment of OYAK by Law

As Turkey became a member of the United Nations in 1945 and of NATO in 1952 and joined the Korean War following those, members of the Turkish Armed Forces became aware of the social opportunities of their colleagues around the world. Then, works were started on what additional social security facilities would be for the members of the army, including housing, and in the years between 1957 and 1960, suggestions were made to establish a military aid organization. The present legal framework of OYAK is based on the *Army Assistance Agency Act* No. 205.[21]

24.5.2 Legal Nature of OYAK

OYAK is, in principle, in the status of a charity fund established by law and as such is an additional social security institution.[22] However, OYAK is not just a fund. As a matter of fact, OYAK, established as a complementary retirement fund with the participation of 65.000 members, focused on preparing a safer future for its members, which are now close to 306.000. In this respect, OYAK is one of the biggest groups of Turkey with its own companies. This development of OYAK is based on the economic activities in regard to the evaluation of funds.[23] The success of OYAK in its economic activities is mainly based on the fact that it stays loyal to the principle of professional management and follows the economic developments and makes the right investments at the right time.[24]

OYAK was established to be a member of the Ministry of National Defence and to provide social assistance to members of the Turkish Armed Forces. The agency is

---

[19]Alper et al. (2015), p. 139.

[20]http://www.oyak.com.tr/TR/kurumsal/oyak-nedir.html.

[21]OG 9.1.1961, No. 10702.

[22]Dilik (1991), p. 12.

[23]*See*: Alper et al. (2015), pp. 181–218.

[24]Alper et al. (2015), pp. 242–243.

subject to the provisions of private law and financially and administratively possesses its self-regulated legal entity (art. 1 Act No. 205).

However, OYAK is not subject to the hierarchical control or administrative tutelage of the Ministry of Defence or any other administrative institution. Accordingly, the Agency is not included in the central or provincial organizations of the Ministry of National Defence.

On the other hand, OYAK does not take a share from the general budget or the budgets of the social security institutions, nor is it a private budget organization that has been allocated by the government. In this sense, OYAK does not use public resources. Similarly, OYAK is not a commercial entity involved in defence industry activities and does not have a commercial relationship with the Turkish Armed Forces.

24.5.3 Structure of OYAK

OYAK's bodies consist of the board of representatives, the general assembly, the board of directors, the supervisory board and the general directorate (art. 2 Act No. 205).

Of these, the general manager is not the chairman of the board of directors; he/she is a natural member and has the right to vote in the decisions of the board of directors (art. 7 para. 2 Act No. 205). The general assembly and election committee elect other members of the board of directors (art. 8 paras 1 and 2 Act No. 205). The board of directors appoints general manager and his/her assistants (art. 14 para. 1 Act No. 205).

24.5.4 Exemptions Granted to OYAK

OYAK is not subject to corporation income tax. The donations to be made to the Agency and the assistance to be made by the Agency to members or legal heirs are exempt from inheritance tax and transfer tax. Similarly, any actions by the Agency are exempt from the stamp duties. In addition, deductions from permanent and temporary members are exempt from income tax (art. 35 Act No. 205).

On the other hand, all kinds of goods, revenues and receivables of the Agency benefit from the rights and priorities granted to the properties of the State. Those who commit crimes against them are subject to prosecution such as those who commit crimes against State properties (art. 37 Act No. 205).

24.5.5 *OYAK Members*

24.5.5.1 Permanent Members

All active officers, contracted officers, military officers, non-commissioned officers, contracted non-commissioned officers and expert gendarmes tasked in the Turkish Armed Forces, members of the retirement system and their spouses who wish to continue the system in case of death are permanent members of the Agency (art. 17 para. 1/a Act No. 205).

Expert officers and all salaried and paid civil servants and personnel working in the Ministry of National Defence, the General Command of the Gendarmerie or companies owning more than half of the capital of the Agency or those participating in it may become permanent members of the Agency if they so desire (art. 17 para. 1/b Act No. 205).

24.5.5.2 Temporary Members

The reserve officers who are serving their active duties are temporary members of the Agency (art. 17 para. 1/c Act No. 205).

24.5.6 *Revenues of the Agency*

24.5.6.1 Deductions

For active officers and non-commissioned officers, contracted officers and non-commissioned officers, expert gendarmes and expert officers, 10% deduction is made. For civil servants and contracted personnel working in the General Staff, the Ministry of National Defence, service commands, the General Command of the Gendarmerie and the Coast Guard Command staff, 10% deduction is made and 5% reserve officers (art. 18 para. 1/a Act No. 205).

The said rate of deduction is 10% of the wages of those who work in OYAK or companies owning more than half of OYAK or participating in it and who have accepted to be permanent members of OYAK (art. 18 para. 1/b Act No. 205).

Except for those who have died before 10 years of membership or during the period of deductions, permanent members who lose their membership are refunded their deductions. However, no deduction refund is made to the temporary members and members whose membership period is not more than three years (art. 23 para. 1 Act No. 205).

The accountants shall make the deductions during the payment of the salary or wages of the member. The depositors shall pay the deductions to the Agency or to the Agency bank account within a month. From those who do not accrue or deduct the deductions from the Agency and do not send them to the Agency within one month, these deduction amounts shall be collected as public receivables together with a 10% delay fee (art. 31 Act No. 205).

24.5.6.2 Operating Revenues

The revenues from the operation of the Agency's assets are included among the OYAK revenues (art. 18 para. 1/c Act No. 205).

24.5.6.3 Donations

Natural and legal persons can make any kind of donations in cash and in kind to the Agency. These donations constitute a quality of revenue for the Agency (art. 18 para. 1/d Act No. 205).

24.5.6.4 Additional Deductions

From those who are permanent members and who want to benefit from the housing pre-accumulation fund, 10% additional deductions are made. These are among the revenues of the Agency, like the other main deductions (art. 18 para. 1/e Act No. 205).

The accumulated additional deductions of the members participating in the housing pre-accumulation fund shall be paid together with the interest in case the membership of the Agency is terminated for any reason (art. 23 para. 2 Act No. 205).

24.5.7 Lump Sum Assistances to OYAK Permanent Members

The pensions and disability and death allowances made by OYAK have the quality of being paid to the members in case of retirement and disability and to the right holders in case of death, and are created in the working life by the members through compulsory savings and are increased by OYAK through management.[25]

24.5.7.1 Retirement Allowance

Permanent members whose memberships are terminated by leaving the organizations they are tasked in for any reason after having been a member of the Agency for at least 10 years benefit from retirement allowance (art. 21 para. 1 Act No. 205).

[25]Dilik (1991), p. 11.

Retirement allowance is the amount that is calculated over the 5% technical interest rate in the savings premium, in response to the period spent by the member in the Agency and the fees paid (art. 24 para. 1 Act No. 205).

24.5.7.2 Disability Allowance

Disability allowance is made in full and continuous or partial disability cases. In full disability, it should be determined whether the member is certainly deprived of the possibility of performing any work due to an accident, disease or disability, whether it occurs within or out of duties, with a health organization report. Partial disability is a continuous but partial disability due to an accident (art. 26 Act No. 205).

Full and continuous disability allowances are calculated as death allowances, that is, 12 times the final allowance (art. 26 para. 1/a 4 and art. 25 Act No. 205). In the partial disability allowance calculation, 12 times the amount of the last allowance will be taken into account and this amount will be multiplied by the disability rates. If the status of the partially disabled member deems him/her to be separated from his/her duty, the amount of retirement allowance accumulating until the date of departure will also be refunded (art. 26 para. 1/b 2-3 Act No. 205).

If the disability is not declared to the Agency in writing by the disabled member or any person related to him/her within one year of the date on which the disability is detected and within five years from the date of the occurrence of the event that caused the disability, the disability allowance request right will be foreclosed (art. 27 Act No. 205).

24.5.7.3 Death Allowance

The heirs of those who died as permanent members of the Agency are entitled to the death allowance (art. 22 Act No. 205). Accordingly, if the permanent member dies while paying fees to the Agency, 12 times the last received allowance amount will be paid as death allowance. In addition to this allowance, the member is granted retirement allowance by taking into account the period from the date of his/her involvement in the Agency to the date of his/her death (art. 25 para. 1 Act No. 205).

Death allowance is paid to the heirs of the deceased member in his/her declaration to the Agency in his/her lifetime (art. 25 para. 2 Act No. 205).

24.5.7.4 Housing Allowance

It is granted to those who want to benefit from the pre-accumulation housing fund and its usage and management procedures are determined by the general assembly of the Agency (art. 20 para. 1/a 4 Act No. 205).

On the other hand, the board of directors of the Agency has been authorized to establish "*pre-accumulation housing fund*" for the purpose of providing permanent members with house ownerships, to buy lands and build houses on these lands, or to sell immovable properties for this purpose in cash or mortgage for up to 20 years and to sell these to them in instalments and with interests (art. 33 para. 1/h Act No. 205).

24.5.8 Assistance to Temporary Members of OYAK

24.5.8.1 Disability Allowance

Disability allowance is valid for permanent members as well as temporary members. In this respect, the foregoing explanations on disability allowances to permanent members also apply to disability allowances to temporary members.[26]

24.5.8.2 Death Allowance

The heirs of those who die as temporary members of the Agency are entitled to the death allowance (art. 22 Act No. 205). Accordingly, if the temporary member dies during the period he/she pays fees to the Agency, 12 times the last received allowance is paid as death allowance. In addition to this allowance, the member is also given retirement allowance based on the period from the date of his/her involvement to the Agency until the date of death (art. 25 para. 1 Act No. 205).

Death allowance is paid to the heirs of the deceased member in his/her declaration to the Agency in his/her lifetime (art. 25 para. 2 Act No. 205).

24.5.9 Assistance to the Members of OYAK in the Pension System

24.5.9.1 Pension

Members who leave the institutions they are tasked in after being a member of the Agency for at least 10 years for any reason may, if they wish, be able to enter the pension system by leaving one-quarter, half, three-quarters or all of the retirement allowance to the Agency (art. 21 paras 1 and 2 Act No. 205).

Likewise, members who will have disability allowance may be able to enter the pension system by leaving one-quarter, half, three-quarters or all of the retirement allowance to the Agency (art. 21 para. 3 Act No. 205).

Again, the spouses or inheritors of those who have died while they were members of the Agency or have entered the retirement system are also entitled to participate in

[26] *See*: above Sect. 24.5.7.2.

the pension system (art. 21 paras 4 and 5 Act No. 205). However, if the member in the system dies, the spouse does not have the right to add the entitled death allowance to his/her reserve (art. 21 para. 7 Act No. 205).

The pension consists of 5% of the annual interest calculated according to the retirement allowance the member leaves to the Agency (art. 24 para. 3 Act No. 205).

Members who are in the pension system can leave by taking their reserves after three years of their entry into the system. However, those leaving the system will not be accepted again (art. 21 para. 8 Act No. 205).

24.5.9.2 Death Allowance

In case of death of the member entering the pension system, the legal heirs shall be paid a death allowance of 10 times the last monthly pension. However, in the event of death of the spouse of the deceased member entering the system while his/her membership continues, death allowance is not made to his/her legal heirs (art. 25 para. 3 Act No. 205).

References

Alper Y, Arıcı K, Özşuca ŞT, Aydın U, Gökbayrak Ş (2015) Tamamlayıcı Emeklilikte Bir Başarı Öyküsü: OYAK. İş Bankası Kültür Yayınları, İstanbul. No. 3298

Dilik S (1991) Sosyal Güvenlik Sistemi ve Ek Sosyal Güvenlik Kurumları. Kamu-İş İş Hukuku ve İktisat Dergisi 3(1):3–12

Şen M (2007) Tanzimat ve TBMM Hükümeti Döneminde Sosyal Güvenlik Hukuku Alanındaki Gelişmeler. In: Erzincan University Law School (ed) Atatürk'ün 125. Doğum Yılına Armağan, pp 55–85

Tuncay AC, Ekmekçi Ö (2019) Sosyal Güvenlik Hukuku Dersleri, 20th edn. Beta Publishing, Istanbul

Tunçomağ K (1990) Sosyal Güvenlik Kavramı ve Sosyal Sigortalar, 5th edn. Beta Publishing, Istanbul

Yurtoğlu N (2016) Türkiye'de Zonguldak-Ereğli Kömür Havzasının Yapısal Analizi (1920-1960). Çağdaş Türkiye Tarihi Araştırmaları Dergisi 16(33):211–256

Chapter 25
Private Pension System

25.1 The Place of Private Retirement in the Social Security System

25.1.1 Feature of the Private Retirement Fund System

The private retirement fund system in Turkey was put into effect as of 2001 with the *Private Pension Savings and Investment System Act* No. 4632.[1] This system, as a complement to the public social security system, aims to provide an additional income to individuals during retirement by directing their savings for retirement towards investment.[2] Thus, the welfare of the retired individual will be increased and at the same time, a long-term resource will be created to increase employment and contribute to the economy.[3]

The neo-liberalization movement has also shown its effects on Turkey in the past. In this sense, it has been observed that the private sector has started to be encouraged in social security along with the efforts of minimizing the State. The private retirement system has also emerged as a product of the transformation in question. Accordingly, with the private retirement system, individuals will not only expect the State to cover all expenses in retirement and will invest in their own future.[4] In this context, the private retirement system becomes an additional social security system established in accordance with voluntary participation and predefined contribution principles.

However, the creation of additional social security applies to those involved in any social insurance program. Because, to participate in the private retirement program, there is no obligation to participate in any program that provides basic

[1]OG 7.4.2001, No. 24366.

[2]Tuncay and Ekmekçi (2019), p. 756.

[3]Çımrın and Durdu (2015), p. 73.

[4]Çımrın and Durdu (2015), pp. 72–74.

T. Centel, *Turkish Social Law*, https://doi.org/10.1007/978-3-030-64704-9_25

(minimum) social security. In this sense, it is not clear whether the private retirement system is a basic social security program or an additional social security program.[5]

On the other hand, the private retirement fund system, which is closely related to a wide audience, is far from being subject to a comprehensive legal arrangement. In this sense, Act No. 4632 has been kept very narrow and, in fact, the regulation work within the scope has been left to secondary legislation. The bylaws, circulars and notifications contained in the secondary legislation reflect the discretion and preferences of the body of execution.[6]

25.1.2 Additional Retirement System Based on Voluntary Participation

The public social security system has three basic functions in terms of meeting social security needs. The first is to provide redistribution of income. As a matter of fact, national income is redistributed through social security from those who work and have income to those who cannot work and are in need. Another function of the public social security system is to cover the damages that may occur, for situations that are unpredictable or for which adequate measures cannot be taken, that is, to bear the insurance function. Finally, the public social security system abandons consumption to meet the desires of achieving a higher standard of living in the future, that is, to achieve a savings function.[7]

A public social security system based on purely insurance is not able to provide all three of these basic functions. In addition to this, in the face of the deterioration of the economic conditions and the decrease in the birth rate and the increase in the elderly population and in the face of the failure to terminate the resulting problems with temporary measures, the system has been in search of an additional system based on fund and providing additional retirement allowances to the social security systems. In this sense, the private (individual) retirement system, based on voluntary participation, provides an additional retirement income for individuals, as well as capital accumulation through retirement funds, and increases the national income and employment opportunities of the country.[8]

Accordingly, the individual retirement system is an additional system for public retirement programs as a result of the evaluation of funds by private companies working under the supervision and inspection of the public, which are composed of individual contributions based on voluntary participation, to provide an additional income to individuals in their old age regardless of whether they work or not.[9] Thus,

[5]Bayri (2013), p. 28.

[6]Ünan and Karayazgan (2009), p. 15.

[7]Alper (2002), p. 13.

[8]Gülver (2011), p. 17.

[9]*See*: Erol and Yıldırım (2004), p. 211; Uğur (2004), p. 16.

the individual retirement system is primarily under the responsibility of the individual, providing an assurance against the social risk of old age, and this assurance is provided by the individual's own savings.[10]

25.2 Institutional Structure of Private Retirement System

The public institution responsible for the functioning of the private retirement system is essentially the *Regulation and Audit Institution for Insurance and Private Pension* (art. 4 para. 1 PD No. 47). In addition, it is foreseen to establish the *Individual Retirement Advisory Board* and *Retirement Monitoring Centre* in order to determine the individual retirement policies and to make recommendations about the necessary measures to be taken for the realization of these policies and to take decisions about the legislative arrangements (arts 3 and 20/A PPA). Also, retirement companies and private retirement intermediaries are important elements of the institutional structure.

25.2.1 Individual Retirement Advisory Board

The individual retirement advisory board is responsible for determining the individual retirement policies and making recommendations on the measures to be taken for the realization of these (art. 3 para. 1 PPA).

25.2.2 Retirement Monitoring Centre

25.2.2.1 Structure of the Centre

The institution that will operate, as the retirement monitoring centre is a legal entity subject to the provisions of private law (art. 20/A PPA).

Retirement companies and insurance companies and other institutions and organizations operating in the life branch may become partners to the retirement monitoring centre. In order to ensure the fulfilment of the duties assigned to the retirement monitoring centre, the companies, institutions, organizations and persons within the scope of PPA are obliged to convey the requested information and documents completely and accurately (art. 20/A PPA).

[10]Gülver (2011), p. 18.

25.2.2.2 Duties of the Centre

The main duties of the centre include:

- Data collection based on surveillance, keeping records in electronic environment and ensuring data security,
- Retaining participant information and retirement contract information sent by retirement companies in electronic environment,
- Performing consolidation of private retirement accounts and funds,
- Preparing surveillance reports and forwarding them to the Ministry of Finance and Treasury,
- Notifying the Ministry of applications contradictory to the legislation and, if necessary, to the Capital Markets Board,
- Keeping records of companies' retirement plans.

25.2.3 Retirement Company

The retirement company means a company established according to PPA and established with PPA and is licensed in the retirement branch to operate in the private retirement system (art. 8 para. 1 PPA).

It is required for the retirement company to be established to fulfil the requirements of:

- Being established as a joint stock company,
- The scope of the activity being limited to the activities specified in the PPA,
- The company's capital being not less than 20 billion TL, the paid-in capital being at least 10 billion TL and the remainder being guaranteed to be paid within three years,
- The issuance of shares in cash and all of the shares being written in the persons' names,
- Compliance of the articles of association with PPA provisions,
- Issuing business plan, system design and feasibility reports,
- Founders having no shareholding in the institutions in liquidation, their activities not being suspended temporarily, not being condemned for certain crimes and having the financial power and reputation required for being a retirement company (art. 8 para. 4 PPA).

The bodies of the retirement company are composed of management and supervisory boards (art. 12 para. 1 PPA).

25.2.4 Individual Retirement Intermediaries

Individual retirement intermediaries refer to persons who mediate retirement contracts of retirement companies or who make them on behalf of the retirement company (art. 2 para. 1/l PPA).

Individual retirement intermediaries must be registered with the "*register of individual retirement intermediaries*" held by the Ministry of Finance and Treasury (art. 11 para. 2 PPA).

The individual retirement intermediary cannot collect money under the names of entrance, contribution or similar fees under any circumstance, cannot exchange money with the participants within the framework of the retirement contract, cannot perform transfers on behalf of the participant and cannot determine the rates of allocation of funds on behalf of the participant.[11]

25.2.5 Retirement Mutual Fund

Individual retirement operates on a capitalization basis as a financing method. In this sense, it is left to the "*retirement mutual fund*" to direct funds to investment and to create portfolio in the capital market. Accordingly, the retirement mutual fund is the assets in the form of a capital market institution which is acquired by the retirement company within the framework of the retirement contract and is established for the purpose of operating contributions that are monitored in the private retirement accounts on behalf of the participants, does not have a legal entity and cannot be established and used outside of the objectives stated in the PPA (art. 15 para. 1 PPA).

Retirement companies have to establish at least three funds with different portfolio structures with the permission of the *Capital Markets Board* (art. 17 para. 3 PPA). Accordingly, the company that obtains operating license in the retirement branch has to apply to the Capital Markets Board to establish at least three separate funds (art. 15 para. 2 PPA).

The fund bylaw is registered in the trade registry of the place where the retirement company's head office is located after it is approved by the Capital Markets Board and is then announced in the Turkish Trade Registry Gazette (art. 15 para. 3 PPA).

[11] *See*: Erol and Yıldırım (2004), p. 249; Gülver (2011), p. 34.

25.3 Participation in the Individual Retirement System

25.3.1 Acceptance of Voluntary Participation

The individual retirement system originally relied primarily on voluntary participation. In this respect, whether the person is insured or working in a job does not matter for the participation in the system. Accordingly, persons with a legal capacity can participate in the individual retirement system. Thus, all-natural persons who have the right to use civil rights have the right to participate in the individual retirement system provided that they sign a retirement contract with the retirement company and pay the foreseen contribution (art. 4 PPA).[12]

In addition, those who paid premiums to the permanent life insurances prior to the entry into force of PPA had the opportunity to participate in the individual retirement system by transferring their savings. For this purpose, life insurance companies have been given the opportunity to transform into retirement companies within five years (prov. art. 1 para. 2 PPA).

Likewise, it is foreseen that the amounts related to the savings and commitments in the associations, foundations, funds, professional organizations or other trading companies that make commitments to the members or employees for retirement are transferred to the private retirement system in part or in full. Then, amendments were made with Acts No. 6740 and 6655 in this legal opportunity granted by Act No. 5684. As of 16/4/2012, the amounts available for domestic and foreign savings and commitments were allowed to be transferred to the private retirement system until 31/12/2015 and then until 31/12/2017 (prov. art. 1 para. 5 PPA).[13]

25.3.2 Adopting Automatic Participation

While the fully voluntary participation principle was adopted at first in the private retirement system, afterwards the right to withdraw was accepted, and the automatic participation principle in the private retirement system was adopted. As a matter of fact, with Act No. 6740[14] aiming at the transfer of resources to private retirement funds, it has been accepted that employees should be automatically included in a retirement plan by adding an addendum to the PPA.

Accordingly, those who are Turkish citizens, those who have lost their Turkish citizenship by obtaining permission to leave and those who are descendants of them up to three generations, who have not reached the age of 45 on 1/1/2017 and who work under the SIGHIA as insured workers or public officials or as workers subject to the private funds of bank insurance companies shall be included in the retirement

[12] *See* in detail: Erol and Yıldırım (2004), pp. 268–269; Gülver (2011), pp. 122–125.

[13] *See* in detail: Gülver (2011), pp. 125–131; Güzel et al. (2020), pp. 852–854.

[14] OG 25.8.2016, No. 29812.

plan with a retirement contract organized by the employer. However, the employer may only include the employee in the retirement plan to be submitted by one of the companies deemed appropriate by the Ministry of Finance and Treasury for the arrangement of retirement plan for automatic participation (add. art. 2 para. 1 PPA).

With the enactment of Act No. 6740 on 1 January 2017, approximately 8.5 million people are expected to be included in the private pension system. In contrast, automatic transition was graded by a decision of the Council of Ministers.[15] Thus, the automatic transition date is based on for the date of 1/1/2017 workplaces with 1000 employees or more in the private sector, for the date of 1/4/2017 workplaces with 250–1000 employees, for the date of 1/7/2017 workplaces with 100–250 employees, for the date of 1/1/2018 workplaces with 50–100 employees, for the date of 1/7/2018 workplaces with 10–50 employees and for the date of 1/1/2019 workplaces with 5–10 employees.

With the same decision of the Council of Ministers, public officials were included in the private pension system. Accordingly, those working in public administrations on 1/1/2018, and those who will take office on that date, will automatically participate in the private pension program on the date of their appointment.

Even though the said regulation seems to be a requirement for participation in the individual retirement system, it is left to the will of the person to participate in this system, which is automatically joined. In fact, the employee may withdraw from the contract within two months of the date on which he/she is informed of his/her involvement in the retirement plan. In case of a withdrawal, the paid contributions are returned to the employee within 10 working days, together with the investment income in their account (add. art. 2 para. 3 PPA).

The automatic participation system is gradually adopted in Turkey. Accordingly, with automatic participation in 1/1/2017, firstly employees of companies with more than 1000 employees where included and then employees and of private sector companies with 250–999 employees and all civil servants were included in the system. Then, in 1/7/2017, enterprises that are active in textile, ready-to-wear clothing, transportation, education, construction, health, food and manufacturing sectors and have 100–250 employees were included in the system. Thus, in 2017 and 2018, 12,194,328 employees in total entered the system. However, 7,782,876 employees have withdrawn from the system by using their right of withdrawal. Thus, 63.82% of the employees in total have left the system.[16] This situation clearly shows that the savings opportunities of the employees in Turkey are limited.

[15]*See*: OG 2.1.2017, No. 29936.

[16]Hürriyet, 26.11.2018, p. 8.

25.4 Retirement Contract

25.4.1 Making a Retirement Contract

Those who want to participate in the individual retirement system must sign the retirement contract. In this context, the retirement contract is a contract regulating the principles, procedures and other rights and obligations of the parties regarding the creating of individual retirement accounts in the retirement company, payment of the contribution to this account, directing the paid contributions to the preferred funds and payment of the money accumulated in the account to the right holders (art. 4 PPA).

The retirement contract can be made either as an *individual "retirement contract"* with the participant or as a "*group retirement contract*" with an organization on behalf of the participant or based on an employment relationship.[17] The individual retirement contract is a retirement contract with the retirement company and the participant as the parties depending on the individual retirement plan. The individual retirement contract as a group is a retirement contract with the retirement company and the participant as the parties depending on the group retirement plan. The employer group retirement contract is a retirement contract signed between the sponsor organization and the retirement company in favour of a participant or based on an employment relationship (art. 4 PPA).

25.4.2 Rights and Obligations of the Parties

25.4.2.1 Obligation to Pay Contribution and Entry Fee

The participant contributes to the individual retirement account to be created in the retirement company in accordance with the principles stated in the retirement contract. Accordingly, the participant may decide that the contribution be shared among multiple funds belonging to the same company within the framework of the conditions to be included in the contract (art. 5 PPA).

The retirement company may request an entrance fee if the participant enters the system for the first time and if he/she creates a new individual retirement account (art. 7 PPA).

The contribution rate in automatic participation is the amount corresponding to 3% of the social insurance premium earnings. The employee can also request the employer to deduct a higher amount than the amount determined in the retirement contract for automatic participation (add. art. 2 para. 2 PPA).

[17] *See*: Gülver (2011), pp. 69–86.

25.4.2.2 Transfer of Contributions to Investment by the Retirement Company

The pension company must transfer the contributions to investment on the second business day following its transfer to the company (art. 5 para. 1 PPA).

If contributions are paid partially or fully to the account of the employees or members of the association, foundation, a professional organization with a legal entity, association or other organizations which is a party to the contracting of the group retirement contract, these contributions and their revenues are followed separately in the individual retirement accounts. The entitlement period of the participant to these savings shall not exceed seven years from the date of entry into the group retirement contract (art. 5 para. 3 PPA).

25.4.2.3 Transfer of Contributions to Another Retirement Company

The participant may request that his/her savings in the individual retirement account be transferred to another retirement company. In order for the participant to make such a request, he/she must have remained in the retirement company for at least one year. In case of transfer request, the retirement company is obliged to fulfil the request within 10 working days after the notification is received and to transfer the information and documents related to the account together with the savings (art. 5 para. 1 PPA).

25.4.3 State Contribution to the Individual Retirement System

Except for those paid by the employer, 25% of the contributions paid to the individual retirement account on behalf of the participant is calculated by the retirement monitoring centre as *"State contribution"*, based on the information transmitted by the retirement companies to the retirement monitoring centre. The said State contribution is paid to the retirement monitoring centre from the savings allocated to the budget of the Ministry of Finance and Treasury to be transferred through the retirement companies to the relevant accounts of the participants. The calculation period for the implementation of the state contribution is a calendar year. The sum of the contributions paid for a participant in a calculation period shall not exceed the total annual gross minimum wage determined for the relevant calendar year (add. art. 1 para. 1 PPA).

Participants who remain in the system for at least three years after the date of 1/1/2013 are entitled to 15% of the amount in the State contribution account, those for at least 6 years to 35% and those for at least 10 years to 60%. Those who are entitled to retirement from the individual retirement system and those who leave the system due to death or disability are entitled to the total amount in the State contribution account (add. art. 1 paras 2 and 3 PPA).

In addition, the State will contribute *TL 1000* once for entry into the system. Those who exercise the right of withdrawal will not benefit from it. The President is authorized to increase or reduce the amount by half. Those with at least 10 years of savings will receive an additional State contribution of up to *five percent* of their savings when they qualify for retirement and leave the system (add. art. 2 para. 5 PPA).

Government contribution has increased interest in the private pension system. As a matter of fact, the interest in the system increased after the start of the state contribution and in May 2019 the number of participants reached *6,814,102* and the fund size reached approximately *60 billion TL.*[18]

25.4.4 Leaving the System Before Being Entitled to Retirement

During the term of the retirement contract, the participant may request to leave the system before being entitled to retirement. The contractual relationship can also be terminated if the participant dies or a disability occurs. The retirement company pays the participant's savings in full within 20 working days from the receipt of the notification, if the participant requests to leave the system before being entitled to retirement (art. 6 para. 3 PPA).

25.5 Conditions to Be Entitled to Retirement

The participant is entitled to retirement after completing the age of 56, provided that they stay in the system for at least 10 years from the date of entry into the individual retirement system (art. 6 para. 1 PPA).

The public social security system recognized the age of retirement as the age of 58 for women and 60 years for men when the PPA came into force. At that time, the retirement age based on the private retirement system had a certain appeal, both due to it being low and the lack of gender discrimination at the age of retirement. This appeal was created to encourage participation in the private retirement system.[19] Accordingly, the said appeal will increase further in the coming years. Because, for the insured workers who will start working for the first time after 30/4/2008, as a general rule, the female worker is expected to complete 58 years of age and the male worker 60 and both to pay at least 7.200 days (art. 28 para. 2/a SIGHIA). No change

[18]*See*: Tuncay and Ekmekçi (2019), p. 775.

[19]Ekmekçi (2005), p. 354.

is foreseen in the age requirement for retirement pension until 2036. After this date, the age requirement is gradually increased. As a matter of fact, the public social security system aims to gradually increase the retirement age in Turkey from the date of 1/1/2036 to 65 years for both women and men.

It is also possible for the participant to remain in the individual retirement system for a longer period by paying a contribution for a minimum period of 10 years.[20]

25.6 Aids Provided by the Individual Retirement System

25.6.1 Retirement Pension

25.6.1.1 Granting Pension in Accordance with the Annual Income Insurance

Pension is granted to the participant within the framework of the annual income insurance contract he/she will make with the retirement company. Accordingly, the annual income insurance means contributions to the insured or right holders for lifetime or for certain periods of time, starting immediately or after a certain period of time provided the insured lives, according to the contributions made collectively or within specified periods (art. 6 para. 2 PPA). In this context, the annual income insurance contract can be arranged within the retirement contract and as part of this contract. This is because the annual income insurance contract does not have to be held separately and independently from the retirement contract between the retirement company and the participant.

25.6.1.2 Determination of the Amount of Pension

The pension shall be determined on the basis of the contributions of the participant in the individual retirement account and the total of the revenues obtained as a result of their usage.[21] Accordingly, the amount of the pension to be paid to the participants may vary depending on the profit of the fund in where the contributions are used. A legal arrangement foreseeing to guarantee a certain pension amount is not found in PPA. In this respect, the participant will be entitled to a high pension if the contribution the retirement company has used is high, a low pension if the profits of the fund are low or if the fund has made losses.

The pension determined according to the annual income insurance contract can be paid monthly, quarterly, semi-annually or annually (art. 6 para. 2 PPA).

[20]Gülver (2011), p. 199.

[21]Ekmekçi (2005), p. 354.

If the participant dies after entitlement to retirement, the amount of the current savings in the individual retirement account will be paid in the form of a lump sum payment to the legal heirs or to the right holders. On the other hand, it is not legally possible for the pensions the participant received before his/her death to pass to the legal heirs.

25.6.2 *Payment of Savings*

The participant who has earned the right to retirement may request that his/her savings in the individual retirement account be paid to him/her instead of being granted the pension. Accordingly, the participant entitled to retirement who wants his/her savings to be refunded can request a lump sum payment, scheduled repayment or pension within the framework of the annual income insurance contract (art. 6 para. 1 PPA). In addition, the participant has the opportunity to have the amount in the individual retirement account shared among the specified options.[22]

The participant who is entitled to retirement may request the lump sum payment of some or all of his/her savings in the individual retirement account.

If the participant requests all the amounts in his/her savings and state contribution account to be paid to him/her, the retirement company is obliged to fulfil this request within 10 working days from the receipt of the request. The participant who wants to collect the savings and the amounts in the State contribution account through scheduled repayment may request a regular payment in monthly, quarterly, semi-annual or annual terms within the framework of a program to be prepared. The participant's right to receive the remaining amount in his/her account at any time is reserved. As a matter of fact, the participant who starts to collect his/her savings in this way cannot pay contribution to the related individual retirement account. However, for the amount remaining in the account, the participant may change the fund allocation or use the right to transfer to another retirement company (art. 6 para. 1 PPA).

25.6.3 *Payment of Savings in Death or Disability*

In case the participant dies within the term of the retirement contract, the right holder may request the payment of the savings in the individual retirement account to himself/herself, and the participant can do the same in the case of disability (art. 6 para. 3 PPA). In this case, it is no longer possible to grant a pension. Accordingly, the right holder will be paid the savings accumulated in the individual retirement

[22]*See*: Güzel et al. (2020), pp. 863–864.

account until the date of death of the participant, and the participant will be paid the savings accumulated until the occurrence of the disability status.

25.6.4 Payment of Savings in Early Withdrawal from the System

Participants in the individual retirement system have the right to withdraw from the system while the retirement conditions have not yet taken place and to request their savings until that time in the individual retirement account. In case the participant requests to withdraw from the system before being entitled to retirement, the retirement company is obliged to pay the participant's savings completely within 20 working days after the notification is received (art. 6 para. 3 PPA).

25.6.5 Future of the Savings in the Subsequent Termination of the Group Retirement Contract

In the event that the group retirement contract is subsequently terminated, it is not possible for the employer, professional organization, association or other organization or group that is a party to the contract to withdraw or make savings on the participant's contribution and savings in the individual retirement account. Contracts to contain provisions contrary to this will not be legally valid. Because, in accordance with the purpose of group retirement contracts and the provisions of the contract for the benefit of the third party, it is necessary to accept that the contributions of the participant in the individual retirement accounts are no longer the assets of the employer or other organizations.[23]

In any case, duration of the entitlement of the participant to the savings in the group pension agreement made by the employer (*vesting period*) cannot exceed seven years from the date of entry into the group pension contract (art. 5 para. 3 PPA). Except for the termination of the employee's employment by the employer for good cause, the participant has terminated the employment contract for good cause or has left his/her job due to disability or disability, or the employer terminated the group pension agreement, went bankrupt or went concordat, the contributions paid by the employer to their own name and account and all of their benefits shall be entitled without waiting for the expiration of the period of entitlement. In case of death of the participant, the payments are made to the beneficiary or legal heirs specified in the pension contract.[24]

[23]Gülver (2011), p. 214.

[24]See: Tuncay and Ekmekçi (2019), p. 782.

25.6.6 *Amount Paid by the Retirement Company Not Being Sought by the Right Holders*

According to the provisions of the retirement contract or annual income insurance contract, if the amount to be paid to rights holders is not sought by the right holders within ten years of the date requiring the payment, the said amount shall be transferred to Central Bank, under the order of the Ministry of Finance and Treasury, with a scale to be drawn up showing the name and surname of the right holders and the amount they are entitled to within six months from the beginning of the year following the tenth year. If the right holders do not seek these funds deposited in Central Bank within two years, they shall be recorded as income in Treasury (art. 6 para. 5 PPA).

25.7 Tax Incentives

It is considered that some tax incentives are provided to encourage participation in the private pension system. As a matter of fact, in the Income Tax Law and Corporate Tax Act, tax facilities and exemptions are provided. For example, 25% of payments made to individual pensioners and those leaving the system due to death, disability or liquidation, and 10% of payments made from other insurance companies for these reasons are exempt from income tax (increase) (art. 1 Act No. 4697).

On the other hand, employer contributions paid to pension companies on behalf of employees, premium payments made to pension companies by the employee himself or his family members are deducted from the tax base. However, the amount to be deducted shall not exceed 10% of the wage earning that month and the annual amount of the minimum wage annually (art. 4 Act No. 4697).

In addition, earnings of pension mutual funds are exempt from tax (art. 8 para. 1 Act No. 5422). On the other hand, payments from the pension company to those who leave early without paying premium or contribution to the system for 10 years are subject to income tax (art. 75 para. 15 Act No. 193).

References

Alper Y (2002) Sosyal Güvenlikte Yeni Bir Adım: Bireysel Emeklilik. Çimento İşveren Dergisi 16 (2):11–32

Bayri O (2013) Türkiye'de Sosyal Güvenlik Sisteminin Kurum ve Kapsam Olarak Gelişimi ve Sosyal Güvenlik Adaleti. Sosyal Güvenlik Dergisi 3(2):18–60

Çımrın FK, Durdu Z (2015) Türkiye'de Sosyal Güvenlik Sisteminin Dönüşümü ve Bireysel Emeklilik Sistemi. HAK-İŞ Uluslararası Emek ve Toplum Dergisi 4(8):60–75

Ekmekçi Ö (2005) Private Pension Fund Scheme in the Turkish Law. Annales de la Faculte de Droit d'Istanbul 37(54):347–355

Erol A, Yıldırım AE (2004) Tüm Yönleriyle Bireysel Emeklilik Sistemi, 2nd edn. Yaklaşım Publishing, Ankara

Gülver E (2011) Emeklilik Sözleşmesi. Der Yayınları, Istanbul

Güzel A, Okur AR, Caniklioğlu N (2020) Sosyal Güvenlik Hukuku, 18th edn. Beta Publishing, Istanbul

Tuncay AC, Ekmekçi Ö (2019) Sosyal Güvenlik Hukuku Dersleri, 20th edn. Beta Publishing, Istanbu

Uğur S (2004) Özel Emeklilik Türleri ve Bireysel Emeklilik. Çimento İşveren Dergisi 18(4):14–25

Ünan S, Karayazgan A (2009) Bireysel Emeklilik Hukuku. Scala Publishing, Istanbul

Part VIII
Non-contributory Regime

Chapter 26
Social Assistances

26.1 Scope of Social Assistances

The main feature of the social assistances is the idea of providing money to Turkish citizens in need of assistance from the State budget.

The Turkish social security system includes both the assistances that bear the nature of compensation and the assistances of a protection nature. As a matter of fact, while the nature of compensation comes forward in assisting the families of needy soldiers, the protection nature is prominent for the social assistances to Turkish citizens in need.[1]

The regulations on social assistance have neither a uniform structure nor a uniform content within the Turkish legal system. In this respect, it is seen that social assistances are regulated by a number of different laws. The disintegration and fragmented structure of the organization and management of social assistances performed by public institutions negatively impacts efficiency and productivity in the provision of social assistances.[2]

26.2 Organization of Social Assistances

The execution of social services was mainly left to the "*Ministry of Family and Social Policies*" and its affiliated organization. In last time, it passed to the "*Ministry of Family, Labour and Social Services*". In fact:

- Developing, implementing and monitoring policies and strategies on social assistances at a national level,

[1]Yuvalı (2017), pp. 105–106.

[2]Bayri (2013), p. 27.

T. Centel, *Turkish Social Law*, https://doi.org/10.1007/978-3-030-64704-9_26

- Carrying out social assistance activities in order to protect family integrity and increase family welfare,
- Carrying out social assistance activities for children, women, disabled people, elderly people, martyrs and veterans,
- Carrying out regular and effective assistance activities for the segments of the society in need of social assistance and protection,
- Coordinating the determination of national policies and strategies for the fight against poverty,
- To supervise the social assistance activities carried out within the framework of the determined principles, procedures and standards,
- Processing, control, monitoring and evaluating information on social assistance activities and beneficiaries through a database to be established in a central system,
- Monitoring the international developments and activities in the field of social assistance and to evaluate them in order to benefit in the works to be carried out, to ensure the implementation of the international conventions and agreements to which Turkey is a party at the national level,

Are among the duties of the Ministry of Family, Labour and Social Services (art. 65 SD No. 1). However, it cannot be said that the Ministry of Family, Labour and Social Services is the only central institution in the field of social assistance.[3]

26.3 Protective Assistances for Citizens Who Have Served Turkey

It is seen that many legal arrangements with social assistance content have been adopted in order to provide assistance to the people who have successfully served and contributed to Turkey in times of war or peace.

26.3.1 Assistance to Families of Soldiers in Need

The recruitment of a person who is a supporter of his/her family may cause the family members staying behind to lose their livelihood because they are deprived of their income. In such a case, of course, the State will need to provide assistance to the rest of the family.[4]

---

[3] *See*: Yuvalı (2017), pp. 239–244.

[4] Yuvalı (2017), p. 146.

In this context, assistance to families of soldiers in need was accepted with Act No. 4109.[5] According to this, it was foreseen that assistances be made for the families of those who were in the military for more than 45 days both in war and peace (art. 1 para. 1 Act No. 4109). This assistance is provided for the mother and father, children, spouse and siblings of the concerned person. However, for this, the person recruited should provide the livelihoods of these people and they should not have other means of providing livelihood (art. 2 Act No. 4109).

Assistance to military families in need continues for the duration of the military service. The amount of assistance will be sufficient to provide the least amount of livelihood in that place and will be determined and implemented by municipal councils in cities and towns, and by board of alderman in villages (art. 3 para. 3 Act No. 4109).

On the other hand, Act No. 4341[6] regulated the free treatment of families of soldiers and officers in need. According to this, in case the families of soldiers and officers recruited get ill, their treatment will be made free of charge in primary health care institutions and State and university hospitals (art. 1 Act No. 4341). In this context, the costs of the drugs to be used in case of outpatient or inpatient treatment of the families of soldiers in need and the vital drugs to be used during the outpatient or inpatient treatment of diseases requiring long-term treatment will be covered by the State (art. 2 Act No. 4341). As the family of the soldier and officer, the spouse, children and mother and father, who will struggle if the soldier or the officer does not provide assistance, can benefit from free treatment (art. 3 Act No. 4341).

26.3.2 Granting Pension to Owners of War of Independence Medal

Act No. 1005[7] has foreseen that Turkish citizens who participated in the national war of independence and received a "*medal of war of independence*", those who participated actively in the Korean wars between 1950 and 1953 and those who participated in the first and second Cyprus peace operations in 1974 by actively being tasked in Cyprus are to be granted pension as long as they are alive (art. 1 para. 1 Act No. 1005).

The amount of the pension to be granted to the owner of the war of independence medal shall be found by multiplying the indicator number of 5.750 by the civil servant salary coefficient accepted by the budget law every year. In the event of the death of the right holder, this pension is given to the spouse at a 75% rate, but in case of remarriage of the spouse, it shall be withheld (art. 1 para. 1 Act No. 1005).

[5]OG 15.8.1941, No. 4887.

[6]OG 22.2.1998, No. 23266.

[7]OG 24.2.1968, No. 12835.

The pensions to be granted to the owner of the war of independence medal shall not be subject to any tax or deduction, nor may they be seized (art. 2 para. 3 Act No. 1005).

26.3.3 Granting Pension for National Service

The provision of granting pension to Turkish citizens who have served Turkey with superior success and diligence, without seeking reward or interest in return, or to their family members who are in need in the event of death, has been accepted with Act No. 3292.[8] The granting of said pension shall be subject to the decision of the President of the State (art. 2 para. 1 Act No. 3292).

In the case of death of the person-receiving pension, the spouse and orphans of the deceased are to be granted pension starting from the beginning of the month following the death (art. 3 Act No. 3292).

The amount of national service pension is equal to the multiplication of civil servant salaries accepted by the budget law every year by the indicator number of 700 for persons concerned, 550 for their spouses, 400 for the orphans and other dependents (art. 2 para. 2 Act No. 3292).

These pensions are not subject to any tax or deduction, nor can they be seized (art. 2 para. 3 Act No. 3292).

26.3.4 Assistance to Those Who Suffer Damages for the Sake of Protection of Public Order

Act No. 2330[9] foresees that armed forces and security forces tasked to protect the public order in peace, prevent, monitor and investigate smuggling and those responsible for storing, transporting, destroying and neutralizing the explosives in their possession shall be compensated and paid pensions if they die immediately or subsequently or become disabled (art. 1 Act No. 2330).

The personal area of application of this pension includes the General Command of the Gendarmerie, the General Directorate of Security and the Coast Guard Command, members of the Armed Forces and National Intelligence Organization, watchmen, forest officers and customs officers, who are responsible for the protection of internal security and public order and the prevention, monitoring and investigation of smuggling. In addition, judicial and military judges, judicial and military prosecutors and assistant prosecutors, local authorities working together with security forces, public officials and civilians whose services were needed during

[8]OG 3.6.1986, No. 19126.

[9]OG 3.11.1980, No. 17152.

the investigation commissioned by the authorities responsible for prosecuting the cases about public order and smuggling are included. In addition, those who assist the security forces by themselves, public officials who have been attacked for the purpose of intimidation of state forces and their attacked spouse, child, sibling and parents have also later been included (art. 2 Act No. 2330).

The legal heirs of the deceased shall be paid cash compensation of 100 times the highest civil servant gross salary. This amount will increase to 200 times for those who are incapable of performing the necessary actions to live and cannot sustain their lives without the help and support of others. In the case of other disabilities, a rate between 25 and 75% of the highest civil servant gross salary shall be taken as basis. Again, those who have been injured in this context will be given cash compensation according to the degree of injury, not exceeding 20% of this amount (art. 3 para. 1 Act No. 2330).

On the other hand, those who are retired by disability are granted a duty disability allowance. The allowances of those who get disabled while receiving a pension will turn into a duty disability allowance. The duty disability allowance to be granted in case of death is transferred to spouses and orphans. Those who are not affiliated to any social security institution are granted duty disability allowance and in case of their death, the duty disability allowance is increased by 25% and granted to spouses and orphans (art. 4 para. 1 Act No. 2330).

Apart from these assistances, the children of the deceased or those who are disabled beyond capacity to work are allowed free education in state boarding schools and educational institutions (art. 7 para. 1 Act No. 2330).

After the adoption of Act No. 2330, two more laws have been enacted to protect public officials for the same purpose. The first one is Act No. 2453.[10] The law in question has foreseen the implementation of the provisions of Act No. 2330 for the persons who die, get disabled or injured as a result of the terrorist attacks they encounter on the permanent or temporary duties abroad (art. 1 Act No. 2453). If the property damage they suffered not covered by insurance companies or foreign authorities, it is agreed that their affiliated institutions will pay the damages (art. 3 para. 1 Act No. 2453).

The other law is Act No. 2566.[11] The law in question further enlarged the scope of Act No. 2330 and has foreseen the implementation of the provisions of Act No. 2330 for the health personnel who get killed, disabled or injured due to their duties in examinations and treatments of persons caught, detained or convicted because of their actions that violated the security and order, and for those tasked in the cleaning of mine fields in smuggling operations and are killed, disabled or injured (art. 1 Act No. 2566).

[10]OG 25.4.1981, No. 17321.

[11]OG 22.12.1981, No. 17552.

26.3.5 Assistances for Those Who Work in the Fight Against Terror

Act No. 3713[12] includes social assistance arrangements aimed at protecting those who work in the fight against terror and anarchy. Accordingly, the provisions of Act No. 2330[13] shall apply to public officials who die or are killed, disabled or injured during or after the end of their duties abroad or in the country due to acts of terrorism. In addition, the total amount of allowances to be granted to the spouses and orphans of the disabled and the deceased who are entitled to allowances shall not be less than the salaries of their peers; if a retiree is killed, the total amount of the allowance to be given to their spouses and orphans shall, by law, not be less than the pension to be granted to them. If it is less, the social security institution as compensation will pay the difference and the amount will be taken from the treasury (art. 21 para. 1/a Act No. 3713).

Apart from that, those injured by acts of terrorism will be treated by the State, and those who suffer loss of life and property will be given priority assistance from the Social Assistance and Solidarity Encouragement Fund (art. 22 Act No. 3713).

On the other hand, the civilians and their right holders who have lost their lives or become disables due to the coup attempt and the acts of terrorism on 15 July 2016 are subject to allowance (art. 7 para. 1 SD No. 667). In addition, these persons and those who are injured due to the said actions are subject to cash compensation.[14]

26.3.6 Assistances to Teachers Serving Turkish Culture

Act No. 168[15] is intended to provide social assistance to Turkish and foreign teachers or religious officials serving the Turkish culture in foreign countries, to them in case of separation from their duties and to their spouses and orphans in case of their deaths (art. 1 para. 1 Act No. 168).

The principles, rates and payment conditions of the social assistance shall be determined by taking into consideration the years of service of the concerned persons, pensions given to their peers and local livelihood indices (art. 2 para. 1 Act No. 168). In order to benefit from this assistance, the person concerned should not receive sufficient financial assistance or pension from any institution or country, not act against the Turkish culture and revolutions and should not leave the country to reside in another country (art. 3 Act No. 168).

---

[12]OG 12.4.1991, No. 20843 (rep.).

[13]*See*: above Sect. 26.3.4.

[14]*See*: Yuvalı (2017), p. 178 and fn. 815.

[15]OG 23.12.1960, No. 10688.

The social assistance to be made is paid from the special portion in the budget of the Ministry of Foreign Affairs (art. 5 Act No. 168).

26.3.7 Assistance to Those Who Suffered Loss During Their Duties

Act No. 2629[16] regulates the compensation to be paid to the Turkish Armed Forces pilots, weapon system officers, navigational officers, tactical coordinating officers, staff of flight crews, task team personnel, paratroopers, submarine teams, atmospheric diving system pilots, divers and frogmen (art. 1 Act No. 2629).

The legal heirs of the martyrs shall be compensated at 100 times of the criterion salary. It is envisaged that those who are incapable of perform the necessary actions to survive and who are unable to continue their lives without the help and support of others are paid 200 times the criterion allowance for the disabled and the others to be paid compensation at rates varying from 25% to 75% of the 100 times the criterion allowance for the disabled (art. 14 para. 1/a-b Act No. 2629).

26.4 Protective Assistances for Persons in Need

26.4.1 Granting Allowance for Turkish Citizens in Need

Act No. 2022[17] aims to grant allowance to Turkish citizens, who have reached the age of 65, do not receive a pension from any social security institution, do not work in a job that requires compulsory insurance, are decided to be in need of social assistance by social assistance and solidarity foundations and who are not granted alimony, as long as their neediness continues (art. 1 para. 1 Act No. 2022). The law in question initially targeted elderly Turkish citizens in need over 65 years of age. As a result of subsequent changes, disabled under the age of 65 and their relatives who take care of them and are with low incomes and those with silicosis (lung dust disease), who lost at least 15% of their income power in their professions were included in the scope.

Accordingly, the person to be paid allowance, first of all, must have reached the age of 65 years. In determining the age of 65, corrections made at the date of birth are not considered (art. 1 para. 3 Act No. 2022).

Taking into consideration all the income of these persons and their spouses, those with an average monthly income per person more than one third of the monthly net amount of the minimum wage and those who are able to generate more than the same

[16] OG 28.2.1982, No. 17619 (rep.).

[17] OG 10.7.1976, No. 15642.

amount are not deemed in need and shall not be given allowance (art. 1 para. 2 Act No. 2022).

Making the limit of neediness based on the minimum wage enabled both the increase of allowances and the extension of the application area of Act No. 2022. Similarly, changes were made in the method for determining the neediness, and expenditures were taken into consideration as well as household income.[18] However, the determination of the source of the expenditures by experts during the social examination is compulsory for an objective determination.[19]

The allowances are granted by the Ministry of Family, Labour and Social Services and paid from the relevant section of the Ministry budget. The ministry and the social assistance and solidarity foundations are authorized to conduct or order an examination of the income, standard of living and assets of the applicants and alimony obligors, if necessary, and to request information and documents from private and official institutions and persons (art. 8 para. 1 Act No. 2022).

The amount of the allowance to be granted is equal to the amount calculated by multiplying the indicator number of 4.387 by the civil servant salary coefficient for those who completed 65 years of age (art. 1 para. 1 Act No. 2022).

Of the Turkish citizens who are in need, for those who are under the age of 65 but over 18 and are with disabilities and cannot continue their lives without the help of another person, the allowance amount to be granted is found by multiplying the indicator number of 4.860 by the civil servant salary coefficient (art. 2 para. 1/a Act No. 2022).

Again, the allowance to be granted to disabled Turkish citizens who are under the age of 65 but over 18 and in need and could not be placed in jobs is found by multiplying the indicator number of 3.240 by the civil servant salary coefficient (art. 2 para. 1/b Act No. 2022). Similarly, Turkish citizens with disabled relatives under 18 years of age who have undertaken their care and have low income will be granted the same amount of allowance (art. 2 para. 2 Act No. 2022).

The starting date of the allowance is the beginning of the month following the written applications of the concerned to the social assistance and solidarity foundations. The allowances are paid in cash on the payment days and periods determined by the Ministry of Family, Labour and Social Services. Allowances paid in cash are not refunded in case of change of status or death (art. 3 Act No. 2022).

---

[18] Yuvalı (2017), pp. 185–186.

[19] Camkurt (2014), p. 103.

26.4.2 *Social Assistance and Solidarity Encouragement Assistances*

Act No. 3294[20] aims to help the poor and needy Turkish citizens and those who have been accepted to or have come to Turkey for any reason, when needed, to make the income distribution fair and to promote social assistance and solidarity through measures to reinforce social justice (art. 1 Act No. 3294).

26.4.2.1 Scope of Social Assistance and Solidarity

Within the scope of Act No. 3294, Turkish citizens who are poor and in need and who do not receive income or allowance from social security institutions and persons who can be put into productive status and will be made useful to the society if they are provided with a small amount of help or education and training are included (art. 2 para. 1 Act No. 3294). The scope that was initially determined in this way was later expanded. Accordingly, the poor and needy persons whose income is less than one third of the net monthly minimum wage, those who suffer from all kinds of emergencies and disasters and the relatives of martyrs and veterans are also within the scope (art. 2 paras 3 and 4 Act No. 3294).

However, it is not bound by objective criteria to identify those who will receive social assistance. Therefore, it is difficult to say that the assistances made are rule-based, rights-based and transparent. As a matter of fact, the increase in the number of donations made during the election periods shows that the concept of cliental comes forward. This results in the consumption of public resources that will realize the social assistance necessary for the whole society outside the purpose.[21]

26.4.2.2 Social Assistance and Solidarity Encouragement Fund

In order to realize social assistance and solidarity services, a *"social assistance and solidarity encouragement fund"* was established at the Central Bank (art. 3 Act No. 3294). The revenues of this fund are composed of the funds to be collected up to 10% from the funds established and to be established, allowances to be put into the budget, half of the revenue of traffic fines, 15% of the revenues of the Radio and Television Supreme Council, all kinds of donations and assistances and other revenues (art. 4 para 1 Act No. 3294).

On the other hand, being counted as *"public receivables"* strengthened some revenues of the social assistance and solidarity encouragement fund (add. art. 1 Act No. 3294).

---

[20] OG 14.6.1986, No. 19134.

[21] Yuvalı (2017), pp. 207–208.

26.4.2.3 Social Assistance and Solidarity Foundations

The provision of resources to be collected in the social assistance and solidarity fund, as cash and in-kind assistance to the needy persons will be performed through *"social assistance and solidarity foundations"* established in each province and district (art. 7 para. 1 Act No. 3294).

The local governors are the natural presidents of these foundations. In provinces, mayor, head of provincial treasury, provincial director of national education, provincial health director, provincial agriculture director, provincial social services and child protection institution director and the provincial mufti is located in the board of trustees; in the districts, the municipality minister, head of the finance office, district director of national education, the district officer of the Ministry of Health, if present the district director of agriculture and the mufti of the district are located in the board of trustees of the foundation. Furthermore, for each activity period, one headman each to be elected from the headmen of the village and the district headmen, two representatives from the presidents of non-governmental organizations and two people to be elected from philanthropic Turkish citizens will work in the board of trustees; a representative each to be elected from the village and neighbourhood headmen of the district, a member to be elected from the managers of non-governmental organizations and two people to be elected from philanthropic Turkish citizens will work in the board of trustees (art. 7 para. 2 Act No. 3294).

26.4.2.4 Exemptions Granted to the Fund and Foundations

The social assistance and solidarity encouragement fund and social assistance and solidarity foundations have some exemptions that are extremely important for implementation. Accordingly, the aforementioned fund and foundations are exempt from corporate tax except for their economic enterprises, from inheritance and transfer tax due to donations and assistances and from all kinds of taxes, duties, fees and funds, foundation auditing expenses and all kinds of working capital fees due to their movable and immovable properties and all transactions they will perform (art. 9 Act No. 3294).

26.4.2.5 Social Assistances and Supports Being Exempt from Seizure

Social assistance and solidarity assistances and project supports cannot be seized even with the person's consent. In addition, these assistances and supports cannot be transferred or assigned to someone else (add. art. 2 Act No. 3294).

26.5 Teacher Support Assistances

Act No. 3580[22] aims to improve the quality of education by encouraging the teaching profession and educational expertise. For this purpose, it is aimed to educate students for free in boarding schools or with scholarships (art. 1 Act No. 3580).

The amount of scholarships to be given to scholarship students and the amount of allowance to be paid to boarding students is determined by the President of the State (art. 10 Act No. 3580).

In addition, the number of books, stationery and other education expenses of free boarding students will be covered by the Ministry of National Education (art. 11 Act No. 3580).

26.6 Supporting Assistances for Successful Athletes

Act No. 5774[23] aims to grant an allowance to the amateur Turkish athletes who have achieved significant success in the international level and, in case of their death, to their spouses and children who are their dependents, and to the national team coaches and trainers of the athletes that have become Olympic or world champions. In addition, the title of "*national athlete*" is given as awarding the athletes, who have achieved outstanding success at the international level (art. 1 Act No. 5774).

These athletes will be granted "*national athlete pension*" from the date when they are at the age of 40 and as long as they maintain their Turkish citizenship, with the decision of the President of the State (art. 3 para. 1 Act No. 5774).

The amount of the pension to be given is:

- In the Olympic games, 200% of the net minimum wage for amateur athletes finishing first individually, 160% amateur athletes finishing second and 140% for amateur athletes finishing third,
- In world championships, 140% of the net minimum wage for amateur athletes finishing first individually, 120% amateur athletes finishing second and 100% for amateur athletes finishing third,
- In Europe championships, 100% of the net minimum wage for amateur athletes finishing first individually, 80% amateur athletes finishing second and 60% for amateur athletes finishing third.

This ratio is determined as 75% if success is achieved as a team (arts 3, 4 Act No. 5774).

[22]OG 4.7.1989, No. 201215.

[23]OG 9.7.2008, No. 26931.

References

Bayri O (2013) Türkiye'de Sosyal Güvenlik Sisteminin Kurum ve Kapsam Olarak Gelişimi ve Sosyal Güvenlik Adaleti. Sosyal Güvenlik Dergisi 3(2):18–60

Camkurt MZ (2014) Yaşlılık ve Yaşlıların Sosyal Güvenliği Kapsamında 65 Yaş Aylığı Bağlanması İşlemleri. Kamu-İş İş Hukuku ve İktisat Dergisi 13(3):71–106

Yuvalı E (2017) Türk Sosyal Güvenlik Hukukunda Merkezi (Kamusal) Sosyal Yardımlar. Turhan Kitabevi, Ankara

Chapter 27
Social Services

27.1 The Concept of Social Service and Its Constitutional Basis

Social Services Act No. 2828[1] defines social services as the whole of systematic and programmed services aimed at eliminating the material, abstract and social deprivations arising out of personal and environmental conditions of individuals and families arising out of their control, meeting their needs, preventing and solving their social problems and improving and elevating their living standards (art. 3 para. 1/a SSA).

In this sense, social services are aimed at individuals who become poor and needy or who become physically or mentally incapacitated for reasons that are not in their control. The purpose of social services is to meet the needs that are required for these people to live a life that is suitable for a human and compatible with their environment. The institutions that will provide social services are state and voluntary private organizations.

As the State's obligation to provide social services, firstly, art. 61 Const. has foreseen the special protection of children, persons with disabilities and the elderly (paras 2, 3 and 4).

Again, the Constitution states that everyone has the right to live in a healthy and balanced environment (art. 56 para. 1 Const.). To this end, the State will ensure that everyone lives in a physical and mental health and will plan and regulate health institutions from a single source (art. 56 para. 3 Const.). The State shall fulfil this duty by utilizing and supervising the health and social institutions in the public and private sectors and may, if necessary, establish universal health insurance by law for the widespread implementation of health services (art. 56 paras 4 and 5 Const.).

In addition, art. 57 Const., foresees the State to take measures to meet the housing needs and also to support public housing initiatives.

---

[1]OG 27.5.1983, No. 18059.

T. Centel, *Turkish Social Law*, https://doi.org/10.1007/978-3-030-64704-9_27

27.2 Principles Related to Social Services

27.2.1 General Social Service Principles

The activities related to social services shall be carried out collectively by ensuring the supervision and management of the State, through the voluntary participation and contribution of non-governmental organizations and the public (art. 4 para. 1/a SSA).

Coordination and cooperation will be established between public and voluntary institutions and organizations operating in the field of social services, and the resources available will be brought into force most efficiently (art. 4 para. 1/b SSA).

In the implementation of social service programs, priority is given to disabled people who are in need of protection and elderly people in need (art. 4 para. 1/c SSA).

In the execution of social services, class, race, language, religion, sect or region differences will not be taken into consideration, and, if the service demand is higher than the supply of services, the priorities will be determined based on the need level and the order of application or detection (art. 4 para. 1/d SSA).

Establishment of social service organizations shall be subject to permission except for those established by law, and they shall be provided to operate in accordance with the determined standards in terms of service, operation and personnel (art. 4 para. 1/f SSA).

The balanced distribution of social service organizations throughout the country will be arranged in a way not to leave any task openings (art. 4 para. 1/g SSA).

Nurseries and orphanages will be grouped according to the age, gender, social and psychological characteristics and the degree of disability of children in need of protection (art. 4 para. 1/h SSA).

Children who are in need of protection will be provided with a job or occupation and will be monitored within the community and supported within the scope of possibilities after the protection decision is taken (art. 4 para. 1/k SSA).

All necessary measures will be taken in order to ensure that the disabled and the elderly who are in need continue their lives in health, peace and security, disabled people receive care and rehabilitation to be able to manage themselves and become productive and those whose treatment is not possible are kept under constant care (art. 4 para. 1/l SSA).

All necessary measures will be taken in order to act together with national and international social service institutions and organizations in natural disasters and to carry out emergency rescue and relief activities effectively (art. 4 para. 1/m SSA).

27.2.2 Principles on Social Services for Persons with Disabilities

SSA firstly determined the principles regarding social services for the disabled. Accordingly, individuals, families and the community will be made aware of the rights and obligations of disabled people, their medical care and rehabilitation will be provided, and their capacity to live on their own in their daily lives will be increased (art. 4 para. 2/a SSA).

Information, service and physical environmental conditions will be made available to the disabled (art. 4 para. 2/b SSA).

Starting from birth, all persons with disabilities will have equal opportunities in education including pre-school age, school age and adulthood (art. 4 para. 2/c SSA).

Employment will be realized together with vocational training and rehabilitation, the appropriateness of employment areas for the performance of persons with disabilities will be ensured, and measures will be taken to facilitate the acquisition of instruments and devices suitable for technology by persons with disabilities (art. 4 para. 2/d SSA).

Social security and income of persons with disabilities will be protected, and their full participation will be ensured in the fields of culture, entertainment, sport and religion (art. 4 para. 2/e SSA).

The participation of the disabled will be ensured in the making of plans and programs for them and during the making of all decisions affecting their economic and social status (art. 4 para. 2/f SSA).

In addition to *Social Services Act, Act on the Disabled* also sets out some important principles regarding social services for people with disabilities. Accordingly, respect for the individual autonomy of persons with disabilities during the fulfilment of services is taken as basis. Discrimination based on disability will not be made, and efforts will be made to ensure equal opportunities for people with disabilities to benefit from all rights and services (art. 4 para. 1/a, c Act No. 5378).

Efforts will be made to preserve family integrity in the provision of services for people with disabilities. Again, care will be taken to ensure the best interests of the child in services for children with disabilities; women and girls with disabilities will be prevented from being subjected to multifaceted discrimination and they will be ensured to enjoy rights and freedoms (art. 4 para. 1/f-h Act No. 5378).

27.3 Organization of Social Services

The implementation of social services today is mainly left to *Ministry of Family, Labour and Social Services* and the organization attached to it. In fact:

- Development, implementation and monitoring of policies and strategies at national level regarding social services,

- Carrying out social service activities for increasing family welfare and for children, women, disabled, elderly, martyrs and veterans and ensuring cooperation and coordination among relevant public and voluntary institutions and organizations in this field,
- Determining the principles, procedures and standards related to social service activities and supervising them,
- Processing, controlling and monitoring the information related to beneficiaries of social service activities through a database to be established in a central system,
- Monitoring of international developments and activities in the field of social services,

Are considered among the duties of the Ministry of Family, Labour and Social Services (art. 65 PD No. 1).

27.4 Services Provided to Those in Need of Protection, Care and Assistance

27.4.1 Services for Children in Need of Protection

The procedure for the determination and protection of the children to be protected is shown in *Child Protection Act* No. 5395.[2] As a matter of fact, necessary measures are taken from the court to ensure that children in need of protection are cared for, trained and employed in social service organizations until they are majors (art. 22 para. 1 SSA). In general, the protection decision continues until the child is a major. However, this decision can be revoked by the court before the child becomes a major if the conditions that cause the protection decision are eliminated, and it can be decided to be continued upon the consent of the child after he/she is a major (art. 24 para. 1 SSA).

The care and upbringing of a child for whom the court rules a protection decision and who needs to be protected can be provided by social services or may be carried out by a "*foster family*". The foster family can be paid in return for the care and upbringing of the child in need of protection, or the foster family can undertake this task voluntarily (art. 23 para. 1 SSA).

The education and training of children at school age in need of protection is carried out in the schools of the Ministry of National Education and other public institutions. Children who do not have the opportunity to attend school for any reason can be employed in public and private workplaces with a wage and have a profession. The amount of the wages of the children employed in such a way as determined by the dormitories shall be paid as allowances. The remaining amount

[2]OG 15.7.2005, No. 25876.

shall be deposited in the account to be issued in the name of the child in the national banks (art. 25 paras 1 and 2 SSA).

The education and training of children in need of special education as well as protection is carried out in official and special education and training institutions of the Ministry of National Education (art. 25 para. 3 SSA).

Girls who are under protection in social service organizations and who marry are given a "*marriage allowance*", for one time to meet their dower needs, which is one and a half times the amount of the highest civil servant monthly wage. This allowance is paid without being subject to any tax or deduction (art. 32 SSA).

27.4.2 Services Provided to the Disabled

Act on the Disabled No. 5378[3] aims to ensure that persons with disabilities benefit from fundamental rights and freedoms, to ensure their participation in social life on an equal basis with other individuals and to make arrangements including measures to prevent disability.

Among the social services to be provided to the disabled, firstly, the provision of support and care services comes forward. According to this, psychosocial support and care services are provided for disabled people to live independently in their environment. In their provision, the biological, physical, psychological, social, cultural and mental needs of the person will be taken into consideration by also taking into consideration the family (art. 6 para. 1 AD).

Another type of service to be provided to the disabled is facilitation and rehabilitation services. Accordingly, facilitation and rehabilitation services are provided to disabled people on the basis of participation and equality in social life. While providing these services, including deciding, planning, executing and terminating the facilitation and rehabilitation, the active participation of the disabled and their families at all stages will be ensured. In addition, it is essential that these services start at the earliest possible stage and are placed in the closest location to the residence of the disabled (art. 10 paras 1 and 2 AD).

On the other hand, it is seen that vocational rehabilitation services are also offered to disabled people. Accordingly, it is foreseen that necessary measures will be taken for disabled people to choose a profession and to receive training in this field. In this regard, vocational rehabilitation programs will be developed in line with the analyses made by the Ministry of Labour and Social Security. Similarly, other public institutions and organizations, municipalities and private individuals will also be able to carry out vocational rehabilitation programs for persons with disabilities (art. 13 paras 1–3 AD).

[3]OG 7.7.2005, No. 25868.

In addition, the task of carrying out works on programs with early diagnosis and preventive services for the disabled has been assigned to the Ministry of Health (art. 11 AD).

27.5 Services for the Protection of Children in Need of Special Education

27.5.1 Scope of Special Education

The principles for ensuring that individuals who require special education can use their right to general and vocational education in line with the general objectives and SD No. 573 regulates basic principles of Turkish national education.[4]

According to this, special education services in early childhood are carried out in houses and institutions based on the informing and supporting of the family (art. 6 SD No. 573).

Preschool education is compulsory for children who are diagnosed with special education. This education is provided in special education schools and other preschool education institutions. The duration of preschool education of children who require special education can be extended by taking into consideration their development and individual characteristics (art. 7 SD No. 573).

Preparatory classes can be opened for children who have completed preschool education and who require special education that have come to the age of compulsory primary education (art. 8 para. 1 SD No. 573).

In addition, individuals who require special education by providing special education support have individual and group opportunities (art. 14 SD No. 573).

27.5.2 Special Education Units

27.5.2.1 Special Education, Guidance and Psychological Counselling Services

In order to regulate, supervise and evaluate the guidance and psychological counselling services and special education services in education and training institutions, it is foreseen to establish a special education guidance and psychological counselling services unit under the chairmanship of the deputy director or the branch manager in each province affiliated with the directorate of national education. This unit will carry out special education guidance and psychological counselling services in provinces (art. 17 SD No. 573).

[4]OG 6.6.1997, No. 23011 rep.

27.5.2.2 Special Education Schools

It is foreseen that special education schools with daytime or boarding schools will be opened for individuals whose conditions require special education in a separate school. Special education classes can be opened in special education schools for students with multiple disabilities. The Ministry of National Education covers the boarding and quartering fees of students and their first-degree relatives for the period of education (art. 18 SD No. 573).

27.5.2.3 Special Education Institutions

Special daytime education institutions can be opened to provide special education support to individuals who require special education, to prepare them for work and profession or to develop basic life skills of those who are unable to benefit from formal education programs and to meet their learning needs. Those who attend business and vocational courses in these areas benefit from the rights such as wages and social security provided to apprentice students (art. 19 SD No. 573).

27.5.2.4 Special Education in Other Schools and Institutions

Individuals who are in need of special education and are eligible for education with their normal peers continue their education and training in public and private preschool, primary and secondary schools. In these schools, auxiliary classrooms are created, and special equipment and training materials are provided to provide special education support to individuals who require special education. For students who need to be educated in a separate classroom, special education classes will be opened in preschool, primary and secondary schools according to their disability status and characteristics (art. 20 paras 1 and 2 SD No. 573).

Part IX
Concluding Remarks

Chapter 28
General Evaluation of the Turkish Social Law System

28.1 Main Features of the Turkish Social Security System

28.1.1 Historical Structure of the Social Security System

The social security system in Turkey seems to have adopted the *Bismarck* model for the most part. However, apart from this premium-based social insurance model, it is seen that non-premium regime institutions are also included.

The Turkish social insurance system had a scattered outlook until the 2000s. This disorganization has emerged both in the organizational structure and in the norms and standards subjected to. Accordingly, the social insurance institutions of employees under an employment contract and self-employed persons are handled under separate laws. Apart from these, the retirement fund has been the competent authority for civil servants and other public officials, and the portions reserved for public institutions in the general budget have met social security assistances other than retirement funds.

The reform movements in 2006 and 2008 aimed to erase this scattered outlook in the Turkish social security system, and previously existing social security organizations were gathered under one roof.

On the other hand, although social security institutions are considered to be autonomous in administrative and financial terms, they have not been able to implement it into practice. The general assemblies of the social security institutions that should be the decision-making bodies became advisory bodies, and the representation of the social partners in the general assemblies could not be carried out effectively.[1]

[1] Ekin et al. (1999), p. 171.

T. Centel, *Turkish Social Law*, https://doi.org/10.1007/978-3-030-64704-9_28

28.1.2 Implementation of Reform Works

The social security system in Turkey, despite the current young population structure, began to give a deficit in the early 1990s. It is possible to sort the following factors as the main reasons for this:

- Very early retirement,
- A large number of borrowing arrangements issued backwards,
- Scattered and insufficient structure of social security institutions in collecting premiums,
- Allowance and income payments being made without premium conditions,
- Extent of unregistered employment against low employment.[2]

In order to overcome these negativities, an intensive reform work has been started in Turkey since 1999.[3] In this sense, firstly, the monthly calculation system in the retirement system was changed, and the retirement age was increased. As a matter of fact, in the past, women could be retired at the age of 38 and men at the age of 43, but the retirement system has been introduced into a process in which the retirement age has been advanced towards the age of 65 in the long term and equalized for men and women. As such, various measures have been taken to increase registered employment through changes in premium-based earnings and premium rates and social security incentives granted to employers.

The scattered outlook of the social security system in Turkey has been criticized for a long time. The presence of the Social Insurance Institution for workers, the Social Insurance Institution for the Self-employed Persons and the Retirement Fund for civil servants and other public officials have led them to have separate laws and to provide different types of social security assistances under separate laws. Similarly, the existence of different social security organizations has resulted in the difference of the ministries they are affiliated with. As a matter of fact, while the institutions of insured workers and independent workers are affiliated with the Ministry of Labour and Social Security, the Retirement Fund remained affiliated with the Ministry of Finance.

It is clear that this outlook is incompatible with the principles of single roof and norm and standard unity in social security. Upon this, the reform laws 5502 and 5510 have been enacted since 2006 in order to collect different social security institutions under one roof and to provide the same norms and standards for different categories of employees. However, these works have only been able to significantly affect those who started to work for the first time after 2008.

As for the insured from the past, transitional problems have started to occur. As a matter of fact, the ongoing obligations against those insured before 1999 and the gradual increase in the retirement age in the long term have continued to increase

[2] *See*: Ekin et al. (1999), pp. 146–172; Erol (2014), pp. 47–55; Gümüş (2010), p. 16.

[3] *See*: Ekin et al. (1999), pp. 179–196.

social security expenditures. However, it can be said now that such problems may disappear in the long run.

On the other hand, the disorganization associated with the non-premium regime is not removed yet. The draft reform of the non-premium regime has not been enacted in spite of the time elapsed. Again, the existence of a fully functioning, planned social assistance system managed from a single centre in Turkey cannot be mentioned. As a matter of fact, there are many social assistance organizations and they do not appear to act in a coordinated manner.[4]

28.2 The Outlook of the Turkish Social Security System

28.2.1 Progress of Social Security Expenditures

Social security expenditures of Turkey continue to rise despite the negative effects of the economic crises in the early 2000s. However, the social expenditures of Turkey are among the countries that are included in the high-income group and the middle-income group. And, the ratio of public retirement and health expenditures to gross domestic product is about two and a half times that of middle-income countries.

The ratio of public pension expenditures to gross domestic product in Turkey is closer to that of developed countries, although Turkey has a younger population structure. However, the high pension practices in comparison with the premiums paid in early retirement and the time worked have increased the pension expenditures of Turkey to even higher than those of countries with high elderly population.[5]

On the other hand, if the income-expenditure balances of the social security system are taken into consideration, it is seen that there is a significant increase in premium revenues compared to previous years. However, significant increases are observed in both insurance payments and health expenditures. There is now a significant improvement in the income-expenditure gap of the social security system. However, the main reason for this improvement is that the State has contributed significantly to the system since 2008.

It can be said that the following factors have especially been effective in the increase in premium revenues:

- Economic growth,
- Decrease in unregistered employment,
- Increase in premium income of the insured working as workers and civil servants,
- The premiums of those who do not have the financial capacity to pay premiums being covered by the State.

[4]Yuvalı (2017), p. 239.

[5]Kalkınma Bakanlığı (2014), p. 3.

On the other hand, it is seen that there is a decrease in the collection of premiums of the self-employed persons.

In addition, the increase in the scope of health services after the implementation of the general health insurance and the transfer of civil health expenditures that were previously covered from the central government budget and health expenditures of the poor to the Social Insurance Institution led to an increase in expenditures.

The contribution of the State to the social security system is quite high compared to the previous period. However, despite the two major reforms made in 2006 and 2008, there was no significant improvement in the ratio of total budget transfers to gross domestic product.[6]

28.2.2 *Loss of Premiums Generated by Unregistered Employment*

The fact that the employment of workers is not declared to SSI or the days or wages they work on are declared inefficiently leads to the loss of income of the social security system. In this context, it is clear that the unregistered employment rate cannot be lowered by incentive or punitive policies applied alone.

On the other hand, the fact that SIGHIA excludes some working groups from the mandatory insurance relationship leads to a decrease in the number of insured workers and the loss of premiums of the social insurance system. Instead, it would be more appropriate for these groups to be equipped with complementary social assistance programs if the pensions in the future are low and fall below the poverty line, and the premium losses will be prevented.

Again, benefiting from the social assistance system is subject to the condition that the person is not subject to the social insurance system. Therefore, people are trying to stay in unregistered employment in order to receive social assistance, and this leads to premium losses.

28.2.3 *Difficulties in Premium Collection*

The fact that SSI cannot collect the premium receivables affects the financing balance negatively. In this regard, the absence of an execution proceeding system for the self-employed persons with premium debts creates a problem. Accordingly, there is no compulsion for the premium payments of independent workers who have not paid any premiums, and the records of the insured persons with debts of five years or more are suspended in the system.

---

[6]Kalkınma Bakanlığı (2014), pp. 5–6.

Similarly, many insured persons who appear to be insured self-employed in the SSI-system do not declare to SSI that they leave their chamber registration or tax liabilities and/or work in another workplace as an insured employee. These premium receivables, which appear in SSI records, do not reflect the actual number of receivables. In order to prevent this, it is necessary to integrate the databases of the previous social security institutions and to ensure the necessary integration of information between SSI, the chambers and the Revenue Administration.

28.2.4 Deficiency in Norm and Standard Uniformity

The reform works in 2006 and 2008 aimed to equalize the conditions for the employees' payment of premiums and their entitlement to social security assistances and thus to create norm and standard unity among the employees. However, these efforts have created some new superiority instead of achieving this purpose.

As a matter of fact, the premium payment facilities granted to employers of workers and the exclusion of the self-employed from the 5-points bonus discount given to them have resulted in not everyone benefiting from the social insurance system. Many examples of this kind arising from the social security legislation bring with them the lack of norm and standard uniformity.[7]

28.2.5 Lack of Effective Audit

In order to increase the registered employment, social security audit should be enabled active. Although nowadays the number of social security auditors has increased, it is seen that they cannot allocate the necessary time to the works related to unregistered employment. Since the social security audit does not pursue a specific audit strategy to combat unregistered employment, the audit does not gain efficiency.

Similarly, since SSI does not have enough officers to monitor the execution proceedings in every district, there is also a difficulty in collecting premiums through enforcement.

On the other hand, since social security inspectors investigate and prosecute abuses in general health insurance, they cannot find the possibility of referring social security audits to unregistered employment in their intensive workload.

---

[7] *See*: Kalkınma Bakanlığı (2014), pp. 31–33.

28.3 The Future of the Turkish Social Security System

28.3.1 Sustainability of the System

The social security system in Turkey has to be in a financially and socially sustainable and efficient structure in the long-term to serve the entire population. Because, the current state of the Turkish social security system shows that SSI has significant financial and social difficulties and is in a structure that is far away from serving the whole of the population equally. It is clear that only increasing the premium income and preventing unregistered work cannot solve the problems of the Turkish social security system.

In this respect, it is necessary to follow some basic policies first:

- Increasing national savings,
- Increasing the employment of women in particular,
- Encouraging elderly people to stay longer in working life,
- Promotion of complementary retirement programs.

28.3.2 Mandatory Policies to Be Followed

Objectives of mandatory policies to be followed should serve to:

- Combat unregistered employment,
- Increase the collection of premiums,
- Avoid actuarial balance-disrupting premium configurations,
- To keep people in working life for longer,
- Increase women's participation in the labour force,
- Ensure norm and standard unity in social insurance programs.

28.3.3 Implementation Strategies

28.3.3.1 Increasing the Number of Registered Employees and the Collection of Premiums

The main reasons for the inability to obtain the expected premium revenues is the loss of registered employment and premiums. It is necessary to increase the number of registered employees and to accelerate the collection of premiums by overcoming them in the short and medium term.

In this context, increasing female employment will accelerate the number of insured persons. However, the legal regulations that will draw women away from working life and encourage them to be bound to home under the name of protecting working women with populist policies should be abandoned. Such policies are negatively affecting employment chances of women.

28.3.3.2 Extending Social Insurance Coverage

The extension of the social insurance coverage will increase the number of insured persons and the premiums to be provided will serve to the cycle of the system. However, it is necessary to simplify and facilitate access to social insurance programs related to them.

28.3.3.3 Intensifying Premium Incentives

The intensification of premium incentives is among the measures that can attract employers to registration. Otherwise, the employer in the unregistered economy will avoid registration as much as possible. This situation causes the loss of premiums of SSI.

28.3.3.4 Enabling the Social Security Audit Network

Unless the social security audit network is enabled, the fight against unregistered employment will not achieve success. However, rather than increasing the number of audit personnel in this regard, ensuring that their activities are mainly directed to unregistered employment will enable active auditing.

In addition, raising the personal rights of social security inspectors and auditors may increase their work motivations (performance).

28.3.3.5 Preventing Low-Earnings Declarations

Earnings declarations made under the actual income to pay low premiums lead to significant premium losses of SSI.

In this context, arrangements are needed to compare the earnings declared to SSI by income tax payers with the income tax base declared to the revenue administration. Similarly, increasing the awareness of the insured on the negative consequences of unregistered earnings would also help to prevent low earning declarations.

28.3.3.6 Ensuring Norm and Standard Uniformity

In order to ensure that employees benefit equally from social security systems, norms and standards that cannot be legally justified must be eliminated. In this respect, the conditions of entitlement to premium and social security assistances of workers and self-employed persons should be equalized, except for those who are protected by their own social insurance programs due to their working conditions.

28.4 Epilogue

In Turkey, social security is based on a mixed system that collects social assistance and social service institutions that are financed by tax revenues, as well as social security institutions that are financed primarily on a premium basis under its roof. Since the 1990s, efforts have been made to initiate a certain transformation with a social security system that is complementary and is based on the operation of private retirement funds, but the savings in this way have not gained much power. The major reform efforts of 2006 and 2008 have not achieved much success in correcting the actuarial balance of the system.

In this context, it is seen that the main problem of the Turkish social security system is developing to close the financing deficits. As a matter of fact, according to current calculations, system deficits are expected to continue until 2040s. To this end, Turkey needs to increase its premium income, which is the main source of financing of the existing social security system, by improving employment and to develop serious incentives and market regulatory policies to prevent unregistered employment.[8]

On the other hand, it should be kept in mind that social security reform does not only consist of reform in social insurance. In the area of social assistances and social services, no reform movement has achieved success. As a matter of fact, fields of social assistance and social service continue their scattered outlook. In this respect, the social security activities to be carried out should include non-premium regime areas in the coming period.

References

Ekin N, Alper Y, Akgeyik T (1999) Türk Sosyal Güvenlik Sistemi'nde Yeni Arayışlar: Özelleştirme ve Yeniden Yapılanma. Publication of İstanbul Ticaret, İstanbul. Odası No. 1999-69

Erol SI (2014) Türkiye'de Sosyal Güvenlik Sisteminin Sorunları ve Sosyal Güvenlik Ahlakı. Kamu-İş İş Hukuku ve İktisat Dergisi 13(3):37–70

Gümüş E (2010) Türkiye'de Sosyal Güvenlik Sistemi: Mevcut Durum, Sorunlar ve Öneriler. Seta Analiz 24:1–21

Kalkınma Bakanlığı (ed) (2014) Sosyal Güvenlik Sisteminin Sürdürülebilirliği - Özel İhtisas Komisyonu Raporu. Kalkınma Bakanlığı, Ankara. yayını No. 2857/711

Yuvalı E (2017) Türk Sosyal Güvenlik Hukukunda Merkezi (Kamusal) Sosyal Yardımlar. Turhan Kitabevi, Ankara

[8]Gümüş (2010), p. 20.

The manufacturer's authorised representative in the EU is Springer Nature Customer Service Centre GmbH, Europaplatz 3, 69115 Heidelberg, Germany. If you have any concerns regarding our products, please contact ProductSafety@springernature.com

Printed and bound by CPI Group (UK) Ltd, Croydon, CR0 4YY
30/09/2026
02225696-0018